Animal-Assisted Interventions for Emotional and Mental Health

Animal-Assisted Interventions for Emotional and Mental Health provides a unique opportunity to learn from a variety of leaders in the field. Leading scholar Dr. Cynthia Chandler and colleague Dr. Tiffany Otting present interviews with pioneering experts from the U.S., U.K., Israel, India, and Hong Kong, revealing key beliefs, values, and ideas that are fundamental to animal-assisted interventions. Their words will inspire and guide current and future generations of practitioners, teachers, and researchers.

Cynthia K. Chandler, EdD, is a professor of counseling at the University of North Texas and the founder and director of the UNT Consortium for Animal Assisted Therapy. She received the American Counseling Association's Professional Development Award and the Association for Creativity in Counseling's Thelma Duffey Award for Vision and Innovation. Dr. Chandler has been practicing, teaching, researching, and supervising animal-assisted therapy in counseling (AAT-C) for many years and is recognized worldwide as a leading expert in the field. She is the author of *Animal-Assisted Therapy in Counseling.*

Tiffany L. Otting, PhD, is a licensed professional counselor in private practice in Georgetown, Texas. She specializes in animal-assisted counseling.

Animal-Assisted Interventions for Emotional and Mental Health

Conversations with Pioneers of the Field

Edited by
Cynthia K. Chandler
Tiffany L. Otting

Routledge
Taylor & Francis Group

NEW YORK AND LONDON

First published 2018
by Routledge
711 Third Avenue, New York, NY 10017

and by Routledge
2 Park Square, Milton Park, Abingdon, Oxon, OX14 4RN

Routledge is an imprint of the Taylor & Francis Group, an informa business

Library of Congress Cataloging-in-Publication Data
Names: Chandler, Cynthia K., editor.
Title: Animal-assisted interventions for emotional and mental health : conversations with pioneers of the field / edited by Cynthia K. Chandler and Tiffany L. Otting.
Description: New York, NY : Routledge, 2018. | Includes bibliographical references.
Identifiers: LCCN 2017054481| ISBN 9780815395096 (hbk : alk. paper) | ISBN 9780815395102 (pbk : alk. paper) | ISBN 9781351113793 (ebk)
Subjects: LCSH: Animals—Therapeutic use.
Classification: LCC RC489.P47 A55 2018 | DDC 615.8/5158—dc23
LC record available at https://lccn.loc.gov/2017054481

ISBN: 978-0-8153-9509-6 (hbk)
ISBN: 978-0-8153-9510-2 (pbk)
ISBN: 978-1-351-11379-3 (ebk)

Typeset in Galliard
by Keystroke, Neville Lodge, Tettenhall, Wolverhampton

I wish to dedicate this book to all my students of the past, present, and future. Their passion for animal-assisted interventions fuels my dedication to this work.

Cynthia K. Chandler, EdD

I dedicate this work to my four-legged family members: Lola, Wally, Stella, and Pearl. Thank you for helping me learn about authenticity and inspiring me to share our work with others.

Tiffany L. Otting, PhD

Contents

Acknowledgments

We wish to thank all the individuals whom we interviewed for this book. All of them were gracious with their time and very forthcoming with their ideas. We would also like to extend our gratitude to all pioneers and experts in the field whom we did not include in this particular volume. We acknowledge that, without the valuable contributions of all pioneers and experts of animal-assisted interventions for emotional and mental health, this field would be significantly behind where it is today.

About the Editors

Dr. Cynthia K. Chandler is a professor of counseling in the Department of Counseling and Higher Education at the University of North Texas, located in Denton, Texas, where she has taught various graduate courses in counseling since 1989. She is a licensed professional counselor and supervisor and a licensed marriage and family therapist and supervisor. She has been involved with animal-assisted therapy practice, supervision, and research since 1999. She is author of the classic book *Animal-Assisted Therapy in Counseling*; the third edition was published in 2017. For her work in animal-assisted therapy, in 2016 Dr. Chandler received the American Counseling Association's Professional Development Award, and in 2009 the Thelma Duffey Award for Vision and Innovation from the Association for Creativity in Counseling.

Dr. Tiffany L. Otting graduated from the University of North Texas, where she specialized in animal-assisted therapy. She is a licensed professional counselor. She has had a private practice in Georgetown, Texas, since 2016.

About the Contributors

Dr. Aubrey Fine of California State Polytechnic University, Pomona. Dr. Fine is well known for his work in the field of animal-assisted interventions for emotional and mental health. Over the years, he has worked in his practice with a variety of animal assistants, including a gerbil, birds, and dogs. He has written several books and presented at a great number of professional venues. One of his best-known works is editor and contributing author of the landmark book *Handbook on Animal-Assisted Therapy: Theoretical Foundations and Guidelines for Practice*. He has spent decades practicing, teaching, researching, and writing in the field.

Dr. Samuel Ross, Jr., and **Myra Ross**, also **Director Michael Kaufmann** of Green Chimneys, New York. Green Chimneys was founded by Dr. Samuel Ross, Jr., and his family. Sam and his wife, Myra Ross, pioneered the idea of a residential therapy farm for animal-assisted interventions for emotional and mental health. Green Chimneys is a place where farm animals have sanctuary and provide companionship for children who are emotionally disturbed and learning disabled. Children's interaction with farm animals and highly qualified teachers and staff assist to motivate children's participation in therapy and facilitate children's emotional recovery and mental development.

Dr. Risë VanFleet and **Tracie Faa-Thompson**. Dr. VanFleet is founder and Tracie is cofounder of the International Institute for Animal Assisted Play Therapy™ Studies. They have collaborated on publications and offer trainings in animal-assisted play therapy. They coauthored the book *Animal Assisted Play Therapy*. Dr. VanFleet has a practice in Boiling Springs, Pennsylvania. She is a licensed psychologist, a registered play therapist and supervisor, a certified filial therapy therapist, supervisor and instructor, and a certified dog behavior consultant. Dr. Risë VanFleet began practicing animal-assisted play therapy with canines as her therapy animals. Tracie Faa-Thompson has a practice in Northumberland, United Kingdom. She primarily works with equines as her therapy animals. Tracie is a social worker and a registered play therapist with the British Association of Play Therapy. Risë and Tracie provide therapy for children and adults with emotional and mental health issues.

Dr. Cynthia K. Chandler. Dr. Chandler is a professor of counseling in the Department of Counseling and Higher Education at the University of North Texas. She is also a licensed professional counselor and a licensed marriage and family therapist. In the year 2000, she started the first training and supervision program for animal-assisted interventions in an accredited counseling program at a major university. She authored the book *Animal-Assisted Therapy in Counseling*. She has provided animal-assisted counseling with adolescents and adults. Her therapy assistants have included dogs, a cat, and horses.

Dr. Sarit Lev-Bendov, Inbar Barel, and **Gal Hakim** of Oranim Academic College in Kiryat Tiv'on, Israel. Dr. Lev-Bendov is a psychologist, animal-assisted psychotherapist, and former director of the animal-assisted therapy training program at Oranim Academic College. Inbar and Gal are the current codirectors of the animal-assisted therapy training program at Oranim Academic College. Inbar is a psychologist who practices couples and family therapy and specializes in animal-assisted therapy. Gal is a psychologist who also specializes in animal-assisted therapy. Both Inbar and Gal teach, supervise, and perform research in animal-assisted psychotherapy. Both of them involve in their practice dogs and a variety of other animals.

Dr. Michal Motro, Tamar Axelrad-Levy, and **Dr. Lauren Wolfsfeld**. Dr. Motro is director of the Institute for Animal-Assisted Therapy and Education at David Yellin College in Jerusalem, Israel. Tamar is assistant director of the Institute. The Institute provides training, supervision, and research opportunities for animal-assisted psychotherapy. The primary medium for interventions is a small zoo with a variety of animals. Dr. Wolfsfeld is head of the Fieldwork Division of the Paul Baerwald School of Social Work and Social Welfare of The Hebrew University of Jerusalem. Dr. Motro and Tamar teach, supervise, and research animal-assisted psychotherapy. Dr. Wolfsfeld assisted in the design of a comprehensive supervision program for animal-assisted psychotherapy.

Rabbi Eitan Eckstein and **Efrat Maayan** of the Retorno Jewish Center for Addictions located near Beit-Shemesh, Israel. Rabbi Eckstein is CEO of Retorno and directs the therapeutic riding program. Efrat Maayan is a psychologist at Retorno and also has a private clinic where she works with persons of a variety of ages and presenting concerns. Efrat Maayan works with a variety of animals. She is founder of the small zoo therapy model in Israel.

Nancy Parish-Plass. Nancy is an animal-assisted psychotherapist and animal-assisted play therapist. She has a private practice on a kibbutz near Haifa, Israel. She is editor and contributing author of the book *Animal-Assisted Psychotherapy: Theory, Issues, and Practice*. She serves a variety of child and adult populations, but has a special focus on neglected and abused children. She works with a variety of therapy animals.

Minal Kavishwar. Minal is a psychologist and the founder and executive director of Animal Angels Foundation in Pune and Mumbai, India. Animal Angels Foundation is India's largest and only registered nonprofit organization, which has introduced and developed the field and scope of human–animal interaction and animal-assisted interventions in India. Their animal angels are dogs who assist in providing services. Animal Angels Foundation has several animal-assisted intervention programs but primarily serves children with emotional and mental health challenges and disabilities.

Dr. William Fan, **Dr. Paul Wong**, **Dr. Rose Yu**, **Steven Lai**, and **Fanny Leung**. Dr. Fan is a psychiatrist and president of the Hong Kong Animal Therapy Foundation. He is one of the first in his country to consider human–animal interaction as a form of therapy for the elderly and the mentally or emotionally disabled. He is also a leading advocate for animal welfare in Hong Kong. Dr. Paul Wong is an associate professor in the Department of Social Work and Social Administration at the University of Hong Kong. Dr. Rose Yu completed her doctoral studies at the University of Hong Kong. Both Paul and Rose have performed the earliest research on the efficacy of animal-assisted interventions for emotional and mental health for Hong Kong populations. Steven Lai and Fanny Leung direct the animal-assisted interventions program at the Chinese Evangelical Zion Church. They serve populations of isolated youth and the elderly. Their animal assistants include mostly dogs and some cats.

Yuen, Sin Nga Gloria; **Ng, Chu Kong Morgan**; **Leung, San Wan Gloria**; and **Wong, Lo Ming** of the Society of Rehabilitation and Crime Prevention. Gloria Yuen and Morgan Ng are senior managers of the Society. Gloria Leung is a nurse who designed and directs the visit with cats program of the Society. Lo Ming Wong is a supervisor of the Society, who does staff management and performs community mental health work in the community, including home visits. Staff work together to provide animal-assisted interventions with dogs and cats to assist persons with mental health illness and also ex-criminal offenders to rehabilitate and reintegrate them back into Hong Kong society.

Yim, Yat Kěuah; **Angie Yu**; **Lily Tang**; and **Lau, Yin Fei Joyce** of Hong Chi Association. Angie Yu and Lily Tang are clinical psychologists, Joyce Lau is a social worker, and Mr. Yim is a service supervisor. Hong Chi Association is the largest organization in Hong Kong mainly serving people who have intellectual disabilities. They operate in over 80 centers, projects, and hospitals for mental disabilities in different grades and different levels. Hong Chi Association was the first to try animal-assisted interventions for those with intellectual disabilities. The animal-assisted intervention programs involve visiting and caring for cats and large land tortoises.

Eddie Lee. Eddie is founder and director of Hong Kong Institute of Animal Assisted Intervention. Eddie, his staff, and therapy dogs work with education and mental health professionals to design and provide animal-assisted interventions for emotional and mental health. They also provide education programs on animal and environmental welfare. They rescue dogs from abandonment in the streets and train and socialize the dogs for adoption, and some of the dogs assist with animal-assisted interventions.

Debbie Ngai. Debbie is founder and director of Hong Kong Animal Assisted Therapy Association, a program aimed to provide professional animal-assisted therapy in Hong Kong for people who are in need. They serve about 90 marginal youths in an at-risk program and about 60 special needs students with conditions such as ADHD, autism, and dyslexia. The animal assistants for this program are dogs. Dogs are well trained and socialized before participation in the animal-assisted intervention programs. This organization also thoroughly trains all participant animal handlers in animal behavior, animal communication, and animal handling.

Introduction

It is not easy to be a pioneer – but oh, it is fascinating! I would not trade one moment, even the worst moment, for all the riches in the world.

Elizabeth Blackwell (McFerran, 1966, p. 154)

Elizabeth Blackwell (1821–1910) was an American physician who was born in England and was the first woman to receive an MD degree from an American medical school in the year 1849. Despite significant professional prejudice and great societal resistance, Dr. Blackwell opened the profession of medicine to women in America and provided care for those in great need (Grant & Carter, 2004; McFerran, 1966). She provided training and experience for women doctors and medical care for the poor. Her words reflect that, although tough challenges face those who do pioneering work, much satisfaction comes from helping others. Pioneers often do not get much benefit from their own contribution, but great joy can be had by making life better for others from new paths that are forged.

A professional field thrives from a robust foundation established by pioneers. Though animal-assisted interventions (AAIs) for emotional and mental health have been presented in professional literature as far back as the work of Boris Levinson in the 1960s and Sam and Elizabeth Corson of the 1970s, the greatest growth in this field is occurring because of the work of pioneering experts of the current generation. While these individuals are still available to us, I (CKC) wanted to preserve the ideas and personality of some of these modern-day pioneers with personal conversations. So I traveled to the other side of the world and the east and west coasts of the United States to interview them. Dr. Tiffany L. Otting, coeditor of this book, accompanied me on my travels and recorded the interviews under my direction. She was, at the time, a doctoral-level student assistant at the University of North Texas. Additionally, Tiffany interviewed me for the book, and we collaborated on our commentary about all the interviews. This book is a compilation of 21 separate interviews conducted with 32 people who are contemporary pioneers in the field of AAI for emotional and mental health. This book includes conversations with pioneers from the United States, United Kingdom, Israel, India, and Hong Kong.

Readers will learn how these individuals make their own unique contributions to the communities they serve within the context of their own culture.

The interviews occurred between December 2014 and July 2016. The content of the interviews is reproduced with as much accuracy as possible. In some instances, especially where English was not the primary language of the speaker, the reproduced interview reflects minor corrections in grammar and syntax that are not meant to change the speaker's intended meaning. We, the coeditors of this book, are very knowledgeable in the field of AAIs, which made the interviews interesting and interactive discussions for a reading audience.

It is clear from the interviews that the contributions of these pioneers further establish the efficacy of AAIs as applied to emotional and mental health. We believe these interviews reveal key beliefs, values, and ideas that are fundamental to the work of these experts and to the field of AAIs. Further, we are hopeful the words of these contemporary pioneers will inspire and guide current and future generations of practitioners, teachers, and researchers of AAI. This book offers a unique opportunity to hear from living legends in a rapidly growing therapy field.

I (CKC) began all the interviews with the initial inquiry of asking professionals to describe their work. I introjected very little during the interviews, only enough to keep the conversations moving. These introjections and follow-up questions varied in content based on interviewees' unique presentation of thoughts and ideas. Interviewees described their role and service within the field of AAIs. Many interviewees volunteered deep background for how they evolved into working in this field. Many shared meaningful stories of the people they had served, and many spoke warmly of the animals that assisted in the provision of service. I ended the interviews in mostly the same way – by asking interviewees to share with current and aspiring practitioners what they felt was most important to understand about this field and to share any final words about the field or their work within the field.

We, the editors, would like to emphasize a point that all the ideas presented in these interviews in this book do not necessarily represent or reflect the views of the editors of this book. We have provided our editors' commentary at the end of each chapter to present our thoughts and ideas about the interviews and our experiences.

Who Is A Pioneer?

In this introduction, we have used the terms "pioneer" and "expert" to describe the people interviewed for this book. One may ask, "What do these terms imply?" According to the dictionary, "pioneer" can be defined in these ways: (1) "one who is first or among the earliest in any field of inquiry, enterprise, or progress"; (2) "to be the first to open or prepare a way"; (3) "to take part in the beginnings of; initiate: to pioneer an aid program"; (4) "to lead the way for (a group); guide"; and (5) "being the earliest, original, first of a particular kind, etc.: a pioneer method" (dictionary.com, n.d.). An "expert" can be defined as "a person who has special skill or knowledge in some particular field; specialist; authority" (dictionary.com, n.d.). All people interviewed for this book meet the definition of expert in that each has a special skill or knowledge that qualifies them as a certain type of specialist in the field of AAI for emotional and mental health. And each interviewee also satisfies, in some fashion, the requirement to be a pioneer, for example, producing a major book considered a classic in the field or being first to develop a major training program for practitioners, or being first in their community to develop a service program attending to a great need, or being first to research an idea or program to further development of AAI in the field or in a community. Meeting the definition of both "expert" and "pioneer" was the first criteria for inclusion as a contributor to this book as an interviewee.

A next major consideration for selecting interviewees for this book was based on a desire for diversity and variety. I (CKC) wanted the book to represent pioneers from a variety of cultures and nationalities. AAIs for emotional and mental health are applied in unique ways based on cultural differences and community needs. AAIs are applied at varying levels of development in different countries and with varying levels of acceptance by different cultures. One aspect of being a pioneer is introducing and developing an unfamiliar idea to a culture that may benefit. Countries, such as India and Hong Kong, may not be as far along in their practice or research of AAIs as other countries, such as the United States and Israel, but practitioners in India and Hong Kong are certainly pioneering AAIs in their own communities, cultures, and nations.

There are many more contemporary pioneers than we had time to interview. Because of this, the most practical additional criteria for inclusion as an interviewee were familiarity, accessibility, and opportunity. From many years of working in the field of AAIs, I (CKC) have come to know or know of several professionals doing pioneering work. I utilized my familiarity with people or their work to decide whom I would contact about interviewing. Also, some of the people who agreed to be interviewed for the book enlightened me regarding other pioneers I should consider and assisted me in making contact with some of these professionals. Unfortunately, I was not able to make contact with a few of those recommended to me. Also, while no one I contacted formally declined to be interviewed for the book, one person showed a significant lack of enthusiasm, so I did not pursue the matter. All other people I (CKC) contacted were enthusiastic about participating.

The doors of opportunity flung open wide for this project, and we ended up with a large number of interviews. After gathering so much material, we decided it was time to publish the work. This book is an effort to further the field of AAIs for emotional and mental health by presenting the ideas of some contemporary pioneers in their own words. Many a time I (CKC) have wished for the opportunity to sit down and have a conversation with professionals I admired. I initiated this project as a gift to myself and completed it as a gift to the world. The people interviewed communicated passion for their work and compassion for humans and animals they work with. Their words are heartening and inspiring. They are a handful of diamonds from a field of valuable jewels. Perhaps this book of conversations with pioneers will lead to similar works. It would be lovely to preserve the ideas and personalities of as many pioneers as possible while they are available to us.

Ethical Considerations

Professionals who work in the field of AAIs are obligated to preserve the safety and welfare of both humans and animals who participate. Practice of AAIs is not possible without the animals who assist. We must honor, value, nurture, and protect these animals at all times. According to Zamir (2006), it is a moral imperative to protect beings that are vulnerable, and this includes animal beings. Preziosi (1997) presented a facilitator code of ethics mandating, among other things, that a therapy animal's welfare must be a priority and animals who assist in therapy should never be forced to engage in any activity. In my book, *Animal-Assisted Therapy in Counseling* (Chandler, 2017), I emphasized constant commitment to the safety and welfare of human participants and animals who assist in therapy. Stewart, Chang, Parker, and Grubbs (2016) presented practitioner competency practices that require, among other things, advocacy for safety and welfare of therapy animals. The International Association of Human-Animal Interaction Organizations provided specific guidelines for considering human and animal well-being in AAIs (IAHAIO, 2014).

We are pleased to report that interviewees for this book expressed great concern and compassion for the welfare and safety of both human participants and the animals who assisted in AAIs. This occurred even though I (CKC) did not inquire about, suggest, or prompt this subject for discussion. The professionals were concerned about protecting and nurturing the animals. The animals were held in high regard and received great care. In fact, many of the interviewees spoke of how working with animals provided additional opportunities to model and educate about animal care and welfare for their clients. Some professionals, such as those in India and Hong Kong, took this a step further through educational and outreach programs at schools and mental health agencies. With these kinds of activities, they aspired to raise conscientiousness toward animals of their entire culture.

Definitions of AAIs

To prepare the reader for the remaining content in this book, we offer some definitions of AAIs. AAIs involve human–animal interactions that are facilitated by a trained professional or a trained nonprofessional volunteer (IAHAIO, 2014). Professional application of AAIs falls into two main categories: animal-assisted therapy (AAT) and animal-assisted education (AAE). In both instances, a professional is involved to develop, guide, or direct AAIs: a professional clinician for AAT and a professional educator for AAE. Also, in AAT and AAE, there are clear goals for intended outcomes, and progress toward these goals is recorded and assessed in some way. Professional clinicians who utilize AAIs for emotional and mental health include psychiatrists, psychologists, counselors, psychotherapists, and social workers as well as nurses who have emotional and mental health training.

Nonprofessional application of AAIs is referred to as animal-assisted activity (AAA). AAA involves social visits with a therapy animal and sometimes providing information about animals. AAA can be beneficial to a person interacting with an animal by lifting mood, increasing socialization, and expanding knowledge. AAA is typically facilitated by a trained nonprofessional volunteer. However, some AAA can also be applied in a service for clinical treatment or education, such as for purposes of healing, personal growth, or development. For AAA to be integrated into a service for clinical treatment or educational gains, a professional clinician or professional educator, respectively, must be involved in the development, direction, or guidance of the AAA intervention.

Perspectives of AAIs

One of my (TLO) perspectives on this project comes from being recorder of the interviews that Cynthia conducted. I recall one interview that included my doing a bit of a dance to avoid a pair of highly social therapy rats from scampering up my pants leg while not interrupting the flow of conversation. In another interview, a professional described the therapeutic impacts of working with a corn snake while removing the corn snake from her habitat to work with on the floor – thus, revealing my fear of snakes and calling into question my learning edge of human–animal relating. Reader, if this book included a chapter on blooper reels, you would read my excited exclamation of "Good Lord!" when the snake was a few feet from me. In a flash of clarity, I fully understood the value of screening our clients for fears and phobias. Moreover, that beautiful snake broadened my perspective of AAIs. I observed the snake and the human interacting with one another in the context of a trusting relationship. For that to occur so intimately, both beings needed to feel safe with one another. Though manifested through different behaviors, the snake demonstrated social interest in her handler in the same way that the therapy rats showed interest in me. Although I have not yet established a relationship with a therapy snake, I now understand that therapeutic opportunities and impacts are possible with a much wider range of animals than I imagined prior to this project.

Our hope as you read these interviews is that you too gain a broader perspective of AAIs for emotional and mental health. From working one on one with canines, to caring for turtles, to cohabitating with felines for therapeutic purposes, we purposely highlight varied perspectives of AAIs within several cultural contexts. These contexts include social norms surrounding the value of animals in societies across the world as well as the perceived worth of individuals with emotional and mental health concerns and disabilities.

As assistant and coeditor on this project, I (TLO) had the privileged perspective of a front row seat for each interview as well as a behind-the-scenes look at the innovations put forth by each contributor. To be first and lead the way requires courage from the perspective of making one's way through a path not yet cleared. From working with children with disabilities, to adolescents with behavior problems, to elderly individuals struggling to find their value in an ever-changing society, the contributors of this book repeatedly call on courage to forge new paths toward healing through AAIs. We hope you enjoy learning from their perspectives.

References

Chandler, C. K. (2017). *Animal-assisted therapy in counseling* (3rd ed.). New York, NY: Routledge.

Dictionary.com (n.d.). Pioneer/expert. Retrieved October 1, 2017, from www.dictionary.com/

Grant, T., & Carter, S. (2004). *Women in medicine: A celebration of their work.* Buffalo, NY: Firefly Books.

International Association of Human-Animal Interaction Organizations (IAHAIO, 2014). *IAHAIO white paper 2014: The IAHAIO definitions for animal assisted intervention and guidelines for wellness of animals involved.* Retrieved October 1, 2017, from http://iahaio.org/best-practice/white-paper-on-animal-assisted-interventions/

McFerran, A. (1966). *Elizabeth Blackwell: First woman doctor.* New York, NY: Rutledge/Grosset & Dunlap.

Preziosi, R. J. (1997, Spring). For your consideration: A pet assisted therapist facilitator code of ethics. *Latham Letter,* pp. 5–6. Retrieved October 1, 2017, from www.latham.org/Issues/LL_97_SP.pdf - page=

Stewart, L. A., Chang, C. Y., Parker, L. K., & Grubbs, N. (2016, June 21). Animal assisted therapy in counseling competencies. *ACAeNews.* Alexandria, VA: American Counseling Association. Retrieved October 1, 2017, from www.counseling.org/docs/default-source/competencies/animal-assisted-therapy-competencies-june-2016.pdf?sfvrsn=c469472c_14

Zamir, T. (2006). The moral basis of animal-assisted therapy. *Society and Animals, 14*(2), 179–199.

Part I
U.S. and U.K.

1 Dr. Aubrey Fine of California State Polytechnic University, Pomona

Dr. Aubrey Fine is well known for his work in the field of animal-assisted interventions (AAIs). He has written several books and presented at a great number of professional venues. One of his best-known works is editor and contributing author of the landmark book *Handbook on Animal-Assisted Therapy: Theoretical Foundations and Guidelines for Practice*. Dr. Fine is professor in the College of Education at California State Polytechnic University in Pomona, California, and has served as practitioner in Claremont, California. He is a member of the American Psychological Association. He has spent decades practicing, teaching, researching, and writing in the field of AAI. Some of the animals he has worked with include a gerbil named Sasha, dogs PJ and Magic, a cockatoo named Tikvah, and a bearded dragon lizard named Aussie. Also, Dr. Fine is an experienced magician and often incorporates magic tricks into his practice.

The interview I conducted with Dr. Aubrey Fine, on October 10, 2015, serves to preserve some of the ideas and attitudes of a foremost pioneer in the field of AAIs (see Figure 1.1). Some of the sources he refers to in the interview are listed in the references at the end of the chapter.

Interview with Dr. Aubrey Fine

Cynthia: We are here in lovely Pomona, California, at California State Polytechnic University. We are visiting with Dr. Aubrey Fine, who is a professor in the College of Education. Thanks for joining us today.

Aubrey: Thanks. I'm honored to be here.

Cynthia: The honor is ours. Please tell us about how you got started in animal-assisted therapy and some of the activities that you're involved in.

Aubrey: Okay. I'm asked that question and I always giggle because I'll even tell you, before I got involved in any of this, I grew up being afraid of animals. Never had an animal in my life. My mom really didn't like dogs and cats so that fear factor was brought upon me. It's amazing that my life was changed.

I always think back of the first dog, and then I'll tell you how I got involved. I never forgot as years went on, although I was apprehensive about dogs, I finally felt that I was ready. My friends had golden retrievers and we [my wife and I] talked about it. We had our first son 34 years ago, and slightly after that son was born, we really just began to talk more about having a dog. Although, when you think about having two babies in a house, a human baby and a puppy, it was an interesting experience. Anyway, I remember the first time we got a golden retriever. It was really funny. Today, I would have never purchased a dog like this, but we were in front of a store and a lady had one golden retriever in a basket. She said that she had sold all of the puppies. She had one left that was sold, but someone said they couldn't pick it up. She wanted to keep it, and her husband said no. I never forgot when I was in front of that woman with the dog, I looked at my wife and said, "Could we have the dog?" It was almost like I became a five-year-old all over again because she said to me, "But it's a major responsibility." I said, "I know that and we've talked about this," but she wanted reassurance, so I kept on doing what a five-year-old would tell a parent. I was "yes" to everything, so when she said, "Who's going to take care of this dog when it wakes up in the middle of the night?" "I will!" Went through this whole process and then she said to me, I never forgot this, she said, "Well, if we get one, if we get this puppy, always remember we'll never have more than one in our family at one time." Of course, that never really came true. We've had a wealth of animals in our home that has enriched our family's life. In retrospect, all the other dogs we've ever got since then, you know there's a lot more thought about how you get the dog, but that was my rookie experience with dogs.

How I got into this field was serendipitous. I was a young college student in Canada and, again, I gave you the story of my mom not liking animals. My first attempt of having a pet was to get a small rodent. Originally, it was a mouse and when I came home, I remember having the cage and everything all ready and she was in a small container, my mother was screaming, "It's a rat. Don't drop it. Don't drop it." She got me so nervous, and she wasn't ready, that I said, "No, no, no. This isn't going to work." I went back to the store and said, "Listen, I'm only giving you back the animal right now, not because I'm giving up on this. I'm going to keep the cage and everything; just give me two or three more weeks to get my family more prepared." He understood and it was fine, but I ended up not getting a mouse. I got a gerbil [Sasha].

At that time, I was a student at a university in Canada, and I was also working in developing a social skill-based program for kids with learning disabilities. This was a large program I coordinated, at probably 80 or so children. You have to look that this is now 1973, long time ago. Number one presenting concern was learning disabilities. We used that term to explain children that today would have ADHD, Tourette syndrome, highly functioning autism, Asperger's. So lots and lots of disorders that were involved in this project. Once I started to get to know my pet, Sasha, all I was going to do was bring Sasha in as my share of the program. I designed the social skill-based curriculum that we were using.

I never forgot a little boy. I tell this story so often that a little boy, who today would have been diagnosed for sure with ADHD. Highly, highly impulsive. He looked at me and said, "Can I hold her?" Now, you have to understand that Boris Levinson [1962, 1969] was doing this work in New York the decade before, yet still not very popularized in regards to mainstream knowing about this. So I had no idea what animal-assisted interventions were. What happened was, when I brought Sasha into share and the boy said, "Can I hold her?" I said, "Sure." I said, "But there's some rules. I'm going to put her in your hands and you have to promise that you're going to be gentle." So there was this boy and Sasha, in her own gentle way, first sniffed his palms, and he smiled. Then she gradually went on his tummy. He looked at me with the greatest smile on his face and he said, "I told you I won't move." That was one of the first times I noticed how in control of his behavior he was. Sasha ended up becoming the mascot of that program. She came often. Kids built habitats for her. They made posters for Sasha.

That was my indoctrination to a field that didn't have any identification to me. I had no idea what I was doing. It was only a little while later that I heard of a gentleman named Boris Levinson, who was doing something similar with a dog. Then, of course, I started hearing little bits of information. I began doing this without any training. But as a young student interested in becoming a psychologist and throughout my career, I've always tried to, one, think of how to interact with patients in ways that make my connection with them easier.

When I was young I learned magic. I'm actually an amateur magician, I guess. I did that, not because I wanted to be a magician, but more so that when you do magic tricks with children it really gets their interest. It took me a very quick amount of time to realize that the animals I brought into working with children weren't magic tricks. They deserve the integrity, the respect, the admiration of people like me to ensure their welfare and care. Even early on I began to get the message, as much as I care about the children that I work with, I really have to make sure that everybody is safe and having a quality experience.

That's how I began. And it's been an evolution of over 40 years now that I've used a variety of animals. Although I told you about the dog story, the reality is I primarily used small animals first: gerbils, bunny rabbits, guinea pigs. Then I went from that to actually using birds. I got trained by a pretty renowned person that knew bird behavior that helped me understand what kind of birds to get. I began using small birds, like lovebirds, that I hand fed. Cockatiels, conures, which I found extremely helpful. Dusky conures are not as noisy. Then, of course, I got into working with cockatoos. All of these animals before my first therapy dog, whose name was Puppy. That's sort of an interesting thing because if you're looking at organizations, like Pet Partners [n.d.] for example, of the 10,000 plus registered teams, almost 9,800 of them are teams that consist of a handler with a dog, not a handler with a bird or other species. I got into doing this a little bit differently, but again it's the connection, how you use that connection with the animals and get that connection with the clients.

Cynthia: You're a leading figure in this field. You've made a lot of contributions. You have a leading book, *Handbook on Animal-Assisted Therapy*. Most of us in the field are very familiar with your book. What would you say the value of animal-assisted interventions is?

Aubrey: We can define the term animal-assisted interventions as having different dimensions like animal-assisted therapy, animal-assisted activities, animal-assisted education, because this area has expanded. But to your question, "What is the contribution that animal-assisted interventions provides?" is a very large question. I think I can break it up in a variety of ways.

One, I see animal-assisted interventions as being a complementary therapy. It's used by a skilled clinician. I think to do this work, number one, you have to be credible in a lot of fronts. You need to be a good clinician and understand the etiologies and the pathologies that you're working with and know how best to help your clients become better. How you do that is an important process. Some people use cognitive approaches. I use a lot of cognitive behavior therapy in the work that I do, but I also use a variety of other ways, and since I primarily work with children I try really hard to make that engagement a valuable experience for them. That's where animals really fit.

Your question is how has animal-assisted interventions supported the work? I think that animals, of course, when you look at the pioneer work of the Corson's [Samuel Corson and Elizabeth O'Leary Corson (1975)], animals truly act as a social lubricant if they're really comforting in working with people. If they're comfortable in doing this, it gets the people to want to engage.

Knowing how to incorporate animals in therapy is probably the first step of getting to this equation of how it can be helpful, because in reality, what was initially found when the Corson's talked about a rippling effect, the fact that having animals in an environment changes that environment, it really does. In the work that I initially started with the little boy and so many other people since, having an animal that demonstrates a sense of comfort and warmth engages them to want to engage with me.

You need to know how to do this, though, because sometimes kids can hide behind what I would call a "body of fur," and then you can miss the information that you want to use or get to. I think of so many examples. I think of children I've worked with that are depressed. I think of a young girl that I worked with early on with one of my early therapy dogs, and she was selectively mute. When she came to visit me, she was a kindergartner, and basically she didn't talk in school. When she was in preschool, no one made a big deal of this because she talked fine at home. When visitors would come in to the home, they just said, "Well, my daughter's shy," but when she went to school, they realized that this is a problem. She's not talking to teachers, she's not talking to kids, so I was referred to this youngster.

Typically I don't meet children the first visit; I always talk with their parents first so the youngsters don't feel uncomfortable. That day, they brought her, and ironically, like most times, Puppy, that was the therapy dog at that time, would just walk down the hallway and greet you. Puppy started greeting this girl and she smiled and chuckled, and eventually I had Puppy come back about eight or 10 feet. I looked at the girl because you could see it in her eyes she wanted the dog back. I just said to her, "Honey, all you have to do is say, 'Puppy, come.'" Of course, the parents are looking at me and saying, "This isn't going to happen," but it did. It was the cold nose, warm heart of a golden retriever that may have caused that.

I told the parents we weren't going to have our meeting because I had already started something. They went into a different room and I sat on the floor. I'm not saying the girl talked a lot, but we interacted, and over a course of time we got her to talk with me and the dog. That wasn't enough, because did I change the behavior in school? No. We now needed to figure out what we could do to make that happen. I said to her, "Would you like Puppy to visit you and your teacher?" For the next several visits we practice, "Well, if Puppy comes, how are you going to introduce her? What are you going to do when we bring the lunch, and how are we going to make sure Puppy has a snack?" Then, of course, that was the first time the teacher heard that child's voice. We reengaged that situation again with children on a playground.

The comment that I'm giving to you is that, number one, people have always asked me, this is going back a long time ago, "Could you have probably got that child to talk without your dog?" And the answer probably is yes. I've worked with children with selective muteism, but on that given day, it was her engagement that acted as the catalyst.

How has animal-assisted interventions changed the way I worked with people, or how does animal-assisted interventions enhance a therapeutic environment? Well, it enhances therapeutic alliance, for sure. One can develop a much stronger relationship with an individual with an animal next to them that is comforting and is engaging. Beyond that, many people never really talked about, what are the wealth of other options that you could use therapeutically that incorporated animals in your work?

Over the last 30 years, I spent a lot of time thinking what I would say "thinking out of the box." Maybe I learned how to think more out of a box, not only for my training in school, but really as the training that I learned in magic, because magicians, in many ways, are always a step ahead and thinking about things that your eye isn't watching. Well, I've learned ways. I've done puppetry where my animals are part of the puppetry. You could talk about play therapy kinds of activities, journal writing. I have children write letters to dogs. I write as my dog to kids. There is also reading stories about animals, talking about animal welfare.

Sometimes it's even talking about similarities that the animals have to the clients that I'm working with, animals that are more vivacious versus animals that are more reserved. Over the years, I've worked with animals that have been abused. Puppy was actually a golden retriever that was abused in her previous life before I met her, and she had some teeth that were damaged. When she smiled at you, you would ask what happened. I had a bearded dragon early in my years that had a tail cut off. You knew something was there, and with children that have had abuse, there was this crossover in conversation. That's not to say that I'm going to look for animals that are abused only because that's how I use them therapeutically. It's looking at the alternatives that are there. I have parents that come in, and when they watch how I interact with the animals, they comment, "I wish I could parent my children like you interact with your animals. You don't seem to get angry with them, you're soft-spoken." These are perhaps skills that I want to show parents. The modeling of appropriate ways of teaching so that we can get across what we need to get across.

Cynthia: It seems a lot of what you're saying is that you value the relationship that can form between an animal and a human, whether that be for strengthening the clients' impressions of the therapist and therapy alliance, to motivate the child and to comfort the child or other client to feel safe to participate, and as a model for parents of children to see what a nurturing, appropriate relationship can look like. It's about strengthening the healing relationship and all the potentialities around that. Animals add to that, especially the ones that can socially engage.

Aubrey: Absolutely. Taking that just a step further, it's also looking at the therapeutic milieu, the environment that makes it richer. You look at the model of Green Chimneys [n.d.], for example, and what makes that environment so magnificent. It's a true living environment where relationships between humans and nonhuman animals are celebrated on a consistent basis. You look at the Bruno Bettelheim [1948, 1950] old work about environments. I think that the environment that I try to work in is a living testimony of my work. I don't really care as much about what the furniture looks like or the pictures; it of course looks nice, but what I'm trying to do is make an environment that's very conducive to connecting with clients, and facilitating their participation in and benefitting from therapy.

In my own clinical office, I have two fish tanks. At one time, I had a half vivarium, half fish tank built, so it was an under-over kind of scenario where we had fish on one part of this tank, and then I had a waterfall and we had small amphibians and little lizards. Parents would come in and tell me that this was the most relaxing part of their week, when they would visit, because it almost had like a brook sound. People pay to get that kind of sound in their homes. You look at the research, what science is helping us understand today after Erika Friedmann and Aaron Katcher's early study in the 80s [1980, 1983] with cardiovascular concerns, is what many people believe intuitively, at least now, that having animals in our lives is good for us.

That's the whole challenge as the field is growing, is a lot of people want much more evidence to explain that what we're saying, perhaps intuitively or qualitatively, can be held up with research and quantitatively. Sometimes, that's harder to do, but I think your comment about the tremendous strength that an animal can bring to the equation of alliance and relationship cannot be misjudged. I think that people really see the tremendous value and strength in that. In so many ways, that's why we're looking at a trained working relationship because I always consider my therapy dogs working with me, almost like Fred Astaire and Ginger Rogers, we learn to dance well.

Cynthia: It's very important for the therapist to know the animal that they're working with. To honor and to respect it, make sure its needs are met, and to understand how to interpret those social engagements that the therapy animal has with the client. That's part of the dance that you were describing.

Aubrey: Right. A lot of people ask, "Why do I believe dogs really can do this very well?" I'm not saying any other species cannot. But when you look at the domestication of dogs, for example, some people believe that it's much longer than 10,000 years but traditionally, people said about 10,000 or 12,000 years. When you're looking at dogs early on in time, when we started to interact with wilder animals like wolves that eventually evolved into what we call domesticated dogs today, these beings that were more able to join our little circle, for protecting, they were more capable of understanding what we wanted in that relationship, they joined our circle. The evolution of dogs has really followed that process. Dogs that read what humans are thinking nonverbally are dogs that seem to be more accepted. Over the last 50, 80 years for sure, you look at dogs or our companion animals in general, going from backyards into our homes, once considered property versus now, many of us consider them our family members.

When I talk about the dance, I've learned to appreciate, one, that therapy dogs need to be well trained in regards to the basic obedience concerns and what they're supposed to be doing in the workplace. On the other hand, there's a portion that I recognize that dogs, number one, seemingly read nonverbal behavior extremely well. That's why intuitively sometimes when they see somebody having some issues, they do things that I can't do. If a client is crying and is feeling a certain emotion, I can't jump over and hug that person. I may offer comfort with words, with a tissue, but my dogs will do that. They will immediately make themselves very close to you. Once you start petting them, they may put their head in your lap. That in essence is that reading of the nonverbal behavior and I think, and I'm going to be a bit biased to say that I think, that I've noticed that dogs do this extremely, extremely well. That's not to say that some of my birds in the early years, when they were involved, didn't do this too. But the dogs, it's much more natural for them.

I think when you're looking at the work of a therapy animal in general, what's changed over the last so many years is that, one, there are people that are really conscious of that side of the equation. As the field grows – and it's an honor to talk with you because you touch many and work with so many other people that will become professionals that will do this work – there needs to be a very clear articulation that it's not all about the humans. That if we can't do this right and protect the quality of life of an animal, recognize when an animal is getting stressed, recognizing the humane way of integrating them to begin with, making sure they get breaks, making sure they get proper nutrition, then we're doing this wrong. That's what scares me.

We've been at a crossroad in this field for a long time. When people say, "Oh, you do animal-assisted interventions? That's a new thing." Well, I told you, I've been doing this for over 40 years. Levinson was doing this in the early 60s. So the trail goes back way, many years.

Have we really gotten to the promised land if we talk about complementary forms of therapy? What's happening is obviously we're seeing many more people interested in this. We're seeing a variety of folks with different disciplines interacting with animals in a therapy way. From a terminology standpoint, I use the term "animal-assisted interventions" because there are professionals who are using this as part of their therapeutic strategies but there are a whole group of people worldwide that are engaging in what we call today "animal-assisted activities." That's not diminishing what they're doing; it's just making sure that it's clear that they're working with people that could benefit from interactions with animals on a nonprofessional, volunteer basis. Animal-assisted activities is a different kind of relationship. Does that mean it's any weaker? Absolutely not. I don't want that to be inferred, but it's different. I've heard wonderful, wonderful, wonderful stories. I could give you one. Many years ago, I have many wonderful stories from talking to thousands of people. But one story that I could just say really quickly was a man in a nursing home. He had a stroke, and he was visited by a woman that had a Husky. When she and the Husky went to visit, to provide animal-assisted activity, the nursing staff told her, "He's really quiet. It can't hurt; go in to visit." When the dog came in with the woman on the first visit with him, the man kind of sat up a little bit. He smiled, didn't talk much. But you could see there was that connection. They kept on doing this a few more times, each time seeing him be much more attentive. Then finally the woman told me in one of her visits, he looked at her and in a very broken English because, one, he was Russian and, two, he was recovering from a stroke, he looked at her and said, "In my country I was a veterinarian. He gives me hope to leave here, the dog."

Animal-assisted activities are a different spectrum, but valuable. I wanted to make sure that was clear. There are a whole bunch of people doing something called animal-assisted education, where they incorporate animals in schools, your main educators, teaching quality issues like caring, empathy, sharing this environment with other species of animals, another different spectrum.

But what concerns me with the professional therapy movement is, one, there are many, many people dabbling in doing this that just think you can bring any dog in or other animals and do this effectively. I'm not sure I agree with that. I feel that if you don't understand how to work in unison with another species of animal, then you're going to have difficulties. The other side to this is that it's not a magic trick. You have to know how your animal is feeling in relating to that work environment. Because the stress they can have may not be appropriate for them. These are things that we need to look at from the clinical side with the growth of animal-assisted interventions, where professionals are beginning to look at this. Who's doing the training? Where are they getting the training from? Is there a level of training that we believe you have to have at least at an entry level to do this? Because right now, that isn't clear.

It's much different than it was when I started doing this 40-something years ago when there wasn't even legitimate books. None of this stuff was there, except for the Levinson piece, which was a legitimate book; I want to make sure to say that. When I say legitimate, there wasn't anything else written on this. Also, what training do you have with animals? I know what I know well, but I go to dog training classes. I learn about reptiles. I learn about birds by going to places that help me understand that better. We need to be able to recognize what we're doing well and how to enhance that kind of training. It's about quality control.

The whole other arena that we could talk about, as I see this field growing is, we know that it works qualitatively, but can we show with evidence that it's more scientific? Now, we're bringing along better research protocols, and I really like that it is helping people answer questions with research that clinicians are really trying to do in their work, research that is translating practice into scientific understanding.

Cynthia: Very well said. Now, I would like for you to take this moment, introspect and share anything that you think hasn't been said and also a special message to those who are training to be practitioners of animal-assisted interventions, either as a nonprofessional volunteer for using animal-assisted activity or a professional performing animal-assisted therapy, to help them understand what they need to about performing their tasks with their animals.

Aubrey: It's one that I could answer in a variety of ways. I'll answer it first with probably the least professional answer, but probably the most meaningful to me. I had mentioned when I was younger I never had animals in my life. Looking back at that experience, I recognized how significant of a void in my life that was, that I didn't celebrate childhood amongst the creatures that inhabit our world. I went all the way to Africa when I wrote one book to try to figure out why I had this kinship. I went to Africa and I saw elephants. I saw cheetahs. I saw lions. My favorite animals are dik-dik, these small little gazelles that just surrounded me. They were just adorable. The more I stayed in Africa, the more I was lonesome for being at home. In so many ways, I was like Dorothy in the Land of Oz. I just had to realize that I didn't have to go to Africa to figure it out. I just followed the yellow brick road home, and it brought me to the place that was meant.

It's an interesting question that I'm asked often. Could I do this work alongside any animal and have the same effect? I really believe that even to do this work as a therapist, let alone doing it with your clients, you have to have a relationship with the animal that you work with. Why I say what I'm saying now in retrospect, it's the relationships that I built with animals over the 40-plus years that I've been doing this that have enriched me as a person. I look back and people say, "Who are your mentors?" My professors of older years would hope that I would say their names. They were my mentors. My family was my mentor. But some of my greatest mentors that taught me patience, taught me diligence, taught me persistence and tenacity have been some of the animals that I've lived along side.

My wife had breast cancer. It was one of our golden retrievers that trained me to walk, to be able to walk 60 miles. So she didn't do the whole 60 with me, but when we trained 12, 14 miles. She was the one that barked away to make me enthusiastically complete. That's the first part. I want people to recognize that as valued as it is with my first commentary is that this is about professionally incorporating animals to make your interventions more effective. This is not fun and games. It's not that I'm bringing my dog in; I'm sitting and talking to my dog while I do this work or my bird or whoever you're bringing along. It's recognizing the wealth of contribution that an animal can help you to perform better what you need to do with others, but that really means competency. That's why I alluded early on that training, forthright preparation, bridging your own academic preparation on how do you integrate animals therapeutically is something that just doesn't happen with hocus pocus. Some people have tongue and cheek literally when they say "Is it the lick of the dog that makes people all well?" I don't want to undermine that comment because it is the work that establishes the relationship, but it's knowing how to use that to get to the next level.

What I hope that we recognize as the field grows, we need to bring along the research part to this for the field to be much more crystallized in regards to acceptance because it's easy for us to talk amongst each other, people that believe in this cause, if I can use the word. To change public policy, to change public awareness, to change new landscapes that will allow us to incorporate animals in those environments, we need to show people that this does work. That not only is it credible, but it's safe for all.

The thing that concerns me more today than ever before is a proliferation of people that are doing this that may not have the insights that we're talking about at either a professional level or at a lay level. Therefore they're doing things that are really not good for people. They're not good for animals. They're not safe for putting lots of animals and people in situations that may not be good for them.

It's exciting to recognize that in so many ways animals can contribute to our well-being. If I can give one more thought, I think of a girl that many years ago, and I won't tell you her whole story, but I met her because she was chronically depressed and she was anxious. Like many of us when we do work with people, sometimes our story ends because we don't know how they'll do 10, 15 years from now because we get them to a certain point and they're well. They're doing better. Then we stop. I have kids that come visit me now as adults, and they always tell me how much they enjoyed the animals. I think of one young lady. She came back to visit because she read about a book that I was writing. When she came back in, it was about five or six years after I had seen her. She had totally changed now. She's doing really well. Did she really come back to visit me? I always say that because I said to her, "Do you want to see her again?"

Her eyes opened up, and now she's almost ready to go to college. She said, "Is she still here? Is she still alive?" I said, "She's not only here. She's the only therapy dog that's here today." I opened up the back door and out came a black Labrador. Her name was Heart. She did that doggy samba with the tail going all over the place. It was the third time that I saw this girl break down into tears. She embraced that dog. She said to me, "It's hard to believe that it was a dog that got me to talk." What I want everyone to recognize is the power of doing this is really not only related to the relationship that's established, but it's knowing how to do this well.

Cynthia: That puts a lot of responsibility on people like us, for those who are following in our footsteps, is to find a way to describe our work succinctly in a way other people can understand what it is that we're doing. The fact that we value the relationship with our own animal. We care for and nurture that animal. The animal trusts us. Then we have the animal engage with our clients. Then there's an engagement between the animal and the client, which is very, very powerful. Then the therapist must know how to utilize that opportunity to help the client progress. That's something that we have to continue to examine, to measure, to define, to describe and teach others how to identify, how to recognize and utilize therapeutic opportunity.

Aubrey: Right. Then you go the other step further in how do we get more of these training options out there because there really aren't many?

Cynthia: Very few.

Aubrey: Although the field is blossoming, we don't have much training guidelines out there, which is of concern. Then the other side to this is the recognition of how do we know what minimal expectations of a clinician doing this work should be?

I don't really always like having big brother or sister look over us, over our shoulder, and saying, "You need to have this level to do this work." On the other hand, I am concerned that we do need people out there that can do this well with the training that they need. We need ambassadors. We need ambassadors to get people to understand, but we also need ambassadors for people that will help them train and supervise so that they can learn how to do this both professionally and voluntarily.

Cynthia: Training and follow-up supervision is vital as they begin to practice.

It's been lovely visiting with you today. It's been an honor, a pleasure. It's been very nice having this time with you. It's been very special. I'd like for you to have the last word. What else would you like to share as your final words for our interview today?

Aubrey: It's an interesting question. Periodically, in the classes I teach I always think of the book called *The Last Lecture.* Also, Carnegie Mellon, supposedly, has an opportunity for professors when they're giving their last lecture when they're retiring; what would they say? Having the last word's an interesting point. Being around the block a couple of times with this area, if I had the last word of what I wanted to say is, we keep on growing. I don't see this field any further than its early adolescence, although it's been here a long time. I want us to grow. I want us to grow to develop a stronger form of efficacy that's explainable both qualitatively and quantitatively. But at the end of the day, I also want to put this in an honest perspective; it's about helping. It's about helping other humans heal and have richer lives. It's an opportunity to help them heal with the richness of "four-leggers," or whichever animals you choose, that really can enable you to be a better practitioner. It's also about preserving integrity, respect, for all parties that are involved.

The last word would really be so much different than when I began my work with my little friend Sasha because when I brought Sasha to the group, again, she was my favorite first companion animal, but I didn't understand what I was doing.

What was a wonderful beginning for my insights may have not worked. The boy may not have related well, or something could have happened. I lead with the commentary that we must, to do this well, look at both sides of the equation. The other end of the leash, the other end of whatever we're working alongside with, the integrity, the respect has to be there. If we're not willing to do that, then I don't know if we really should be doing this at all.

Cynthia: Thank you so much for your time.

Aubrey: Oh, it was wonderful. Thank you, it was great fun.

Editors' Commentary for Chapter 1

A striking aspect of this interview that is difficult to capture through text alone was the warmth with which Dr. Fine spoke about the animals with whom he worked. The glimmer in Dr. Fine's eye was obvious as he described his relationships with Sasha the gerbil, Puppy the dog, and other therapeutic animal helpers. His words and affect remind us that, at its core, animal-assisted work is about relationships. In particular, relationships between clinicians and the animals, relationships between clients and the animals, and most remarkably the integrated relationship between clinician, client, and therapy animals. Moreover, in animal-assisted therapy a clinician has many opportunities to model nurturing, kind, and compassionate relationships for clients and their families through the clinician's relationship with the therapy animal.

Dr. Fine's acknowledgment of "the other end of the leash" could be easily correlated to empathy for "the other." We believe that this is the first place to start for someone who is curious about or is planning to integrate animals into one's therapeutic practice. Think first, not about the positive impact for clients, but about any potentially harmful impacts for the therapy animals. If one could see through this lens of "the other," one might be more likely to see the grave importance of human training when integrating animal-assisted interventions. As clinicians, we hold the most power in this triad of clinician–client–therapy animal. Therefore, we are tasked with the responsibility to maintain the emotional and physical safety of our more vulnerable counterparts, the client and therapy animal. We echo Dr. Fine's admonishment to "protect the quality of life of an animal, recognize when an animal is getting stressed . . . making sure they get breaks, making sure they get proper nutrition." To that end, we encourage those who are considering integrating animal-assisted interventions to receive proper training in risk management and animal advocacy. We recommend that people receive introductory training from organizations such as Pet Partners (n.d.), receive advanced training and supervision from one or more professional experts, and adhere to guidelines for human and animal well-being, such as the IAHAIO White Paper 2014 (IAHAIO, 2014) and the American Counseling Association's Animal-Assisted Therapy in Counseling Competencies (Stewart, Chang, Parker, & Grubbs, 2016).

Dr. Fine spoke of the complexity of animal-assisted interventions and the need for training, supervision, research, and oversight in the field. To this point, we highly recommend that current and future practitioners of animal-assisted interventions obtain advanced training and continuing education from established experts of animal-assisted interventions.

References

Bettelheim, B. (1950). *Love is not enough: The treatment of emotionally disturbed children*. Glencoe, IL: Free Press.

Bettelheim, B., & Sylvester, E. (1948). Therapeutic milieu. *American Journal of Orthopsychiatry, 18*(2), 191–2016. doi:10.1111/j.1939-0025.1948.tb05078.x

Corson, S., Corson, E., Gwynne, P., & Arnold, L. (1975). Pet-facilitated psychotherapy in a hospital setting. *Current Psychiatric Therapies, 15*, 277–286.

Fine, A. (Ed.). (2015). *Handbook on animal-assisted therapy: Theoretical foundations and guidelines for practice* (4th ed). San Diego, CA: Academic Press.

Friedmann, E., Katcher, A., Lynch, J., & Thomas, S. (1980). Animal companions and one-year survival of patients after discharge from a coronary unit. *Public Health Reports, 95*, 307–312.

Friedmann, E., Katcher, A., Thomas, S., Lynch, J., & Messent, P. (1983). Social interaction and blood pressure: Influence of animal companions. *Journal of Nervous and Mental Disease, 171*, 461–465.

Green Chimneys. (n.d.) Home page. Retrieved October 5, 2017, from www.greenchimneys.org/

International Association of Human-Animal Interaction Organizations (IAHAIO, 2014). *IAHAIO white paper 2014: The IAHAIO definitions for animal assisted intervention and guidelines for wellness of animals involved*. Retrieved October 6, 2017, from http://iahaio.org/best-practice/white-paper-on-animal-assisted-interventions/

Levinson, B. (1962). The dog as a "co-therapist." *Mental Hygiene, 46*, 59–65.

Levinson, B. (1969). *Pet-oriented child psychotherapy*. Springfield, IL: Charles C. Thomas.

Pet Partners. (n.d.). Home page. Retrieved October 5, 2017, from http://www.petpartners.org

Stewart, L. A., Chang, C. Y., Parker, L. K., & Grubbs, N. (2016, June 21). Animal assisted therapy in counseling competencies. *ACAeNews*. Alexandria, VA: American Counseling Association. Retrieved October 1, 2017, from www.counseling.org/docs/default-source/competencies/animal-assisted-therapy-competencies-june-2016.pdf?sfvrsn=c469472c_14

Figure 1.1   Dr. Aubrey Fine is the editor and contributing author of the landmark book *Handbook on Animal-Assisted Therapy: Theoretical Foundations and Guidelines for Practice*. Photo copyright of Aubrey Fine (used with permission); photographer Tom Zasadzinski.

2 Dr. Samuel Ross, Jr. and Myra Ross, also Michael Kaufmann of Green Chimneys

Green Chimneys was founded by Dr. Samuel Ross, Jr., and his family. Sam and his wife, Myra Ross, pioneered the idea of a residential therapy farm for animal-assisted interventions for emotional and mental health. Green Chimneys is a place where farm animals have sanctuary and provide companionship for children who are emotionally disturbed and learning disabled. Children's interaction with farm animals and highly qualified teachers and staff assist to motivate children's participation in therapy and facilitate children's emotional recovery and mental development.

The program began on October 27, 1947, when the Ross family purchased a 75-acre dairy farm in Putnam County, New York, to house a private boarding and day school and summer camp where children could interact with farm animals. "An emphasis was placed on the integration of the children with farm animals, nature and the environment" (Green Chimneys, n.d.). Over the following decades, Green Chimneys continued to grow and offer a variety of services to a diverse population. In 1974, the school expanded to become a residential treatment center for children with emotional and behavioral issues. Green Chimneys now includes a 50-acre Hillside Outdoor Education Center, located less than a mile from the main campus in Brewster, New York. The Green Chimneys farm expanded to include a wildlife conservation and rehabilitation program that houses a large collection of permanently disabled birds of prey and assorted wildlife. In 2000, Green Chimneys opened a new multimillion-dollar education facility for day school with state-of-the-art classrooms for both residential and day students. The Brewster campus has several structures, including classrooms, gymnasium, playground, learning center, dining hall, residence halls, greenhouse, wildlife center with several aviaries, dog kennel, barns with indoor and outdoor pens, horse stables, small and large corrals, and large fenced pastures. There are also small and large herb and vegetable gardens. In residence, there are dogs, camels, llamas, sheep, goats, chickens, rabbits, pigs, cows, horses, donkeys, and a peacock. Today, Green Chimneys serves a multistate area and continues to expand (Green Chimneys, n.d.). Green Chimneys is an internationally recognized program that also provides internships for a few lucky students from around the world who want to benefit firsthand from the vast training opportunities offered by this wonderful program.

We were able to visit Green Chimneys one weekend when they sponsored a conference on human–animal interaction. We found Green Chimneys to be an incredible place with dedicated staff assisting many children. The various types of animals there receive great care from paid and volunteer staff. We were fortunate to attend one of the more meaningful activities of Green Chimneys, releasing a rehabilitated hawk back into the wild. Before leaving, I had the honor and pleasure of interviewing founder, Dr. Samuel Ross, Jr., and his wife, Myra Ross (see Figure 2.1). Dr. Ross authored the book *The Extraordinary Spirit of Green Chimneys: Connecting Children and Animals to Create Hope* (2011). While at Green Chimneys, we were fortunate to also have an interview with Michael Kaufmann, who is the director of Green Chimneys services. The interview I conducted with Dr. Ross and Myra Ross took place April 24, 2015, in Dr. Ross's office on the Brewster, New York, campus of Green Chimneys.

Interview with Dr. Samuel Ross, Jr., and Myra Ross

Cynthia: Thank you for joining us today. Why did you start Green Chimneys, what is your philosophy, and what do you accomplish here?

Sam: Well, in 1947, I was on my way to the University of Montreal, and we stopped off at a school for very young children. My grandfather and my father were in the car and I was there and I said, "I want to open a school for very young children," and my father said to me, "What do you know about running a school?" I said, "Dad, I've been to school all my life and I think I know how to run a school and I don't like what I saw here today." So he said, "Well, when you get back from Montreal we'll talk about it." And when he picked me up in Montreal and we headed home, he said to me, "What are you going to do next week while you're home?" I said, "I thought we're going to go look at property." And he said, "What property?" I said, "The property we're going to buy to open a school." So he said, "Okay, here's the deal. You can see three pieces of property, and if one of those really interests you and you think it's the proper place, we'll consider it. But if not, you go back to school, graduate, and that's it."

So I got a realtor from Mahopac, which is in this county, and he took me around. We saw three places, and at the third place I said, "Boy, this is it," and it was Green Chimneys. My father paid $38,500 and we bought the school, this farm. The idea was to surround young children with animals so that they would have something that would love them and they would be able to love. Because I felt that separating young children, having them live away from home, they needed to feel that they weren't being given up, that they were away but they were still in contact with family and they had good people taking care of them.

Myra: What you didn't mention is that you spent many years in different schools as a young child, and you always had a dog with you. I was afraid of animals. I was afraid of dogs. I was almost bitten by a great big dog when I was a little girl, and that was a traumatic incident, really a traumatic event. Anywhere I saw a dog, if I was walking down the street, I would keep crisscrossing in order to avoid it, until an old woman sort of desensitized me and I realized that dogs, and not just dogs but having animals, are very helpful to young children.

We never thought about the therapeutic impact of dogs. We did know that having animals was comforting to the children. It wasn't called animal-assisted therapy that way back. That was not in our heads. But as we began to work with more challenged children, we found out that sometimes the standard therapies just don't work. They just don't really do what is needed to open them up. Even in the admissions department when we would be interviewing children to come to either our day program or residential, and the child would be very nervous and scared, and one of us, one of the interviewers would say, "Would you like to come up and see the horse?" We'd take the one child, we'd go up, see the horse, pet the horse's nice velvety nose, go back to the office, and then the child would be ready to talk. There's a magic there that exists that is wonderful for kids. It's also great for staff. The other important thing in this animal-assisted therapy is, it isn't just the animals. It is the people who are up there taking care of the animals. It's the relationship of children and staff and animals that can work almost magic with some very difficult-to-reach children.

Cynthia: We had the pleasure of taking a tour of your facility, and we saw a variety of animals. What do you think the importance is of having a variety of plants, the gardens, different types of animals, the wildlife center, the horse barn?

Myra: I think the value of that is that for every child there is something. You know, we used to say, "If we can't figure out something that will help the child move from where he or she is when he comes, then we're not doing our job." For some children, it isn't the horses, but it could be the garden, it could be the big organic garden down the road, but we have to find something for every child. And with a variety of opportunities, it usually happens.

Cynthia: You were speaking earlier about a young man who exemplified the kind of individuals that you serve here. Very gifted, has some difficulties, autism, and yet you saw his brilliance. He wrote you a letter and he talked about how at other schools, he was just weird. He came here, and he was no longer weird anymore. He felt like he belonged. It was a place he could thrive. Tell me more about that story and other similar stories.

Sam: We have a great interest in this young child because he is extremely bright, and he's blossomed here. What makes the difference is, here he felt from the very beginning, that he was being accepted. He was really stunned by being bullied elsewhere, and he felt that the other children were picking on him. Here, he feels comfortable and belongs. He's always trying to do something nice. That really makes the staff feel good. Here, he's very bright and doesn't bother anybody else. That makes a big difference.

One of the things that he has been doing of late is that he was not acting well with his parents, and I said to him, "Listen, if you're going to act up with your parents, it's going to be difficult for us to really think that you're such a wonderful person." I said to him, "Can we make a little pact? I'll do a pinky thing with you, but I want to hear good reports about you." And he's turned around. He listens. He feels that he's accepted here. I think it's the acceptance that makes a big difference in his life. In other words, we've reached him, and he's reached out to us and is accepted.

Myra: You know, we have children who are really very different. It doesn't matter because everyone here has an issue and they all know it. If somebody is picking on someone else, one of the staff is going to say, "I don't think that's a good idea because it's going to come back at you." They have to learn that there are differences and that's what the world is like. There are differences in humanity's ability to accept people for what they are and not look at the differences. Some of the children look a little stigmatized, and it's okay. We run the gamut of every psychiatric diagnosis known to God and man. We really do. We have them all. But what we want to do is go beyond the diagnosis, not get married to it, and see what are the child's strengths and what are the child's disabilities. People want to know, what are the various psychiatric diagnoses these children have? We're not hung up on the diagnosis. What we're looking for is, what is the child all about? What are the child's strengths? What are the child's areas of weakness and what can we do to help move that child along so the diagnosis can change. A lot of children come in with rule-outs. Rule out this diagnosis, rule out that. Some children come in without any diagnosis. As far as we're concerned, they all have issues that need to be addressed. That's our job. To address the issues and help them move along and get back into a more normal schooling and educational situation.

We have children who come on many psychotropic medications. There's always a lot of controversy about medications. Our goal is to reduce them. If they're coming out of hospitals, they are on multiple medications. We don't change anything the minute they come in, but as they're in here there are psychiatrists looking at them. We want to reduce medication because, you know, every medication has an outcome. Some very positive, and sometimes not so good. It's just constantly changing what we're doing so that we can really get the best out of each child.

Our goal is to get them out of here. They come in and our focus is, what's the discharge plan? Whether it's a day student or resident, what is the plan for discharge? Are the families ready for the children to come back? Some families are not ready and need help. Our job, the social workers are the primary ones, is to work with the families and give them some skills in how to deal with certain behaviors that make it difficult to have the children at home.

Sam: One of the things that we have now that we didn't have for many years was the ability to take a child into the residential program, do some repair work, and send the child back home. Then, the child could commute during the day and come to school so that we really had the opportunity to work with the child over a longer period of time, but not keep him out of the family. We're also spending a great deal of time lately working with the parents because you can't work with the child and not work with the family, and help them to understand the child and make room for the child in the family.

Cynthia: What are some of the things that the animals help you teach the children that are so important in life?

Myra: One thing is that many of our children have had significant losses in their lives and really have never been able to grieve. Living on a farm, you know the cycle of life; animals get sick, sometimes animals die. In the horse stable, every horse has its own place and if it's the death of a horse, the children will go into there, put pictures of the horse, write notes to the animal, put flowers there and go up there with their social workers and learn to say good-bye. It's a life lesson. They see that the life goes on. They see good parenting by some of the animals, you know, when babies are born, and they're there and they see it. It takes a little of the mystery out of that. They're learning a lot just by observing what's going on there.

Sam: A couple of years ago we had a teacher die during the night, and it was very sudden. When the children heard about it the next morning, on their own they went to the classroom where he was the teacher, and they decorated that classroom in the same way they had learned to decorate for a horse. It's very interesting. You get to feel that the children are listening. We thought that we would never take high school students because we thought they would be beyond what we have to offer, but we found a little mix the last two years, and the high school students really want to do what they have to do and they get a lot by being here.

Cynthia: The children participate in helping to provide care for the animals, right?

Sam: Absolutely. They have chores. One of the things we talk about is agricultural science when they go to the farm, or farm science, so that they understand that the animals have to be fed before they have breakfast in the morning; then they go and do that. We have a kennel with rescued dogs. The idea is to find them forever homes. The children know that they have responsibility for those dogs.

It was very interesting. Three children were talking to me about their vacation. One said he'd been to Disney World and how it was. The other one said he'd been sent to some other kind of park. The third one said to me, "I stayed here. I didn't get a chance to go home, but I got a chance to take care of the dogs because there weren't many people here to do that." It does have an importance to the job. The animals are accepting. Yes, they have to be careful because there's certain animals that don't have good manners and don't know what their behavior should be, but the children understand this. It works out very well.

Myra: They also understand that if you're kind to the animal, the animal will be kind to you. If you're kind to another peer, the peer will be kind to you. There are lots of lessons. It's really nice early in the morning when I go up to the dining room to see what's going on with the kids, that you see some children coming in later and sitting with the farm staff. What happens in the morning early, because the chores are done early in the morning, is one of the farm interns will go up to the dining room, pick up the child, they would go do the chores, then the child would come back and sit and have a little later breakfast and just hang out with the staff for a while. All of that is just good stuff and makes the kids feel like they have a purpose.

Cynthia: So the kids are learning lessons about life; they're learning a lot of lessons about relationship. From your many years here in this beautiful program that you've created, what is your perspective around why they can finally learn some lessons about how to relate to people by learning to relate to the animals first. How does that work?

Sam: Well, you know, we try to get the child to work with a particular animal and then find another child that's interested in that particular animal, so now they're working on something that they're sharing the opportunity. Then the animal can be pulled backwards a little bit and the two can form a relationship. It's also something that they can remember for long periods of time. Children come back here after many years, and they want to run up to the barn. They've been gone for 14 years, and they want to see the goat that they used to take care of. Well, the goat isn't there anymore, but they understand what happened. It's like a geriatric ward because we don't butcher anything on the grounds. So the children see some of the goats and things they may have known, but maybe not a particular one.

The other thing that happens here is that it gives the children an opportunity to show off because as they participate in 4-H [a youth development organization (4-H, n.d.)], or as they participate in the sale of vegetables or something, they get a sense of belonging, a sense of caring, a case of sharing. Before they were feeling, based on what people would say, "You're no good, you're not going to amount to anything."

Cynthia: I suspect that as they start to build some confidence and feel safe here and accepted here, that allows them to take risks to explore the difficult issues in their life and allows them to take that risk that helps to facilitate a healing that was before sort of stuck.

Myra: We have social workers who have a dog in the office with them. It helps the child relax and talk. Our job is not to cure. We never say we cure the children. You know, some parents say, "Here's my child; fix them up and then send them back when he's ready." And we say, "We don't cure your children; we only intervene where they're on a downhill trend, and we give them skills and we work with them so they're ready to go back into the greater society." That's the goal for us, to get them in here and out of here. They're not here forever. They're not our children, and they're not here forever. Some will be here for many years, and others will be out of here in two years and will have done well and are ready to move back. There's no easy answer. It's all very individualized. It's individualized for the children as well as with the families.

Sam: One of the things that I tell staff, they say, "Wow, this child is so troubled. This child is so difficult." And then I say, "Well, wait until you see the next one," because people are not going to send us children that have no problems. School systems are not going to be able to send children here that are academically perfect or whose behavior is wonderful and attitude is wonderful. They're going to send us a difficult child that isn't making it in the present setting. There's two misplaced, conflicting pressures involved with children who come here. One is the parents saying, "Let's repair everything and get him back home." And, two, the school system that says, "We couldn't do anything with him. Don't push him out faster than he has to go."

Cynthia: In taking the tour today, we saw such a variety of animals. I can imagine it would be difficult for a child not to be curious enough to want to try and interact with some of the animals, from horses to pigs to camels to llamas.

Myra: And chickens. Did you ever see a child walking around petting a chicken or a duck? It's unbelievable. I mean, they learn real empathy. We had a sick frog. I don't know how you know a frog is sick, but this is a classic here. The sick frog went with a staff member up at the farm, and they went to the vet and he gave the sick frog . . . I don't know what he did, but the frog got better. Even a frog is important, and the life of a living thing is important.

Sam: Our head of the wildlife program has been here 27 years. He started the idea that when the birds recover, those that recover, that they could be released. We started then when the children were going home, and was a permanent move, that the bird would be released and they would do it. Children look forward to that. They look forward to the Birds of Prey Day because, first of all, it brings thousands of people onto the campus, but not only that, they get to show off the animals. They get to show off at the 4-H fair.

          Something recently happened that really got everybody thinking. A bird fell out of the tree in a town about 14 miles from here. Of course, the bird was brought down here to recuperate, and then the bird did recuperate. So the idea was it was close enough, why not take that bird back to the same place and let the bird have the release there? So the children went there, and they released the bird; the bird flew up in the tree, you could count to 10, and another bird came and sat down next to that bird, and then the two birds flew off together. And the children got the message that the bird recovered and the mate was waiting for the bird and now they're reunited. It's almost like for them that, "After I'm better, I'll be reunited with my family." There's so many things that we can teach the children by pointing out what life is like.

Cynthia: Learning about the cycle of life. And it's in a form that's easy to understand because the animals have a richness about them that's simpler. There's not a lot of emotional baggage like we have mixed up in families. It's very simple, it's very immediate, and it's very honest. When something is simple, immediate, and honest, it's easier to learn from that by example. That's what you provide here, a lot of honesty and opportunity to learn and grow.

Sam: That's a very cute thing you've said because a lot of our children, as Myra said before, are on medicine. They wonder why they're taking it. When the vet comes to take care of the animal, they get the message, we have to give this to this animal because we want the animal to recover and they become more accepting to why they should take their medicine.

Myra: A lot of the children come in with all kinds of "I don't like this" and "I don't eat that" and "I don't eat vegetables. "I don't eat, I don't like." If they're growing it in the garden, it's amazing to see them once they're harvesting stuff and eating the fresh raw vegetables down in the big garden when they're harvesting the corn, they're eating the raw corn. They're learning to change their palates so they become very much less fussy about what they will or will not eat or what they say "I'm allergic to." Which of course they're not always allergic; they just don't like it. They're learning a lot of stuff that, you know, it's not in the treatment plan that this child will learn to eat vegetables, but it happens.

Cynthia: It's the natural environment that's so healing. I hear you say that if they're working with the plants that they eat, they're working with the horses and cows and chickens and camels that they can form a relationship with, that's natural. Human beings are natural. I think if we get too far removed from that we stop being natural, and we don't know where we're going and we get confused and we have difficulties. But if you bring this back to nature, that facilitates the healing because we are natural too; we're animals too, and we need to be around plants and we need to be around animals and that helps the healing process.

Sam: Once in a while we get an animal here that has been terribly abused, and many of the children can relate to that. We had horses that we couldn't ride because they were so badly abused that you couldn't even put shoes on them anymore because their feet were all cracked and damaged. They also see now that we're rescuing dogs from a shelter and that, if you train them and prepare them, they'll make their way to some home and they'll live in that home forever. We don't call it adopting the dog; I want to have them know that they're going to a home forever. It's just a play on words, but it has a meaning that the dog is going home. You've done a great job of training that dog, and now the dog is going to be accepted in a home and he or she is going to be there forever.

Cynthia: I'd like for you to say anything else that's on your mind about helping people understand the healing and learning environment that you have here at Green Chimneys. Is there anything that we haven't covered that you'd like to say?

Sam: Yes, I think there's one more thing that you haven't covered that's very important. We are a not-for-profit, large operation on a lot of acres in Putnam County, New York. A lot of people will tell you that in certain communities people say, "Not in my backyard." We've worked very hard to overcome that kind of an attitude. The best way that we've done it is that on Saturdays and Sundays between 10 in the morning and three o'clock in the afternoon, people can come with their baby carriages, park in the parking lot, which is not completely empty but has more spaces than it does during the workweek, and come in here and attend any kind of an event or just come to walk and visit with the animals. I have to tell you that it's not something that we regret doing because it has given us recognition in our community, and financially, it's a very smart move because when we have our summer camp, people are not afraid to place their children in our summer camp.

Now, with day students, it's the same thing. The day students need it, and they understand why they're here. We have a nursery school. It runs 12 months a year. People know we hire in the local community, we care for children in the local community, and we have community services for the people that are here so that they too can benefit from our presence. And I guess one of the most important things, the hiring. We have a lot of staff that live in this community.

Cynthia: Myra, is there anything else that you'd like to share?

Myra: I think we covered about everything. I think a lot of it, you know, we talk about, "What's the magic?" The magic is in the relationships. The relationships between children and staff, between children and animals and all of it, and I think that's what makes it work. If there's not relationship, there's no change.

Cynthia: Green Chimneys focuses on relationship, and that becomes a very healing relationship. A mechanism for healing and learning and growing.

Myra: It's not 100 percent. Nothing is. You know our staff come here, but they're not coming here for the big bucks because the pay that we can give is nothing comparable to what they can get in the local schools. There's something about being here that attracts them and keeps them here.

Cynthia: There is now an institute at Green Chimneys founded in your name, right?

Sam: The board founded the institute, and they honored us by naming the institute for us. Myra and I are married 60 years, so we've been here 60 years together. They honored us with that institute. If I had a chance, I would have called it the Myra and Sam Ross Institute. But the board called it the Sam and Myra Ross Institute.

Myra: Which I approved.

Cynthia: You have the internship program, which is supported by the institute. Tell us a little bit about why you think it's important to have that internship program supported by the Sam and Myra Ross Institute.

Sam: Well, one of our board members is very vocal about this. He said to me the other day, our kind of training for professional staff and for young people who are seeking their future, this place is a learning and a teaching place for adult learners as well as the children. When you put those two things together, you realize that the training of staff has to be very thorough because a lot of our people have never worked with children who have some of the problems that are displayed by the children who go to school here.

We realize that there's constant turnover in a place like Green Chimneys; so you have to be very aware of what our needs are, and the training of future staff is a bonus and we do very well at it. In fact, today at our conference, we have a human–animal interaction conference today; one of the interns from back in 1985 is a member of the group that's here today.

Cynthia: You're really contributing to the future.

Myra: It's great because you get young people out of college and are getting their PhDs and come here as either clinical psychology interns or social work interns and OT [occupational therapists], and they come in, they're very enthusiastic. They've got an energy that maybe some of our veteran staff don't have that energy, and they add a lot for the program.

Sam: You have to be open to work with people. You have to make demands, but you have to be reasonable and understanding that they have needs, and you have to take care of their needs as well because if the staff is not good, and if the staff doesn't feel good about the program, you're in trouble.

Cynthia: All right, one final word about Green Chimneys. What would you like to say? Then we'll close it off.

Sam: Well, you know, at 86 years of age and having been here since 1947, I wish I could predict what it's going to be like 10 years from now. But I have to be understanding that a new voice has to be heard. We only hope that the strong programs that have made a difference will continue for many years to come.

Myra: Basically the same and that the culture that this started with will continue to be the culture because it's very easy to change things to the point where it's not really what you recognized it to be. I think the Institute's job is to make sure that the focus that we've been talking about this whole weekend will continue regardless of who is there because there's a lot of transitions that will be happening as we all move on to wherever we're going next.

Cynthia: Your hopes are that the value of human–animal interaction and facilitating healing and growth and development will continue to be fostered at Green Chimneys forever.

Myra: Absolutely.

Sam: It goes beyond what you just said. It's that we hire people that understand that because if we don't do that, it won't be here.

Cynthia: Keep it going.

Myra: Keep it going.

Sam: I think that it's so well entrenched that it gets better and better. And we try different things all the time.

Cynthia: I want to thank you both so much. This has been a very special experience for me. Your sharing today has been very valuable, and it will be shared with my students and others who may actually come to Green Chimneys someday to be an intern or staff member. I know that you're very dedicated and you're very busy and this is a very special moment.

Myra: The specialness of something like this [the conference] is that we're seeing people, friends who have been here for prior years, and it's amazing how many people can come back.

Cynthia: From all over the world.

Myra: From all over the world. We have attending the conference persons from Japan, we have Holland, we have Germany, we have . . . I don't even know it all.

Sam: Israel, India, Italy, we could keep going. Finland.

Myra: In some sense, it's almost like a reunion for many people. It's great.

Sam: Thank you very much for giving us this opportunity.

Myra: Thank you.

Cynthia: Thank you for your time. Thank you so much. It's been an honor.

The interview with Michael Kaufmann took place April 25, 2015, in the horse barn on the Brewster, New York, campus of Green Chimneys (see Figure 2.2). Michael is the director of Green Chimneys Farm and Wildlife Center/Sam and Myra Ross Institute. He provided additional information about facilities and programs.

Interview with Michael Kaufmann

Cynthia: Would you tell us about Green Chimneys?

Michael: Absolutely. It'd be a pleasure. Green Chimneys is a residential treatment school, day school, for children with psychosocial disabilities. We're in Brewster, New York. We're about an hour and 15 minutes outside of New York City. We've been here since 1947. It's a very old program with a lot of history. Currently, we're serving 200 children. As I said, they have psychosocial disabilities, which is everything from autism spectrum to attachment disorder, mood dysregulation. Ages, they are about five to 18 years old. We serve mostly boys, but we also have girls. Nobody really quite understands why more boys get referred to services like ours.

We are positioned between a psychiatric hospital and a special education classroom. When the children come here, on average they've been psychiatrically hospitalized twice. They are at a high level of fragility. The parents, the families, are very concerned about them. The school systems don't know how to educate the child in the public school. The placement source for Green Chimneys is a public school. The children come here, the average length of stay is about two and a half years, three years, which is not terribly long. To some people, it seems like a long time. From admission to discharge, the goal is to have the child go back into their family. It's not about having them stay with us on the farm and live forever with the animals. The animals, and us, and a staff of 600 professionals, try to make sure that the kids go back home significantly improved. It's interesting, our discharge rate right now is 80 percent of the kids go back into their families a lot better. That leaves 20 percent that don't do so well and that will need to continue to have higher levels of care, sometimes lifetime care.

What's interesting is our kids, in terms of IQ, are all over the place. We have children who are academically brilliant, but socially lacking. They can't get along with peers. They can't get along in school or at home. We have a very mixed student body. Also, see many economic backgrounds. They come from all over New York State. We currently don't serve kids from all over the country. Some people think we do. Wish we did. There is only one Green Chimneys, and we're here in Brewster. Of course, it goes back to the dream Dr. and Mrs. Ross, who in 1947 wanted to have a farm with animals and kids. Decade by decade, it has grown to the point of where we are today.

Cynthia: Tell us about this beautiful facility we're standing in right now.

Michael: We're standing in our horse barn. We have a pretty large farm. We have five areas to our farm. We have two gardens, which I always mention first because horticulture therapy, working with plants, is significant at Green Chimneys. We have our traditional farm animal barn, where we have cows, goats, sheep, chickens, and Bactrian camels. We took in two of those a couple of years ago. That was fun. The horse program is a mixed program of interaction with horses. It's a riding program. At the base of all our animal programs is building a relationship with the animal. We find that's a very significant thing for the children.

The next area I want to mention is our wildlife rehabilitation center. We specialize in birds of prey, eagles, hawks, owls, vultures. The idea is that we take in local birds that are brought to us by the police, the fire department. We try to heal the birds, get them better and back into the wild. The other animal program that we recently started is a sheltered dog interaction program, which basically relies on a partner shelter bringing dogs to us for six weeks. The dogs live with us on campus, interact with the children. The children take care of the dogs. Then the children help place the dogs into permanent homes. We have about 300 animals, which is a significant amount of animals to take care of. We try to make a real point not to talk about "using" the animals in therapy, interactions, and education. We want to partner with animals. We involve animals. Animals work with us. The animal welfare component here is very important for the children, for our staff. We try to make sure that, in the interactions with the children, the animal really benefits also.

Most of the animals come here for life. When we take in a farm animal, when we take in a horse, we do try to make a full commitment. As I mentioned with the wildlife, the goal is to get them back into the wild. If we can't repair a broken wing, then the bird may stay with us in captivity for life also.

Cynthia: That part of the rehabilitation, healing an animal and helping it return to the wild if it can, is very beneficial for the kids here.

Michael: What I sometimes like to say is there's a metaphor at play in each of the animal areas. In the teaching barn with the farm animals, it's more about learning to build a close relationship with an animal. All of these animals are domesticated. They can be handled. They can be touched. A healthy touch is a very important lesson to learn. They all have names, stories. The children can attach to the lamb that was orphaned and came here, to the old sheep that is slowly nearing the end of life. The life cycle in that barn is very important.

Here, in this barn, in the horse barn, it's more about congruent message sending to a very large animal. Horses are obviously very imposing and can be dangerous due to their size. The children really start to understand what the horse is sending out with their ears, with their body language. They learn how to send messages to the horse, what they want the horse to do. Possibly take it for a walk or eventually ride it. You get some sense of mastery out of this. There's really nothing like getting on that horse for the first time. "Look, it's listening to me. I'm pulling on the rein and the horse knows what I want." That's a lot of self-esteem building.

Of course, at that point I must say, we're very dedicated to evidence-based work. Unfortunately, in human–animal interaction, a lot of what we do is evidence informed at this point. Research is not conclusive how animals benefit kids, how a program like ours really works. We know it works. In terms of data, we're still trying to put the pieces together.

Back to the metaphors in wildlife. That's what your question was. When we have an animal with an injured wing, a hawk let's say, and the children come into that area. What we try to really show them there is that wild animals do not need people the same way as the farm animals do. The wild animals are less likely to want to interact with us. They don't want to be pets. We don't even name those animals out of respect due to their wildness. The children can feed them. They can do some medical treatments. Really, we try to stay away from them as much as possible. That's setting boundaries.

For our children with mood dysregulation, with autism spectrum, learning about boundaries is critical. Because while some children are very reluctant to come at you, some of them are always on you. They're always in your space. Learning different spatial relationship with different animals is a very subtle thing we do throughout the program. Really, one of the messages that's really critical in a human–animal interaction program is that the animal doesn't always have to be what we want it to be or where we want it to be. In our setting, the animals can opt out too. If a goat or a horse really does not want to participate on a day, they don't have to. Just because we want to pet the goat today, if the goat doesn't feel like it, that's the goat's choice.

Cynthia: He can walk away.

Michael: He can walk away. That sounds a little fuzzy maybe, but that just requires knowing your animals. Anyone who works with animals in an educational–therapeutic context, you better know your animals very well and what their capacity is, what they're comfortable doing. That goes back to your animal selection, about which animals work in your program.

Cynthia: We understand that you have a school here. We saw that on the tour yesterday. Tell me about your school. You have an occupational therapy program too.

Michael: From admission to discharge, every child has a treatment plan, an academic plan. The social worker is at the center of the treatment team, but all of our staff, including the farm staff, we are part of the team and regularly feedback information of how the child is doing in the program.

For the residents who live here, at eight o'clock in the morning, school starts. Eight to three they have school. They have a homeroom teacher. Class sizes are eight students, 12 students, three adults in every classroom, teacher's aides, a lot of adult–child ratio. The school day just goes from eight o'clock until three o'clock. The children, during the day, go to the different farm areas. You might have garden class at nine. At 10, you have a reading class. Then at 11, you go to the horseback riding area and work with the horses. All these animal programs are woven into our school.

The school is a state-mandated accountable school, so we do have academic testing and academic pressures, which can be very hard for some of these students, who really are struggling behaviorally and are really not at a point of doing academics. Working in the animal areas often is a transition from being an academically failing child to slowly learning again how to learn. Because really, that's what it's about.

Cynthia: The children learn things like compassion. They learn how to connect in relationship. They learn empathy through working with the animals. That helps facilitate their sense of well-being, which allows them to feel like they fit in and feel accepted here. Not being accepted in their other environments, before they came here, really hindered their sense of well-being, their growth and development. That sense of acceptance here and ability to connect with another sentient being like an animal, which is a little bit easier to do than connect with a human, sometimes jump-starts or facilitates that growth and development for them, that they need so much.

Michael: I like that word, "jump-starts," because when a child is admitted to our program, often, I've mentioned, they've been hospitalized psychiatrically. They've been tested. They've had a therapist ask them questions, maybe two or three therapists. Here, they come to another place. It's a strange place. We have a health center. One of the first things that happens is that somebody makes sure they're healthy. Then they know it's a school. On the first and second day, suddenly you're in a barn surrounded by sheep and goats. You really don't know what to make of it because this is obviously not just another hospital or another school. This is something different. Realistically, a lot of the kids when they come into the farm for the first time are afraid of the animals. What it does is it totally takes them out of themselves. It allows them almost this little bit of a clean break. Most children, we find, have an innate curiosity about a horse, about the sounds, about a snake, whatever animal they see. That's really the open door.

We actually, during our admissions visits, have the children walk through the farm with a social worker who is part of our admissions team. What we see is how that child behaves with their parents. How are they in the barn? Are they totally fearful? Do they have absolutely no fear? Are they overly impulsive? Do they listen to directions? Do they ask questions? How verbal are they? Simply walking through the barn with the child without even the child knowing that an assessment is taking place, you can tell a lot about that child.

Once the child is in the program, we have social workers who clinically work at the farm. They will come up with the child to walk around the farm. It may not be a focused session with one animal, but just by walking in this environment, the therapist can connect much easier with the child. That makes our work easier. It's even more cost effective. We are a business. It's a nonprofit business. Our goal is to treat the children to get them home as fast as possible.

The example I like to use is, if during the first session, the social worker is trying to engage and the child doesn't even say anything, then that was a wasted session that we paid for. If that takes two or three sessions like that, we've wasted time and we've wasted money. But, if during the first session, we're here at the stall looking at the horse, and all we're doing is just looking, the child might say, "What's he doing? Why is he doing this? That's a funny sound." To which then I can say, "Well, yeah, he's eating his dinner. Have you had dinner?" "Yeah, I had dinner." "Did you like dinner?" Before you know it, a conversation is happening, which then builds the relationship with the therapist, or the teacher, or the dorm staff too. That's equally important.

Cynthia: The animals serve as a bridge to help build the relationship with the teachers and the therapists so that they can actually be more effective.

Michael: Exactly. You know from academics, I've learned the term social glue. Animals really are that. You see that with anyone who goes to a dog park with their dog. Everyone will talk to you. Everyone says hello. You talk to strangers that you normally would never talk to because they also have a dog. Some people even feel they can find a date by walking a dog around a park or something.

Cynthia: I really appreciate your time. I want you to have the last word. What else do you think people need to know or understand about Green Chimneys and how it is so socially and emotionally beneficial?

Michael: I think the most important thing to remember is that animals are not cure-alls. They're not magic vitamin pills. They are a way for people to connect and celebrate a living world. There's a lot of other ways that you can do it. At Green Chimneys we made the choice that nature-based interactions are something we build into our work. I really want to underscore that, for us, it is talented staff, trained therapists, professional childcare staff, certified teachers, farm staff that know how to take care of animals, veterinarians who provide good care. All of that makes the animals be able to do their work and to make their contribution. Really, if you're really going to help people, you have to have the whole team in place. Everybody working together.

Cynthia: Thank you, Michael. I really appreciate your time.

Michael: You're very welcome. Absolutely.

Editors' Commentary for Chapter 2

Dr. Samuel Ross is truly a visionary. He was one of the first in the U.S. to recognize how animals can benefit children in a learning environment. He pursued his dream by buying a farm and turning it into a school. His vision expanded over time, with the assistance and support of his wife, Myra, to include services for children with behavioral and emotional needs. Today, with the assistance of dedicated staff, community support, and generous donors, Green Chimneys has state-of-the art facilities where the children and the animals live and indoor and outdoor learning spaces where children learn and receive emotional support services. They include areas for gardening and human–animal interaction.

Green Chimneys is considered a premier learning and therapy environment for children with emotional and mental health concerns. It is located in a rural area with large grassy pastures interlaced between forested, rolling hills. The surrounding topography, along with a variety of animals and gardens at the facility, makes this a terrific therapeutic milieu. Green Chimneys is a sanctuary for animals and children. It is a place where animals live out their lives comfortably and safely. The children learn, grow, and heal by gardening; interacting with animals; providing care for animals; and engaging with talented teachers, therapists, and animal experts. Interacting with nature, the plants and animals, helps children with challenges grow and heal in ways not possible inside the confines of more traditional school and therapy environments. Through gardening and interaction with animals, the children experience positive social interactions, gain self-confidence and self-efficacy and learn to trust others and then to trust themselves. This helps to fulfill an important part of the mission of Green Chimneys, to help children so they may integrate back into their families and live a more socially and emotionally satisfying life. It is our opinion that every practitioner of animal-assisted interventions for emotional and mental health should make at least one visit to Green Chimneys.

References

4-H. (n.d.). Homepage. Retrieved October 6, 2017, from http://4-h.org/
Green Chimneys. (n.d.). Homepage. Retrieved October 5, 2017, from www. greenchimneys.org/
Ross, S. B., Jr. (2011). *The extraordinary spirit of Green Chimneys: Connecting children and animals to create hope*. West Lafayette, IN: Purdue University Press.

Figure 2.1 Dr. Samuel Ross, Jr., and Myra Ross. The Ross family founded Green Chimneys in the state of New York. Photo copyright of Dr. Samuel Ross and Myra Ross (used with permission); photographer Joann Coates.

Figure 2.2 Michael E. Kaufmann, Director, Green Chimneys Farm and Wildlife Center/Sam and Myra Ross Institute, in the state of New York. Photo copyright Michael Kaufmann (used with permission); photographer Christina Horn.

3 Dr. Risë VanFleet and Tracie Faa-Thompson of the International Institute for Animal Assisted Play Therapy™ Studies

Dr. Risë VanFleet is the founder and Tracie Faa-Thompson the cofounder of the International Institute for Animal Assisted Play Therapy™ Studies (n.d.). They have collaborated on publications and offer trainings in animal-assisted play therapy. They coauthored the book *Animal Assisted Play Therapy* (2017). Dr. VanFleet has a practice in Boiling Springs, Pennsylvania. She is a licensed psychologist, a registered play therapist and supervisor, a certified filial therapy therapist, a supervisor and an instructor, and a certified dog behavior consultant. Dr. Risë VanFleet began practicing animal-assisted play therapy with canines as her therapy animals (see Figure 3.1). Tracie Faa-Thompson has a practice in Northumberland, United Kingdom (see Figure 3.2). She primarily works with equines as her therapy animals. Tracie is a social worker and a registered play therapist with the British Association of Play Therapy.

I interviewed Dr. Risë VanFleet and Tracie Faa-Thompson on April 25, 2015, when we were in Brewster, New York, attending a human–animal interaction conference, and where Risë and Tracie were among featured speakers at the conference.

Interview with Dr. Risë VanFleet and Tracie Faa-Thompson

Cynthia: Risë and Tracie, each of you practice animal-assisted play therapy. Why don't you tell us about your work?

Risë: I work out of Boiling Springs, Pennsylvania. It's a small, south-central Pennsylvania city. I do mostly animal-assisted play therapy. I am a licensed psychologist. My degree, my doctorate, is in human development and family studies. So I like to think in very integrative, multidisciplinary kind of ways. I have been trained and I have been a registered play therapist supervisor for many years. I've done lots of play therapy with children. I also have traveled around the world training other mental health professionals to do play therapy. My favorite activity is filial therapy, where we train the parents to do special play sessions with their own children. I learned that directly from its founders, the Guerneys [Bernard and Louise Guerney (1989)]. I've been doing that for many, many years. I have written several books about filial therapy and child-centered play therapy and lots of articles and chapters.

Quite a number of years ago, I dabbled with animal-assisted work in the past without really knowing what I was doing, but I never did very much of it. What kind of got me started in combining animal-assisted therapy with play therapy was a dog that I acquired from a rescue who was very, very playful. Her first client was a cat. By playing with the cat, she actually brought this cat out of her shell and really kind of made a big, big difference in this cat's life, that I had been unable to do. At the same time, I was seeing some clients for a therapist in our practice who was diagnosed with cancer and was out for about a year, and one of the children that she was seeing had a horrific abuse history. He had done well with play therapy. We had done filial therapy with his foster family. Everything had been going quite well for him, but he still had so many issues, and he did have some issues with hurting animals. So I got the idea to involve my dog, Kirrie, who was extremely playful, in the process. That was kind of the beginning of a big adventure that I'm still on. I only had one or two sessions, and even though I had lived with dogs my whole life, I realized I needed to know a lot more. So I then moved into dog training and dog behavior work. I immersed myself in that world to learn more about how to be a positive dog trainer. So I'm also a certified dog behavior consultant, and I work with troubled dogs once in a while. But my big passion for a long time now has been animal-assisted play therapy where we use playful interactions to help children, families, adolescents, really people of all ages with various types of emotional, social, behavioral problems, kind of process them through the power of play.

Cynthia: All right. We're going to get into a lot more detail about your philosophy and some of your practices here in just a moment. Tracie, tell us about your work.

Tracie: I'm Tracie Faa-Thompson. I've got a master's in social work. As you can hear from my language, I'm not from over here. I'm from the U.K. [United Kingdom]. I live in a very, very rural area, which is lovely, and it's great for doing equine-assisted psycho-therapy. I've also got a master's in play therapy and a master's in criminology. And I've worked in ride-with-disabled for the last 30 years at my own ride-with-disabled association to work with adults because everyone wants to work with the children. These children got older and adults weren't cute anymore, so I started my own ride-with-disabled. And from the outset it hasn't just been the children and the adults riding the horses; it was horse management and stuff like that as well as caring for the horses and riding them.

As a social worker, I started to work years ago with children who'd been severely sexually abused. They didn't have a learning disability or a developmental delay. I'd take them along to meet the horses and do work on the ground with them. It started off with a girl maybe about 20 years ago, and she was a teenager and she'd let boys have sex with her because she thought that's what love was. I started working with horses, and a horse that was very, very tickly. When you would touch him down in the genital area, the horse would kick out. I'd say, "You know, that's him protecting himself. He just knows he hasn't got the relationship." So we worked through the animal that way without any formal sort of training around it or any sort of basic idea of what I was doing. But I'd been around horses all my life. Unless I'm on vacation, I've never had a day in my life without at least two or three horses in my life, so I know them pretty well.

Just from there, in 2006 I did the EAGALA model [Equine Assisted Growth and Learning Association (n.d.)] and that formalized some of my training. And I thought, well, I can take part of that knowledge and use it. And someone rung me out of the blue and said, "I hear you know about equine-assisted psychotherapy. Here's $30,000." This would be in 2007. "Would you like to start a program?" So I did. That was a year-long program. It was a ride-for-the disabled. It was built with English national lottery money. It was like a two-million pound, purpose-built facility, which was lovely. It had lovely stables and lovely horses and everything you need. But from the therapeutic part of it, it wasn't very good because it was like having therapy in a room and then someone walks into it. No privacy. So I decided since I've got a really lovely home with horses, let's try it at home. We've got loads and loads of space.

After that, Risë and I met each other in 2006 at a filial training. We realized that we had a lot in common, and that's where we decided to take this further. There is a lot of animal-assisted therapy around there [U.K.], which is wonderful. But as a play therapist some of it, for me, was a bit grown up. I wanted to bring the play element into it. So that's where the collaboration came from to do animal-assisted play therapy.

Cynthia: You say your practice is in the U.K. Where is it located?

Tracie: It's in Northumberland. Where, if anyone's interested in Hogwarts and Harry Potter, it's where a lot of the filming's been done in the Alnwick Castle. We've got lots and lots of castles, and it's on the English–Scottish border. There's still a war of independence between the English and the Scots at the moment. It's been going on for hundreds and hundreds of years. It's a very rural area, but it's very, very beautiful. The whole atmosphere is a huge estate that enables us to be out in nature and the countryside, working mostly outside rather than in the barn.

I don't like working in barns unless it's absolutely pouring rain or snow because horses are naturally claustrophobic and working inside takes the naturalness out of the whole process. Horses can't teach when they're in the barns because there's nothing for them to eat. It just doesn't feel as natural for me. I know a lot of people do some excellent work in barns, but for me personally, it's not the way that I want to work.

Cynthia: I'm going to toss some key words at both of you, and I just want you to spontaneously take these key words and run with them, as they relate to your practice and your philosophy and why you think animal-assisted therapy works. Okay? Nature, relationship, and what would be the third word?

Risë: For me play.

Tracie: Partnership.

Cynthia: So for you, Risë, it is nature, relationship, and play. And for you, Tracie, it is nature, relationship, and partnership. So run with those.

Risë: For me, I mean, I think nature is something we have become quite divorced from. Even when I was a kid we had woods in the backyard. So I've spent a lot of time in nature myself and love wilderness areas. I spent a lot of time in Alaska hanging out with wild bears, bears in the wild, taking photographs and doing a lot of things that I find really fulfilling for myself. But I see lots and lots of kids and families, people of all ages, who really don't have that connection anymore. I think what animal-assisted therapy of any kind helps us with is to start to reconnect with that natural world.

Sometimes the way we approach our animals is not all that natural, but hopefully, when we're doing therapy work, we are being a little bit more natural. We're trying to help clients understand that these animals are different beings. They're different species. They think and act, there's similarities, but there's also differences.

For me relationship is everything because nothing really happens in a vacuum. I am trained as a relationship psychologist. Relationship is something I'm thinking about all the time. I think there's lots of relationships when you're doing therapy, especially when an animal is involved. You have the relationship between the therapist and their animal if it's their own animal that they're involving, which is typically the case I think. There's the relationship between the therapist and the child or the family. It's not necessarily just the child. There's the relationship between the client and the animal. Those are all things you want to facilitate and use in a way that allows people to start to see what a positive, healthy attachment is all about. To me I'm always thinking about attachment processes. How do we build relationships? Because if our relationships are strong, I think we're stronger. I mean, we can overcome an awful lot of problems if we have the right kind of support in our lives. I think the animals provide some of that for us in animal-assisted therapy. But, it's not just that the animal is there. There is someone who has to be facilitating that and witnessing it and guiding it so that it can move in a healthy direction.

Then the play part for me is all about safety. We live in a very serious time and people take themselves very seriously. A lot of people, whether they're kids or adults, feel anxious or depressed. We're pressured with all the things that go on in life, and we have lost sight of play. Play is a very natural thing. It's part of our brain. Jaak Panksepp [2007] has talked about play as being one of the primary emotional systems of the brain, and it's a reparative thing. It's hard to be anxious and playful at the same time.

We use play in the therapy work to actually lighten everything up. We can look at ourselves better from a little bit of a distance and not feel like we're going to be judged. For me, playfulness, probably part of it comes from a personal experience. I used to be kind of a shy kid and would worry a lot about what I was saying and how I get into conversations and things like. But my parents were playful and that was a very helpful thing. I rediscovered play somewhere down the line. But once I got into play therapy I realized this stuff is so powerful. It can be as light as just a light tone, just a tone of voice that's a little bit lighter that allows the safety to be there. Or it might be doing something that's really quite playful or quite imaginative. Especially for children, play is how they process the world. If we aren't able to connect on that level, I think we're missing some really important pieces of it.

Final point about play is, animals like to play too. Dogs, like humans, play into adulthood. They don't always play as much as when they were young; that's true of us as well. But there's lots of play that goes on if we allow it to stay there and be alive. Having the animals be involved in a playful environment is really beneficial. It replenishes everybody, I think. It just makes this nice interaction. Therapy happens; sometimes profound therapy happens. But at the same time, it's that safety has been established through that playfulness in the context of that relationship. Of course, the animals bring all this nature to us.

Tracie: For me, like as I said before, I don't like to work in a barn, and I like to have it as natural as possible. My horses, when they're doing the work, they can eat, and kids love nothing better than when the horse farts. They think it's absolutely wonderful. What's more natural than the horse farting? And then they poop themselves, and the kids say, "Oh, that's gross." I've got six boys [horses] and they'll drop the penis, and they [clients] think that's gross as well. It's all nature and they all love it, and it really does break down barriers and that helps with the relationship. Just being out in the open and being in the fresh air, being with animals that aren't trained to do anything specific other than be a horse, and just love the interaction – that brings the relationship part.

It brings partners. Rather than being a standoffish therapist and being all grown up, the kids start to partner with you, as well as with the horses, and the trust is there. I say it time and time again, you know; the horses can be running around, the kids are running around and, you know, now ask the kids to do something and they'll do it. Because they trust you. It's a trusting relationship and partnership. And I feel absolutely warmed that these kids trust me to keep them safe and the horses safe. Things work out all right because these kids put trust in me, even when they usually don't put trust in things.

I like the whole being outdoors and being in the elements because life isn't room based, and it isn't safe. And sometimes, you know, we'll be out there and the wind will get up, and the horses will be like running round. And when it's really, really windy, the kids get all hyper as well, and they go running round. And what's more natural than wind, in whatever form? Because life doesn't fit into boxes. And we get a lot of distractions. And that's what happens in life. And to be able to deal with that through relationships, through maybe, you know, if the horse is running round and you might get a lot of contact with a child, you just made that connection because they smile and stuff. That's what it's all about. And I find, for me personally, it is more difficult if you're working within like a square box whether that's a barn or a room-based thing.

Risë: I might tag onto that. There was one equine program that I did at a local college. It all went really well. These were all students in transition, so that was the focus. We did a variety of activities, ground-based activities, and I, with another local person that I was working with, facilitated a lot of things. And the horses would throw in the unexpected. Like a little tiny bar that one horse wouldn't go over. And the woman he wouldn't go over the bar for was actually a horse person. The challenge caused her to think about how she was facing the next barrier in her life.

So that was all happening, and the very last day they all said, "Could we go into this big field and just hang out with the horses?" What they ended up doing and it was all very safe, but they were running with the horses. There were about four horses, and I think we had seven or eight women. At the end, we kind of debriefed. They said, "That was so freeing. Just to be able to run with an animal." I mean, it was tons of space, and they and the horses seemed to be loving it. They seemed to love it. That freeing, that freedom, I think we're missing this a lot. I like your way [speaking to Tracie] of kind of thinking about how we live in these boxed rooms all the time and there's so much more to life than that.

Tracie: I'll just tag onto that as well because our kids, you know, where I'm trying to talk to schools and parents and all that, I'll say now the horses are loose, the kids are loose. They'll think, "Well, how on earth can you control these kids? Where's the boundaries?" But there are loads of boundaries. But if we're always putting in the boundaries for the kids, they'll never learn to self-boundary, to think about themselves. They're so focused on this little thing here that the peripheral vision is gone. You know, when you're working with horses in particular, they can come out of anywhere, and the kids have got to learn to be safe for themselves and look out for each other. And that's the relationship part for the kids as well with each other, to look out for one another, which is really, really important.

Getting the vision going from this little square box here on whatever they play, video games or whatever, to being out and having to focus on the much wider world and being more aware and being more natural and free. Kids will say and parents say, "I feel more alive when I'm here." Which is really important. When they first come, it's just like tunnel vision and every man for themselves. And it's really, really important that they learn to say "Oh, see who's next to you and watch out for so and so" and learn to like look out for. I think this is a really, really important lesson because we're very good at getting tunnel vision. None of us would be here if we couldn't make relationships and we couldn't have partnerships.

Cynthia: Tracie, you were talking about how by having the freeness with the horses, running free and the kids running free, there are boundaries there but you allow the kids to learn about those boundaries themselves and set them for each other and look out for each other. And that's part of the importance of the relationship and the partnership.

Tracie: Absolutely. We put so many boundaries on children. Our expectation is, especially the children I work with, is that they can't do it for themselves, and the things at school and at home are ever so tighter, tighter, tighter, tighter that, when they're out here, they're really, really free. And then they've got to learn to look out for themselves and to look out for each other as well, which is something that happens when they start to work in teams. They start to work together where there's never ever been any of that kind of connection before and any of that kind of partnership or relationship.

It's really, really important in life that they start to think for themselves because what happens when they first come is, I'll say, "There's the horses. What do you think of them?" And we'll talk about them and stuff. Then I'll say, "Right, you know, go put the equipment on them, and we'll bring them into the other end." They'll say, "I don't know how." And I'll say, "Tracie's not being rude, but if you ask me to do something for you, Tracie will say no. It is not about Tracie being rude; it's about if I do everything for you, you'll never learn yourself." Because you see some of the teachers, actually, when they come, they want to do it for the kids. It's actually not helping them at all because soon as the teachers start doing, the children stand back and it's done for them.

Sometimes, in the beginning, the whole hour-and-a-half session will be taken up with just trying to get the head collar on the horse. They're all trying to do it individually and not working as a team. Then I say, "Oh, my goodness, sorry guys, but that's your session up for the day." They say, "Oh, we never got to do anything." I say, "Well, you know, who chose to do that? You know, who chose to not work as a team and to muck about and to give up? Who chose that?" They very quickly learn. And, by about the fourth session, they've got it done in 10 minutes because they need to take responsibility for themselves. I think often our kids don't. In one sense they have too much responsibility, you know, on social media, and it's like all out there. And in another sense, some of our kids, my kids, 14 and 15 year old, they can't make a cup of tea for themselves. They can't make a sandwich because everything is all done for them. This is the first opportunity of actually being responsible for themselves and responsible for another animal. At the end of the session, we spend 10 minutes grooming the horses, saying good-bye to them and thanking them for the session that we've had. They take them back to the field, and they say good-bye and then they give them the carrot, and they absolutely love that because that's a nurturing bit. It's also a release of oxytocin [a mood-lifting and wellness and social-enhancing hormone] in the kids and a release of oxytocin in the horse. They're very, very proud.

I've got two white horses and two black-and-white ones, and they love to see how clean they can get them. They have a competition to see who can get the cleanest horse. A little bit of competition doesn't do any harm. It is part of the process. Sometimes, the teacher will say, these kids are calm for three days after having that whole process and seeing it right through. My kids have always got to bring the horses to the session to where we're going to be working. They're never set up for them. They're never brought in. They've got to engage the horses when they're in the field. If they can't succeed, well, you know they've got to try harder. My horses are mostly their own, have their own mind.

Cynthia: Through your work with dogs and equines, I hear a lot of very important messages about facilitating healing, growth, and development through an aspect of nature. You talked about play helping us get back to nature because play is natural. And also when you're playing, you're not engaged in the fear, the anxiety response. It seems as though all these things that a person might need, whatever that might be – whether it's to grow, to heal, to develop social skills, overcome fears, overcome trauma, learn to cope with some sort of diagnosis – that engaging in the process with the animals helps create the atmosphere that makes change a lot more viable. It adds a dimension that lets us facilitate that process with especially those who are challenged by this. That, without the animals, you can do play therapy but sometimes that's not getting through to some kids. Then, when you add the animals, that finally gets through.

The animals are helping bring back a sense of nature, the natural. I am hearing you say that people and children who have lost their sense of self need to go to that place of naturalness, to find their own sense of relationship with nature, before they can really get to that point where they can heal, to have that atmosphere for greater healing.

Risë: I think that's a really nice way of putting it. I know in our practice and the work that I've done, I've worked with lots and lots of different types of problems and family problems as well. I think that naturalness really is very special in a way that nothing else can work. I mean, I'm a really good play therapist. I'm a really good filial therapist. I mean, that's my main specialty. I've always said I love filial therapy. It's my first professional love. But the animal-assisted play therapy, and animal-assisted therapy in general, is like right next to it because there is just something – a qualitatively different thing that happens.

In addition, I think, to the naturalness is also the social lubricant effects of animals. I work a lot with kids in foster care or who have been adopted, so they have huge amounts of trauma and attachment problems and things in their lives, and I know about how long it takes with some of these kids or kids with those kind of backgrounds in general to be able to trust another person whether it's a therapist or foster parent or adoptive parent. It's a process. I mean it takes time. I've just never seen things happen so quickly as they do with the animal. The animal opens the doors in a way.

Then, kind of by juxtaposition and the fact that I'm there and allowing it to happen and sharing actually part of my life, which is one of my own animals, with them, by almost default, then they start trusting me a little bit more and that happens quicker.

What I have seen is that it enhances anything I might do in play therapy to have the animal there, if you have the right animal and the animal is properly suited for what you're asking that animal to do. I mostly work with dogs. I think what I see is this opening up happening very quickly. I'll give an example.

I had a girl who was 15. She had a lot of serious problems. Her family had a lot of disruptions and things in it. She came in. She wanted to work with the animals. I mean, she had agreed to do that, but she came in with no eye contact, earphones with music in her ears, kind of sullen and just kind of like "Oh, here's another adult that's kind of pulling a game on me maybe." My dog, by her default, is to jump up. Now, she's got a really good sit for greetings and rarely does jump up on people, but in this particular case, when the girl came in, the dog jumps up, gets all tangled up, pulling out her earphones. But the dog was like so happy to see her. She felt that. She took the headphones and everything out and put them aside. Never came in with them again. So the dog, Kirrie, taught the kid to take out her earphones. Not literally, but it was really kind of amazing.

She was a child who wasn't sure what to trust. But she did great work, and she had some marvelous dog-handling skills. She was also seeing another therapist in another practice for her regular therapy. I always wondered if I'd gotten through to her. About two years later, after I had discharged her because we had finished our program, she contacted me. Said she was doing a project in high school, a final project or something, and she wanted to learn about dog training. And so we've had some continuing contact where she wants to be able to work with dogs, and she has the talent for it. It was nice to kind of find out later that our work together did matter. Our connection was through the dog, but it was obviously a connection with me that she could come back. I think there is that natural piece that the dog just naturally helped her away from her electronics, and it worked nicely.

Cynthia: With nature we also get honesty. Animals are explicitly honest in their relationship with us. We know that whether with a child or an adult, it's that immediate honest relating that seems to be so powerful because children may be suspect of another person because of betrayal or because they see or experience people hurting people. And they understand if a dog is in my face licking me, that dog likes me. There's no ulterior motive.

Risë: Yeah.

Cynthia:	It's the absolute implicit honesty in the way animals relate to us, I think, that also makes it so powerful.
Tracie:	And the spontaneity as well. You know, because you might set something up and you never know what's going to happen and what's going to come out there. And you celebrate everything that comes out. You might think at the time, you know, that wasn't great, but kids will go away and process it and they'll come back and they'll be resilient. You know, you can't get that from a child playing with a toy. You don't get that spontaneity and that kind of feedback like you do with a live animal, that social lubricant, like when my horses give a kiss. Kids will go up to a big, thousand-pound horse, and the horse with its lips will come over and give an ever so gentle kiss. And the kids, they love it, but they hate it at the same time because it's like this big slobbery horse on you. You can see them like getting bigger in self-esteem and stuff like that. It's the whole interaction that you can never get without the animal. And I work with multiple horses as well, so it's the whole having to be aware of around you and not so focused in on yourself. You've got to be aware of so many things, and that's what our kids have gotten. It's just like raising awareness. It's like an awakening. It's like lots of stimulus but in a nice way, and that's not electronic stimulus. It's not like a focus in; it's like just a blossoming. You see these kids blossom week in and week out with the horses.
	I've got a boy coming at the moment, one of a group of seven, and his school teacher says, "Here, he's always running around and he's always like so happy and stuff. So I need to bring his other teacher out because this boy at school sits in the corner and cries and won't be reached." He's been there since January, and they haven't got one peep out of him. Well, I can't shut him up, and he's been like that from day one with the horses.
	It's just the freeness. It's the freedom and being able to be authentic, and the animals are authentic. They don't care whether the kids got the designer clothes on or whatever; as long as the child's happy to be there, my horses will be with them. Then you get kids who come in who are really angry, and my horses will stand and express "Well, I'm not going to be close to you." They pick up on attitude.
Risë:	I would like to build on that a little bit too because I think that is honest feedback. Occasionally, I hear people talking about animal-assisted therapy or animal-assisted activities and saying "Animals give us unconditional love," and actually I don't believe that's true.
Cynthia:	I don't either.
Risë:	I think most animal experts will probably agree with us because they [animals] have a stake in things, and if we do something like you [Tracie] just said, if we act in particular ways, the animals

back off or they're going to express "I'm not comfortable with this." That's why reading body language is important. I think it's the honest feedback, immediate like you just said, that is the most powerful piece of this. They like us. They want to be with us, especially dogs; I mean they've been domesticated over thousands and thousands of years. They're built, it's kind of wired into them to want to connect with people. It's there, and if we treat them nicely, they appreciate it. Just like we do. But if we don't treat them so nicely, then they do not appreciate it.

Some of the kids we work with have never experienced empathy. So to have an animal show interest in them while at the same time the therapist is giving some empathic responses, that's a good thing. We also want them to develop empathy or pull it out of them wherever it might have been squished away.

If a child, say, approaches a dog too head-on and the dog turns his head or backs away, oftentimes, the way I'll handle that is just to say, "Hmm, I just noticed as you were doing this that the dog backed away. What do you suppose is going on with that?" The kids will have their responses about that. Sometimes, they're clueless. Then I'll say, "You know I noticed this and the dog did this. Do you suppose she's feeling a little uncomfortable?" So I can kind of gradually help them notice more and more about how the dog is responding. Very often the empathy just eventually erupts. I've had many children who, because we focus all the time on how the dog is feeling by the body language, by watching what the dog is doing, that they start to watch that themselves.

I've had so many kids that you'd never expect in any other form of therapy who will just come out and say, "I think Kirrie's got a little bit of blood on her lip" or "I think Murray's tooth is loose," and it may or may not be the case. But to me, I capture those moments as a sign of empathy. The way I capture those moments is, for example, "Oh, thank you for noticing that. That's a wonderful thing that you've noticed, and you did just the right thing by letting an adult know. Let me check it out." So we take it seriously, and you can reinforce the intent. And sometimes they're right, and I missed it. Other times, you know, they're may be projecting something.

Cynthia: Take a little bit of time, each of you, and talk about the most important thing you want people to understand about the value of incorporating animals in a work that will emotionally benefit people.

Risë: Okay. A couple of thoughts come to mind with that. One is not so much the benefit but the process of doing it. To me, I think we're talking here a lot, and I suppose other people have too, about how valuable this is and it is incredibly valuable I think in a way that nothing else can be. But at the same time it takes a huge amount of training and education about the animals, about our interactions with animals, how to train animals, how to facilitate all those interactions that happen. And always keeping our eyes on the needs of the child but at the same time the eyes on the needs of the animal.

That part of it, the idea if you have a really nice, friendly, wonderful dog or really nice, friendly cat or whatever animal you might want to use, it's not about just taking that animal into work with you. It's much more about your developing your relationship, understanding and getting the right kind of training and experience and supervision, just like you would with any other specialty in our field to do that kind of work.

The nice thing about all that, gets back kind of to your point, is it's very exciting to do all that. It was wonderful when I first learned about dogs licking their noses as a sign of stress. I had never seen it before in my life, and I've lived with dogs my whole life; I decided okay I'm going to watch for it. Within 30 seconds, honestly, I saw one of my dogs licked her nose, and it was a stress response kind of thing. I thought, wow, I've missed a whole world. It's exciting to learn all this stuff and it is well worth it. Then, once you learn it, you keep learning, but then you're able to apply it to your practice in a lot of different ways. I really think the day is coming where we're going to see lots more of this, but my big hope is that people have the right education and understanding. I think that people think this is simple, but I think it's very far from being simple.

Cynthia: I think it's one of the most advanced therapies we have.

Risë: Yes. I agree. I would agree.

Cynthia: Thank you for sharing that. I think those were very important points.

Tracie: I think, going on from what Risë said, it sounds really simple, but you haven't just got the relationship between the horse and the child or the child and the therapist, especially when I work with multiple families and multiple horses. It's like juggling all these balls together, and it's really, really complex. But it's absolutely fascinating as well. Sometimes to stand back and allow it to be and just to have that space to let things happen and to be strong enough to let it happen and to allow, and not to go in too quickly and not try and protect or put your own stuff on it. Things can just happen in ways that you wouldn't expect in this work.

Every time I work, it's like the first time. It's like going out there and thinking, "Oh, wonder what's going to happen today." I expect the unexpected in this work and embrace it and think it's the most wonderful thing ever.

I've got a lovely dog as well; I've got four dogs, but I've a lovely German Pointer Cross Labrador, and he sometimes just comes out and hangs out with the kids and the horses. The kids love it. He's part of the team as well. We've got like huge balls for the horses, and when the dog was an adolescent, he was going through the area and the unexpected happened. He tried to jump on the ball, and he was trying to hump it basically, and he kept on falling off and jumping on and humping and the kids were absolutely fascinated by that. One of the 15-year-old boys said, "Mind, he can go for a long time." And you laugh along with the kids and you think, "Well, this is life." These kids know things that we as children didn't know; they've been exposed to so much. But for them to be able to share in a safe way through the horses, through the movements, that's what's really freeing. With this, you can run around, you can be very, very free. My kids go away physically exhausted.

As Risë was saying, you need to be well trained, and you need to be thinking about what's in it for everybody. It's a therapy that has something for everybody. It's just wonderful going to bed at night thinking, I have been part of this amazing thing. Risë and I, we were talking, someone asked us, when do you see changes, and we both said separately, typically after session four. You know, it takes four sessions, and when you think, you know, in normal therapy or in play therapy without animals, you've got no idea when you're going to see changes. But things just happen so much quicker with animal-assisted therapy.

Risë: We were talking about significant changes. I mean, you see little changes right from the beginning.

Cynthia: But you see those real breakthroughs; they happen fairly quickly.

Tracie: Real breakthrough. Yeah.

Cynthia: Around four sessions.

Tracie: Absolutely.

Risë: And they last.

Tracie: They last. And they build on it.

Risë: It carries it on, yeah.

Tracie: It carries on. It gets better and better. There's a breakthrough, and then it just goes on and on.

Cynthia: It can happen faster, and it can also reach individuals that haven't been . . .

Tracie: Reached before.

Cynthia: Reached by what we call other therapies, traditional therapies that don't involve animals. It's quicker and more immediate and helps people reach goals they might not otherwise reach.

Tracie: With the horse, you can work with multiples; you can work with family groups. And unlike with room-based therapy, because people have space to interact, they will project onto the horse because it's safer projecting onto the horse. When I first started, we were doing some observations, and I said, "Do any of the horses remind you of yourself or anyone in your family?" And this young girl says, "They remind me of my mom and dad." And there was a white horse standing that way and a black horse standing that way, bums towards. I said, "Well, what is it about your mom and dad that they remind you of?" She says they didn't speak to one another. Then she says, "My dad's not black mind." I said, "Oh, I didn't think he was because the black horse was black, you know." I said, "I didn't imagine he was, but thanks for letting me know that." It's just like the laughter and, you know, the things that come out, the spontaneity.

Risë: It allows the honesty of the kids to come out too.

Tracie: It does.

Risë: You know, whatever's on their mind, they're not censoring it or worrying about how it's going to be received.

Cynthia: Which is one of the reasons why I think we've been discussing why it works so quickly is if they can feel safe enough to get to their honest place quicker; then they're going to heal quicker.

Risë: Yeah.

Tracie: It's the whole whatever they say and whatever they do and whatever happens, the horses will accept them. There's a total acceptance that these kids have never had. And we accept them as well, but they're not used to humans accepting them. And there's total acceptance about whatever they bring. Unless, of course, you know, that they're frightening the horses or something like that, and then they'll get immediate feedback about what their behavior is doing to the horses right away. It's immediate, the feedback. I think that helps as well, which you can't get that with a toy or with an adult. Like when kids are saying things where they might want to shock you, and you're sort of like keeping a deadpan face. You get immediate feedback from an animal because he's just reacting as an animal and the kids see that and that can have a huge impact on them.

Cynthia: Any last words to share?

Risë: I hope you're interviewing yourself [to Cynthia] because you have contributed so much to this field. I really appreciate being part of this project, and certainly your work has been marvelous for all of us and look forward to what you come up with next.

   As long as I'm able I'm glad to be a resource for people that are interested in all of this. I mean the filial therapy has always been rewarding because you see the changes happen in the family, you see the parents really changing. This animal-assisted therapy is rewarding in a somewhat different way, but you still see magic, and it's not really magic. I mean, I don't get into the whole woo-woo stuff.

Cynthia: There's a mechanism behind it.

Risë: Yes. There's a mechanism behind it. We don't always understand that mechanism, but it's really very, very special. And when you know that you've facilitated that, you helped that happen. Maybe I'll just add that it isn't just the animals doing this. I think sometimes I hear people say that "Oh, horses took care of this and the dogs took care of that." They bring something very special to this, but it's our skill as a therapist that has to be there. Whatever form of therapy we do, it has to be there because we can make or break a particular situation in terms of whether it's actually therapeutically beneficial. So sometimes, we get kind of caught up in the animals. They're good things to get caught up in, but at the same time we can't forget that, you know, we're there for a job and it's a skill that we have to allow this whole thing become therapeutic rather than just hanging out with animals.

Cynthia: You know, we're all three practitioners and we're all three trainers.

Risë: Mm-hmm [affirmative].

Cynthia: And one of our challenges is teaching. How do we teach other people what it is and how to do it, because it is the therapist's ability to recognize an animal's response and to point that out. So the therapist is a vital facilitator paying attention to all relationship dynamics. So we who aspire to practice this the way we practice it, we have to teach others how to observe, how to recognize, how to identify, and how to respond to all that. It's a very complex process, and so I think that's where we are in the field right now is finding new and better ways to teach it, to train for it, to keep it going, to understand it better, to teach people to be more effective facilitators, as they could be.

Risë: I think that's really true. And I think one of the weaknesses, even in the research as well, is maybe in the way we sometimes teach this – we don't always define what we're doing. I think in many instances we probably do, but I think we need to continue to define what we do. You know, we're not just sitting around petting animals; there's a lot of different options and so forth.

We have a fairly involved training program for practitioners that want to come back and get that education after they've been out practicing for a while. I mean we teach a lot of different components. We pull together aspects of what we've developed, a competence-based certification. But where I see the real change happen is through supervision. When they can show me a video and we talk about the video because one of the things I notice about myself, and I've noticed it now with people that I'm supervising, is that when you first start doing this there's so much to keep track of you forget some of your well-known clinical, well-worn clinical skills. And it's almost like you go back and realize, "Oh, I forgot to empathically listen to that."

So I can see that now in the people that we've trained, and we're doing supervision and supervision groups with, I think, people really need that supervision for it to start coming together. Because we're all kind of doing our things, and there's probably lots of overlap and other things that are quite exciting that we want to hear from each other. I think it is a great way for us to move forward.

Tracie: I think there's a level of unconscious incompetence as well where people don't know the things that they're doing aren't right, and they don't know what they don't know. And it's like I think there's a big level of that in the U.K. I'm not sure about the U.S.

Risë: I think everywhere.

Tracie: And when people come on our training courses, they're sort of like, "Wow, you know, we didn't know that we didn't know that." And we're all learning because it's quite new. It's ancient because people have had relationships with animals for years and years and never labeled it as therapeutic or anything like that, but it's new because it's active. Everyone would be fine if you just had to go hang out with a horse or a dog for a week or two, but it doesn't work like that. It's got to be the active dynamic of the therapist facilitating the process. If you just put a kid in the barn it might be very, very nice, but you've got to, especially in the beginning stages, initiate that and to bring out those thoughts that these children can't articulate.

Most of the kids I work with, they've been round horses, but they just don't see them as sentient beings. Most of them have got dogs, but it's very, very different. It's a different relationship. It's the change in the dynamic of seeing the dog or the horse or whatever as a sentient being, a partnership, you know, something that's valuable, something that they can really, really connect with.

Cynthia: Thank you for your valuable time.

Risë: And I do hope you're interviewing yourself [to Cynthia] or having someone interview you. And I want you to leave that in if you're editing it, that I said that.

Cynthia: Well, I just want to thank each of you for your very valuable insights today and for taking time out of your busy schedules to spend with us. It's been absolutely wonderful.

Risë: As well for us too. I mean, it's really wonderful. We don't often get the chance to sit down together but I always have fun when we do it and just really appreciate your warmth and all that you've provided for all of us too. So we'll all keep plugging away and continue to help build this into a viable, really solid type of intervention that we can continue to be proud of, and so it will grow.

Tracie: Thank you for inviting me as well from the U.K., and it's been an absolute pleasure to meet you at last because I've heard so much about you from Risë and obviously read your books as well, so it's great to make that connect and I'm honored.

Cynthia: Well, thank you so much, again.

Risë: You're welcome.

Tracie: Thank you.

Editors' Commentary for Chapter 3

Dr. Risë VanFleet and Tracie Faa-Thompson spoke eloquently of the benefits of animal-assisted play therapy. The incorporation of the animals provides for more natural social interaction that can accomplish much more than the confines of therapy without animals. It is not as emotionally threatening to interact with an animal being as it is with a human being because the adult or child client may have a negative history with one or more human beings. Interacting with and relating to the therapy animals, this client–animal partnership, provides greater opportunities for the client to recognize and reflect upon their social and emotional challenges. And the medium of play with the animals, as compared with just traditional talk therapy, allows for greater freedom of symbolic expression. This combination of play therapy with animals can assist a client to reach deeper into the self and pull to the surface, to the conscious level, in the immediate moment, the social issues and emotional challenges that need to be expressed and processed with a therapist. There is increased therapeutic opportunities and decreased client resistance with animal-assisted play therapy, as compared to play therapy without animals or traditional talk therapy.

Both Risë and Tracie spoke of the complexities of animal-assisted play therapy. The number and type of psychosocial dynamics that are presented by both the human clients and the therapy animals are so plentiful that it can be difficult to see them all, and it can be difficult to recognize their value. Then there is the consideration of what to say, if anything, and when to say it so to be of benefit to the client. Both Risë and Tracie addressed the need for training and supervision for beginners of the practice of animal-assisted play therapy. They both provide this training through their institute, offering workshops in the U.S., the U.K. and as they travel around the world.

References

Equine Growth and Learning Association (EAGALA). (n.d.). Homepage. Retrieved October 5, 2017, from www.eagala.org/

Guerney, L., & Guerney, B. (1989). Child relationship enhancement: Family therapy and parent education. *Person-Centered Review, 4*(3), 344–357.

International Institute for Animal Assisted Play Therapy™ Studies. (n.d.). Homepage. Retrieved October 3, 2017, from http://risevanfleet.com/international/

Panksepp, J. (2007). Can play diminish ADHD and facilitate the construction of the social brain? *Journal of the Canadian Academy of Child and Adolescent Psychiatry, 16*(2), 57–66.

VanFleet, R., & Faa-Thompson, T. (2017). *Animal assisted play therapy.* Sarasota, FL: Professional Resource Press.

Figure 3.1 Dr. Risë VanFleet is the founder of the International Institute for Animal Assisted Play Therapy™ Studies. Photo copyright of Dr. Risë VanFleet (used with permission); photographer Craig Carl.

Figure 3.2 Tracie Faa-Thompson is a cofounder of the International Institute for Animal Assisted Play Therapy™ Studies. Photo copyright of Tracie Faa-Thompson (used with permission); photographer Risë VanFleet.

4   Dr. Cynthia K. Chandler of the University of North Texas

I, Dr. Cynthia K. Chandler, am a professor in the Department of Counseling and Higher Education at the University of North Texas (UNT), located in Denton, Texas. At UNT, I have been teaching full-time, graduate-level courses in counseling since 1989 (see Figure 4.1). I am a licensed professional counselor and supervisor as well as a licensed marriage and family therapist and supervisor. I started practicing and teaching animal-assisted counseling back in 2000 because I wanted to share the nurturing gifts of my pets with my clients and students. The first dog that I worked with as a therapy animal was Rusty, a red and white, curly furred cocker spaniel. He and I worked together providing pro bono professional animal-assisted individual and group counseling as well as group recreational activities with adolescents at a local juvenile detention center. I volunteered my professional animal-assisted therapy services there for over six years, eventually incorporating into my work at the detention center my cat Snowflake in 2001 – he was short haired, pure white, with one green eye and one blue eye – and then my dog Dolly in 2004; she was also a red and white cocker spaniel. I also initiated and cofacilitated the first equine-assisted counseling for juveniles in this detention center by partnering with a local equine therapy center for several years. Rusty and Dolly also assisted me in providing volunteer disaster response services to survivors of hurricane Katrina in 2005. I am currently registered as a handler-animal team with the organization Pet Partners (n.d.) with my dog Jesse. She is shades of buff and tan, with a few white highlights, and has long, flowing fur. I am also a licensed instructor and handler-animal team evaluator for Pet Partners. Jesse and I helped to start a volunteer animal-visitation program at three hospitals in Denton County, Texas, and we were one of the first therapy teams for each of these hospitals. We still visit staff and patients at one local hospital on a weekly basis.

In 2000, I developed and offered the first animal-assisted counseling training course and supervision at any counseling program at a university in the U.S. that was nationally accredited by CACREP (Council for Accreditation of Counseling and Related Educational Programs). Rusty, Dolly, and my current dog, Jesse, assisted me in training students and supervising counseling interns at the university and in the field. Also in 2000, I founded the Consortium for

Animal Assisted Therapy (n.d.), a service that provides international networking, local trainings, distance learning programs, handler-animal team evaluations, supervision of interns, and research by faculty and students. In 2005, I published a classic book in the field of animal-assisted interventions titled *Animal-Assisted Therapy in Counseling*; the third edition was published in 2017. In 2015, I developed the first theory that explains how animal-assisted counseling and psychotherapy actually work. I cofounded the Animal-Assisted Therapy in Mental Health Interest Network for the American Counseling Association (n.d.), and I am a member of the International Society for Anthrozoology (n.d.).

My association with companion animals is long and continuous. Since I was very young, growing up in a modest household in west Texas, my family always had a pet dog in our home that was a mixed breed rescued from a shelter, and often an adopted stray cat as well. We often visited my grandfather's farm in the panhandle of Texas, where he kept a horse to help him manage his small herd of cattle. My siblings and I were allowed to groom and ride the horse for recreation. So from an early age, I experienced the companionship of dogs, cats, and horses. When I was a young woman in my early 20s (I am now in my early 60s), I adopted a buff-colored puppy from a litter of cocker spaniels my uncle owned, and I named the puppy Muffin. I raised and trained Muffin. From her companionship, I fell in love with the playful and lovable personality of the breed, and I have had at least one cocker spaniel in my home ever since.

I wasn't originally going to include myself in this interview project of pioneers, but several people, including the coeditor of this work, Dr. Tiffany L. Otting, said it would be a mistake not to. Tiffany conducted my interview. She was a doctoral-level graduate student assistant at the time of working with me on this project. Tiffany Otting (see Figure 4.2) focused her doctoral study on animal-assisted counseling and completed her doctoral dissertation investigating the credibility of constructs of my human–animal relational theory. I was honored to be her major advisor. Tiffany's dissertation is titled *Human-Animal Relational Theory: A Constructivist-Grounded Theory Investigation* (Otting, 2016). So now, here is Tiffany interviewing me, on July 6, 2016, at a counseling clinic of our department at the University of North Texas.

Interview with Dr. Cynthia Chandler

Tiffany: Thank you, Dr. Chandler, for taking time to do this interview. I know that those who are interested in the world of AAT will want to hear from you about your experiences. And those are the kind of questions I'd like to ask you about today, your experiences and just what you'd like for the world to know about animal-assisted therapy. So could you tell us a little bit about your experience in the field and some of the work that you do at the University of North Texas?

Cynthia: Well, I got interested in animal-assisted therapy back in 2000 and just wanted to share the love and companionship that my dogs provided for me with the rest of the world. I received permission from the University of North Texas and my Department of Counseling to start a program to train and supervise counselors in animal-assisted therapy. And also, I started volunteering in the community, providing individual and group counseling, that is, animal-assisted therapy, as well as recreational animal-assisted activity at the county juvenile detention center. Since then, I've also volunteered in a number of different places. I volunteered at various hospitals in the community and did disaster and crisis response with animal-assisted therapy. I started the Consortium for Animal-Assisted Therapy in the year 2000 because I realized there was a great need to train professionals in this modality, and I also started a graduate course to train student counselors in animal-assisted therapy here at the university.

The field has grown a lot over the last 17 years, but when I was just getting started, there were no other universities out there offering this type of training in animal-assisted therapy for counselors. We were the first counseling program, accredited counseling program, in the U.S. affiliated with a university that started a training program in animal-assisted therapy. So we were the very first. A few other universities have started doing that since then, which is really good news.

I've worked with cocker spaniels doing animal-assisted therapy because I fell in love with the breed. I've had various cocker spaniels over the years. I've also worked with my cat, Snowflake, and I've done some equine-assisted counseling. So it's been a wonderful journey, and it's been a lot of fun. I've met a lot of people. I've traveled the world. I've been able to see the wonderful programs that are happening all over the world and met a lot of wonderful students and had a lot of wonderful animal teachers.

It was my dog Rusty that really taught me the power and the value of animal-assisted counseling. As we started doing it, I quickly realized the social magnetism animals have with clients, especially in the ways they help clients feel safe and comfortable, and how interaction with animals can challenge clients to recognize what was happening inside of them, the emotions and attitudes of the clients. Because the animals would attend to them or signal them, either move towards them or away from them, depending on what was going on inside of somebody. Observing that social dance between the animal and the client, the animal and myself, and seeing how the animal contributes some powerful dynamics to the therapeutic triangle, to the therapeutic alliance. By valuing these animals as social beings that appreciate a social relationship, and that signal the ebbs and flows of a social relationship, this has allowed me to be able to share that message with the rest of the world. I teach others how to recognize what an animal is trying to tell us in their body language and their vocalizations because animals care about other animals and other people that they're with. Animals socially engage with people to receive and give nurturing touch, and animals also will signal and communicate some very valuable emotions they perceive in others or experience in themselves.

Tiffany: So building off that a little bit, can you tell us about who's with us today and maybe what might be going on with our dynamics?

Cynthia: Well, this is Jesse, and she's my most recent therapy dog. She's the only therapy animal I work with right now. Jesse is my family pet. All of the dogs and the one cat I worked with were my family pets. Jesse volunteers with me at a local hospital, and she also comes up to the university and visits with students and goes to my classes with me. She works with me in providing animal-assisted supervision for my students. She also works with me when I occasionally practice counseling for clients at our on-campus clinic.

Tiffany: I notice that she's sleeping now.

Cynthia: She's very relaxed. She was just visiting with a number of children who are coming up here to the university clinic. She's been visiting with a number of them this morning, so she's pretty tired out.

We are sitting in one of our therapy rooms, which is dedicated to animal-assisted therapy. This is a counseling room in the development center, which is part of our University of North Texas counseling program clinic. We have three rooms that are dedicated to working with animals. We have about 15 total therapy rooms in this clinic, for both individual and group counseling, but two or three are dedicated for work with animals. That makes it easier to control for people who might have allergies, and we have posted outside the counseling room door "allergy alert, animals participate in these rooms." This particular room was set up with a nice couch, which allows a dog to lay next to a client if a client enjoys having closer contact with the animal. So we allow the dogs up on the couch to lay down and visit with our clients.

Tiffany: And you've developed a theory regarding human–animal interaction. I wonder if you'll tell us a little bit about that?

Cynthia: Yes. It all congealed for me in the spring of 2015. It's my journey through 15 years at the time of involvement with animal-assisted therapy, but it all came together when I was early in my travels of the world to interview other animal-assisted therapists. You see, as a profession, we were all relying on the only terminology that we had at the time to try and explain the power of animals engaged in assisting with therapy. We talked a lot about the human–animal bond. But to me that was too global of a concept. It's a correct concept, but it's too global of a concept. For me, it doesn't really pinpoint the moments that happen in the room, the therapy space, that are so powerfully therapeutic. And I felt that's where we as a profession needed to go. As a teacher, a researcher, and a practitioner, I have this need to be able to pinpoint what is happening, to recognize and then teach others how to recognize and value the specific dynamics that an animal adds to the therapy. So I had thought for many, many years, "How do I communicate this? How do I teach this?" So the pieces came together for me in 2015. I call it human–animal relational theory, HART; this is my theory [Chandler, 2017]. It describes how the moment you bring an animal into the therapy space there are a series of human–animal relational moments that are occurring. And through the constructs of my theory, what I can help a counselor do is to identify which of those moments are most significant. When does an animal signal something about a client? Or when does a client make a connection with an animal? Or, when does an animal make a connection with a client? At what special time? And for what special reason? Between the animal signaling, or the connections being made, or even if there's just a moment where the client may desire a connection greater than what might be occurring, it's a significant relational moment. Or maybe there are a few significant relational moments within all the series of relational moments that might occur within a counseling session. Some of these moments will really stand out. And they'll touch something deep within a client. And it's like a doorway that opens wider, and emotions go deeper. It helps the client go deeper within themselves to explore. Like silently reflect, "What was going on inside of me just now that the dog recognized that I needed a dog in my lap right now? The dog woke up, walked over to me and laid in my lap. What happened in me just now?" And when you query a client about that, they'll like, "Well, you know, at that moment I was feeling this" or "I was thinking about that."

A therapy animal is very accurate in signaling the internal experience of the client. We're not absolutely sure why. But not only do they hear and see what's going on with a person, we speculate they can probably smell it. And they can probably even taste it because their taste enhances their smell. Animals smell those hormones that are changing in a person's body, hormones associated with emotions. Animals not only help a therapist recognize the more overt things that are happening with a client in the way they respond, but they also help us recognize those things that are not so visible because they have some better sensory detection. They have this very powerful ability to smell and taste emotional change within a person's body. Animals are also very sensitive to the way things feel; they have a keen kinesthetic sense of what is going on around them. Most especially, dogs and horses can perceive emotions and express a reaction with immediacy. Other animals can too, but dogs and horses are especially keen at doing this.

Tiffany: Is there an example you can think of, a time when you've seen that happen with Jesse or any of the other animals you've worked with?

Cynthia: Oh, so many opportunities to share, to help somebody remember what a significant human–animal relational moment is. I call it a SHARM, as an abbreviated acronym. Look for those SHARMS. Look for those more significant moments.

There was a time when I worked with a teen in counseling, and he had a severe anger problem. He had explosive anger with his teen-aged peers in the juvenile detention center. The center thought they were going to have to send him to a more restrictive facility because of his anger. Staff knew that he liked animals. He had often mentioned missing his dog back home. And so they asked me to work with him in individual counseling. He was nonresponsive to all the other counselors, and so they asked me since I did animal-assisted therapy. I was a volunteer counselor at the facility, and they asked if he could work with me and my dog Rusty. When I would bring Rusty into the therapy room, this teenager would smile, a rarely seen behavior for him, and he would talk to Rusty in a way that he wouldn't talk to any person. And already, just through the greeting, from the moment that he was greeted by the animal, he became different. It touched a deeper place within him. A sense of safety, of comfort, of enjoyment. His fear was released. He became very responsive to therapy with Rusty involved, and he began to share things with me he wouldn't share with any other counselors. Whenever he would get to a moment where he was very subdued, and you could tell it was getting very, very difficult, very painful for him to speak, Rusty would sit up and he would look at the client, maybe start licking his hand or face. These moments stood out. And I reflected them. And the client felt supported by Rusty, so he would share something very painful, something he resisted sharing before but felt safe to share now. While he expressed very difficult concerns, Rusty would either rest his head on the client's lap and fall asleep while the client petted him or sometimes would sit next to the client and snuggle against the client's shoulder. There would be many times when this young man would be affected by Rusty's response to him. You could tell by the look on his face, the look in his eyes, that he was processing inside himself. He was affected by how Rusty was relating to him. I think that we have to value the internal processing that's going on, the private processing of the client. There's effect; there's impact even if there's not an external dialogue with a therapist. There would be times though that I would want to initiate an external dialogue, some external processing to ensure that the moment was not lost – just in case the moment might be lost otherwise. I worked with the client for 12 weeks before he was able to successfully and consistently manage his anger. Most of the success with him was because of his connection with Rusty. He had experienced horrible abuse in his life that explained why he was so angry and did not trust humans. By the third counseling session, he ended that session and every one thereafter by kissing Rusty on the top of the head and whispering in Rusty's ear, "I love you, Rusty." Close to the end of our work together, the client shared with me, "I did not trust you at first, but I watched you carefully with Rusty and saw how you loved and cared for him and how Rusty loved and cared for you. He trusted you. And I trusted him. So I figured I could trust you too."

There is benefit from pointing out to a client that something significant just happened involving a therapy animal. For instance, to say, "Rusty just sat up from his nap and licked your face." You can simply reflect this and see how the client responds. Or you can be more direct and follow with a question, "Did something change inside of you? Is there something going on inside of you Rusty is picking up on?" It is sometimes important to capture that moment that might otherwise be lost. There's certainly great value in a counselor initiating external dialogue or a client initiating external dialogue. Equally so, there's great value in internal or private processing going on. Processing the moment, that's a very important part of my theory. It's not just that we need to identify the significant human–animal relational moments; we also need to recognize the value of the internal and/or external processing. I call that human–animal relational processing, or HARP. Truly, it is the combination of a SHARM and the HARP that gives us the human–animal relational therapeutic impact, which I call HARTI. It's a little simple formula that I devised to help practitioners, and teachers, and researchers value and put together the most important constructs and see how they go together in a session: SHARM plus HARP equals HARTI [SHARM + HARP = HARTI]. You take a significant human–animal relational moment, plus the type and quality of the processing that occurred at that moment; it's going to determine the therapeutic impact, the human–animal relational therapeutic impact. If you keep the formula in mind, it is a nice simple guide. Of course, that isn't the end all of the theory. There are more constructs to the theory. But that is the heart of my theory, valuing these significant relational moments that occur, valuing the internal and/or external processing that's going on that's going to have therapeutic impact. Meaning that the processing is of some benefit or value to the client. And it is not the number of SHARMS that occur in a session that is of importance but rather the quality of the internal and external processing that occurs regarding a SHARM that most affects potential therapeutic impact. This is why the counselor must be very skilled at facilitating this type of therapy.

SHARMS can be nurturing relational moments with an animal or can be challenging relational moments with an animal. Within my theory, therapy animals play two primary roles. These are not the only roles they play, but two primary roles are certainly identified. One, an animal serves as nurturer. And two, the animal serves as emotional distress detector. Animals provide comfort and nurturance, which helps the client feel safe and more comfortable. The animals also will signal when they are perceiving or experiencing distress. If you act in a way that the animal doesn't feel comfortable around you, that animal is perceiving a stressor. Maybe they will act nervous or pull away, or try to calm you down, or whatever. Also, when they perceive that there's distress within a client or distress even within a counselor, they will signal that. They may try to move towards a person to calm the person down, to comfort you so that you're no longer distressed. They may choose to pull away from a person because the distress is too much; they're not feeling safe. They're like, "I don't know if I want to nurture this right now. I think I'll pull away a little bit." They'll either move towards or away from a stressor or stressed person, trying to make themselves feel better or whoever is experiencing the distress feel better. Again, animals serve in the roles as a nurturer and emotional distress detector. Those are two incredibly powerful roles they play.

My theory is very consistent with the science of relationship described in previous literature [Handlin et al., 2011; Odendaal, 2000; Odendaal & Meintjes, 2003; Olmert, 2009; Panksepp, 1998, 2005; Uvnäs-Moberg, 1998a, 1998b, 2005]. The desire for mammals, both human and nonhuman, to relate and the behavior of relating is referred to as the social response system. The social response system also interacts with the stress response system. All mammals, such as dogs, humans, horses, and so forth, share a similar social response system and stress response system. Because of their social response system, animals are designed to be social initiators and to seek the reward of social nurturance from interaction and play. The more domesticated they are, the more likely they are to do this with humans. And their stress response system is designed to have animals signal when there's emotional distress, that is, that something needs to be attended or avoided.

Tiffany: What might one look for? You call them emotional distress signals. What might a counselor or a client look for in an animal who's working in therapy to call attention to some things as distress?

Cynthia: There are three primary categories of animal communication I look for that reflect experienced or perceived stress: calming signals, displacement signals, and alerting signals. Calming signals are described throughout literature on animal communication. Some examples of calming signals in a dog would include a yawn, looking away, licking lips, rapid eye blinking, sniffing the ground, and so forth. For horses, you can add to that list empty chewing, pawing the ground, and some other behaviors. They're basically communicating there's distress being perceived or experienced. They're perceiving or experiencing distress. It could be coming from maybe a client, a counselor, or from something else in the environment. Displacement signals are sudden changes in body posture or position. For example, a dog sleeping next to a client suddenly sits up and looks at the client, or a horse backs away from a client. Alerting signals are just that; the animal is alerting that something needs to be pointed out, addressed, or attended to. This could come in the form of a vocalization from the animal or some behavioral manifestation, such as a dog pacing back and forth between the counselor and the client, or a horse redirecting its attention, or even an animal being repetitive or persistent with its behavior, as if trying to communicate, "Over here, focus over here. Focus on this. Focus on me. I am communicating something important."

Horses are herd animals; dogs are pack animals. They are designed to be part of a complex social system. They bring that into their relationship with humans. They have been domesticated with humans for thousands of years and are capable of including humans as extended herd or pack members. We need to be able to recognize animals' signals and appreciate those signals.

That's some ways an animal assists us in animal-assisted counseling. They can detect things that we can not necessarily detect. They can send us those signals immediately, and that gives us more information. Plus, they can provide comfort and nurturance. This is all very powerful in a counseling session. I know that you have worked with your dog Wally, in the past. He is profoundly talented in his ability to signal something needs attention. Share a story about him signaling, how he likes to signal that someone needs attention.

Tiffany: When we first started working, I actually thought it was going to disqualify him from being a therapy animal. He is a very vocal, verbal dog. We were working with a teenage client, who part of what she was coming into work for was social anxiety and a real obstacle in just verbalizing whatever it was that she wanted to share, whether it was getting a need met at school, needing to go to the restroom, or just making new friends. She was having a really hard time with that. Ironically or maybe not ironically, she was paired with a dog, my dog, who has no qualms about being verbal. In our sessions, she would clam up and not really want to talk. It wasn't her idea to come to counseling. She was being recommended by her parents. There wasn't a lot of communication verbally, but there was a lot of nonverbal communication happening from her. Wally just started barking in the room, not in an aggressive way, just a high-pitched, "Hey, hey, listen, listen to me." At first, I thought, "Oh no. He's scaring this client, and we're in a clinic with 20 other rooms. Everybody can hear him." Then, I think, he was aware of my own anxiety about that, which heightened his stress level.

Thankfully, I had you for supervision to discuss what was happening there. You very astutely noticed that he was calling something to attention. If I would acknowledge him, then maybe the client and I could figure out what was going on. The next session, when that all started again, I said, "Thank you, Wally. Thank you for letting us know something needs attention." I explained to the client. "When he does this at home, it's a cue to me that, hey, something needs attention." I asked the client, "I wonder what he's noticing between us that needs attention?" Of course, she's 14, so she's like, "I don't know." We worked through that. We had some conversations about that, and probably four, five weeks down the road, same client, she had her cell phone and it buzzed during the session. She picked it up and then turned it over, put it back under her leg, and tried to reengage with me. Wally started barking again, and he hadn't done it in a while. He started barking at her, and she said, "I know what that is."

Cynthia:	She said that about Wally, his alerting signal?
Tiffany:	Yeah, she said, "I know what that's about," and then started to tell me this story about her social life that she hadn't told her friends, she hadn't told her parents. It was really part of the crux of why she was in counseling, was her fear of communicating.
Cynthia:	The whole story unfolded simply because she recognized Wally coming over and signaling, "Something needs attention," with his barking. That opened up this whole other area for her to explore, that she hadn't shared with anyone else.
Tiffany:	Yes.
Cynthia:	She had grown to value the dog's signals.
Tiffany:	And recognize them.
Cynthia:	And respond to them.
Tiffany:	She [the client] was doing the work.
Cynthia:	It's like the dog cued her and she like, "Okay, you got me. Okay, so here it is."

Tiffany:	Yes.
Cynthia:	That's pretty powerful.
Tiffany:	Yes, and he didn't bark much after that with her. She felt safe then to communicate with both of us. We got a lot of work done.
Cynthia:	That's something fascinating that needs a lot more exploration. When an animal signals that there's this emotional response, it's like an emotional pressure that they're sensing, perceiving through smell or feeling. It's probably the hormones that they're smelling or tense energy they are feeling. Also, there's a pressure that builds up in someone when they're really anxious. For example, when a person is bordering on the precipice of resistance [not sharing] versus opening up, there's this pressure. The dog is signaling that through alerting signals, like a bark, or by persistently looking at a client, or looking back and forth from client to therapist, which I have seen Wally do. I recall my dog Rusty would lay his head on a client's knee or lap and just stare at the client with his big brown eyes until the client started crying, opening up, and talking more. Rusty had powerful counselor eyes. We know the animals are sensing something. They're perceiving something important. When the counselor facilitates, "Hey, what's going on with the animal, what are they picking up on," or the client initiates it on their own, "I think I know what the dog is signaling," then the client responds with an important catharsis. They open up. They move over the precipice of resistance and they start to share. What is so fascinating is, as soon as they start to share, the animal senses that the pressure's going down inside the person, and the animal calms down very quickly.
Tiffany:	He relaxes, yeah.
Cynthia:	Relaxes and often falls asleep, even if the client starts to cry and share very emotional things, because the animals senses, "Okay, it's being dealt with." The catharsis process itself is one in which the animal can actually reflect for us, "Okay, it's being dealt with. The issue is being dealt with. The pressure is releasing." I have seen this when working with my therapy animals. My client may be crying, but they're talking about the important concern. They're dealing with it. They're facing it. It's a lot of emotional pain, but the animal's okay with it because they sense, "Hey, it's being dealt with. They're finally facing it." It's like the client is over that angst of avoiding the issue. Sometimes, a therapy animal will just lay down and go to sleep when a client starts a catharsis, reassured the issue is being dealt with. But sometimes, I would see my therapy dog or a therapy horse I was working with respond with further nurturing behavior, more physical contact, maybe snuggling, when the client opens up, thereby reinforcing the depth of a client's sharing. Once a client started the emotional catharsis, my dog

Rusty would move his head from the client's knee or lap up onto the client's chest or shoulder and press against the client. This comforting behavior reassured a client, who responded by sharing even deeper things they really needed to share.

The pressure builds up through the avoidance, the resistance. Then the animal helps the client recognize, "You know, there's resistance here. There's pressure. You should just get into it." Then the pressure starts to subside, and then the animal reflects calmness again, and maybe even engages in nurturance. It's the great anxiety or tension in a therapy space that animals often alert us to.

Tiffany: It sounds like part of what you're saying is that the animal can often be a reflection of the internal experience of the humans in the room.

Cynthia: Absolutely. Animals will signal through their body language, or as in Wally's case, vocalizations, that there's anxiety that has to be dealt with. It could be a painful journey for a client, but the pain of not dealing with an anxiety, of holding it in and not processing through it, not moving towards healing, is greater. The animal is very uncomfortable with that; they really sense when there's tension or distress. And this tension or distress could sometimes be a client's resistance to healing, that a client is holding on to anxiety. Animals don't like that and act like, "You need to deal with this." Once the process initiates and the client starts to deal with it, the animal is like, "Okay, good." They'll often lie down and go to sleep or maybe comfort a client.

Tiffany: That's something we've seen consistently with the dog that I have worked with, Wally, you with Jesse, and also just students that we've supervised or colleagues that we've worked with, and even around the world now. It's not an isolated event. That is something that has been consistent across culture, across age of client, across breed of dog, across animal. To me, that's powerful.

Cynthia: Yeah, you have to address these moments because that helps the client address something that really needs to be attended. The animals are signaling to us, "That needs attention," and that helps us counselors be aware and the clients be aware. Then the clients start to deal with it, and the animals signal with a relaxed or nurturing behavior, "Okay, it's being dealt with."

That's one of the most powerful things to overcome in therapy, is a client's resistance to healing. That's one of the greatest gifts that the animals offer us, is that they signal that the resistance is there through the role of emotional distress detectors. This helps both clients and counselors, like, "Okay. All right, the dog is sensing that something's there. What do you think it is?" It's really interesting the difference between me just saying, "Hey, I think that there's something going on with you," when there's not an animal in the room – I'm still experiencing resistance from the client. When you bring an animal into the room or you're standing there next to a horse and say, "You know, I think this horse is signaling distress through its looking away and its empty chewing, so there's something going on." Clients value that because they know animals don't lie. Animals don't make stuff up. And they're not going to judge a person for anything other than the relationship they have with that person.

Tiffany: Talk about specific, measurable, observable therapeutic impact.

Cynthia: Time and time again, I experience when I say like, "The horse is signaling something that needs to be attended to," the clients just open right up. Whereas, when an animal's not present and I say, "I think there are things that need to be attended to," the client is like, "Yeah, I don't know. I'm not sure."

Tiffany: "I'm not going to tell you."

Cynthia: When the animal in the room or therapy space is signaling something and you point that out, and they're like, "Yeah, I know what the dog is talking about. I know what the horse is signaling," and then they get into it. They get the affirmation that "Yes that needed to be attended to." Even through tears, the client may sit there and pet the dog or the horse, and the dog or the horse may be very calm at this moment because the animal realizes, "Okay, good. They're dealing with it."

We really have to have a theory like human–animal relational theory. The field needs a theory to help understand these constructs. Human–animal relational theory is not meant to take the place of any other counseling guiding theory. It's actually meant to overlay. It's like a meta-theory to overlay. For instance, if you're person centered, stay person centered when you do animal-assisted therapy. You can overlay human–animal relational theory with your own counseling guiding theory, your own style of doing counseling. Human–animal relational theory will help a counselor and client recognize all these different and important relational moments. There are some SHARMs, significant human–animal relational moments, that are more common than others. The theory helps describe them, identify them, explain what to look for, explain how to identify and how to process it. That overlays whatever your existing guiding theory is. If you're gestalt, stay gestalt. My theory just helps a counselor utilize a primary counseling guiding theory within the framework of animal-assisted therapy and make it more powerful and potent because you have an additional guide on what to look for, what to value, what to identify.

Tiffany: It seems like the SHARMs would be pretty consistent across the board, but the HARPs, the human–animal relational processing, that might be particularly dependent on a counselor's guiding theory of how they might intervene or how they might choose to process with the client.

Cynthia: Sure. Different counseling guiding theories have different focus areas, and so how you choose to move your client towards healing might look a little bit different. The processing probably will be framed a lot within your primary guiding theory of gestalt, existential, Adlerian, person centered, psychoanalysis, and so forth. Human–animal relational theory helps you within that moment to recognize those valuable therapeutic opportunities that are occurring, to recognize this is a therapeutic opportunity and think "I want to remember this for later processing in this session or later processing in another session" or instead, "I think it's valuable to bring it up right now, so I'm going to bring it up right now, use some immediacy."

You may be immediate with your processing. You may delay your processing, but the important thing is to value the significant relational moments that occur. What is it telling you about the client? How and when do I share that with the client for the benefit of the client? I have found that most of the time, it's most valuable to go ahead and share it in the moment, but there have been other times that the client and the animal interacted in a way that gives me information that I might want to hold on to privately just to understand the client better or maybe even share with a client at a later time.

Timing is always an important thing to consider, when and how to share. The more you practice, the better feel you get for that, the whole idea of being able to value and utilize what these animals are providing. The most frequent question asked of me when I first started teaching animal-assisted therapy is, "What do you do with the animal in the room? What happens?" Though I could answer that over the years in different ways, I think I have the best answer for that today. It's presented best through human–animal relational theory. It's to look for the human–animal interaction as more than just "Oh, isn't this cute?" or "Oh, isn't this fun having an animal in the room?" or "Oh, doesn't it just feel good to pet or play with an animal?"

Tiffany: So after all of your years working in animal-assisted therapy, teaching animal-assisted therapy, researching animal-assisted therapy, what words would you like to impart to current and future animal-assisted therapists, practitioners, researchers, educators?

Cynthia: Animal-assisted therapy, in the counseling field, in the psychotherapy field, is a very powerful medium. We are discovering new things about its potential every year. There's new research, and practitioners are coming up with new ideas. For example, I came up with a new theory. As long as we value the contribution that the animal is making, then the potency of the field will continue to grow. It's not just that the animal is in the room, the therapy space; it's how the animal is acting and interacting in the therapy space. Whether it's sleeping, which is very comforting, or signaling distress, or licking your face, or laying in your lap, there's a lot of powerful things that are occurring with an animal that nurtures or signals distress.

What animal-assisted practitioners have to do is be able to understand the animals, appreciate the animals, value them as contributors to the therapeutic process, and recognize the number of therapeutic opportunities their presence and interactions create. You have to understand animal behavior. You have to understand animal communication. You have to find a way to integrate all of that into what you already know as a counselor, and all the while when practicing, maintaining the safety and welfare of all humans and animals involved in animal-assisted therapy.

It is an advanced form of therapy. It's very complex, and that's one of the things that a lot of people miss. Some people think it's as simple as "Okay, I have the education and credentials to practice counseling and psychotherapy, so now, I'm just going to bring my dog to work." From a risk management perspective, that's not a good idea. You really need to know what you're doing to protect the safety and welfare of the animals and humans involved, but also, it is a complex form of therapy, one where you need training. You need knowledge to be able to recognize what the animal is communicating and to be able to understand how to process that, internally as a therapist and externally with a client.

It's an advanced form of therapy. It should be integrated and practiced under supervision initially. Your supervisor should have some training and experience in animal-assisted therapy; the more, the better. Animal-assisted therapy is very powerful. What we understand about it now is profound, and knowledge is continuing to grow as we contemplate what animals can detect through their senses and communicate with their behavior. We still don't realize or acknowledge everything that animals can detect or communicate, but there is appreciation for their abilities.

Everything we are finding out from studying animals, like animal communication, animal social interaction, and animal integration into counseling and psychotherapy, everything that we're learning through investigation and practice, is supporting the power, the benefit of animals assisting in the therapeutic process. So it's much more than just taking your animal to work. You need to understand the science behind it. You need to study some theories about it, and you need some supervised practice.

It is very powerful, and it is helping us have breakthroughs with our clients much sooner than we would without an animal present. And it's helping us have breakthroughs that are much deeper with clients. So the efficacy of animal-assisted therapy is that it facilitates quicker and deeper processing and, therefore, more opportunities for recovery with certain clients. It doesn't seem to matter what age. Just about every age is appropriate for animal-assisted therapy.

There are a variety of animals that are very powerful cotherapists; maybe that's using that word too liberally, but there's a large variety of animals that work well within a therapeutic setting. So as long as you have the proper training and understanding of animal-assisted therapy, then you and your clients will do well. But you cannot assume that it is simple. It is complex. It is difficult. It does take practice, and supervision, and training. But once you get that, it's one of the most powerful counseling and psychotherapeutic mediums that I have ever practiced and witnessed.

Tiffany: Wow. Well, I want to thank you for doing all of this work and kind of leading the way in the field, for being a mentor that can open those doors to the powerful therapeutic impact of animal-assisted therapy. So on my personal behalf, "Thank you." But on behalf of the scores of other folks that you've impacted around the world, I know that they are thanking you with me.

Cynthia: I thank you for the interview.

Tiffany: You're welcome. And thank you, Jesse [who is still sleeping blissfully on the couch].

Editors' Commentary for Chapter 4

We have divided our commentary for this chapter into two parts since both of us were involved with the interview. First, I (CKC) elaborate on a few points for clarification. Then Tiffany provides her perspective. When I (CKC) speak of resistance in my interview, I am not limiting that to clients' resistance to a therapy process. I speak of resistance as a type of emotional intensity, that is an emotional friction or emotional pressure that can be distressful. Metaphorically, this is like resistance one experiences from dragging a heavy object across a surface or like building pressure against the walls of an inflating balloon. There are many forms of personal resistance, both within oneself and between self and others. Resistance may have many different manifestations, including self-criticism, self-doubt, fear, distrust, anger, avoidance. There are many types of emotional intensity from either positive or negative experiences, but when intrapersonal or interpersonal resistance (friction, pressure) occurs it is distressful. Distress is accompanied by a biological and sometimes behavioral response that many mammals (human and nonhuman) can detect through their senses. However, nonhuman mammals can often detect distress much better than humans because animals have some sensory perceptions that are more advanced, such as enhanced olfactory and kinesthetic sensitivity (Correa, 2005; HeartMath, 2006). Furthermore, nonhuman mammals will most often respond to distress they perceive in themselves or others with immediacy and authenticity as part of their innate survive and thrive biology (Panksepp 1998, 2005). Mammals' response to perceived distress in another may involve their moving toward the being in distress in order to tend, that is, to help alleviate the distress, or mammals' response to perceived distress in another may involve moving away from the being in distress in order to avoid. Mammals also give or seek out nurturance for social reward, and not just under circumstances of distress (Panksepp, 1998, 2005). Nonhuman mammals can be both emotional distress detectors and nurturers for each other as well as for humans with whom they socially engage (Chandler, 2017). Incorporating nonhuman mammals into counseling and psychotherapy can be of great benefit for humans, yet we must always be very mindful of preserving the safety and welfare of animals who assist in therapy.

I (TLO) am fortunate to have worked with Cynthia Chandler for several years. Having traveled the world with her, I have learned a great deal from her about incorporating animals into therapy. A salient lesson in her teaching and supervision is the welfare of those involved in the therapeutic process. In particular, Cynthia values equally the experiences of all beings involved in animal-assisted interventions. Like other contributors to this work, she is inclusive of the contributions of animals in therapy as more than mere reflections of human experiences. Chandler acknowledges human–animal interactions as authentic relational moments among sentient beings who are neurologically wired for connecting with one another.

Animals, mammals in particular, spend a lot more time using the parts of their brains responsible for survival, such as the brain stem and midbrain (Perry & Hambrick, 2008). For mammalian-brained animals, such as canines or equines, emotional intensity can not only be uncomfortable; it is experienced as a threat to safety (Bekoff, 2007). They alert us when a situation feels unsafe or needs attention. Just as one's companion animal may alert of an intruder or threat to the home, a therapy animal can alert us of emotional intensity that is intrusive or threatens the relationships in the therapeutic milieu. When the humans in the therapeutic milieu are incongruent, therapy animals feel uncertain about what will come next. Therapy animals feel the safest in congruent, predictable relationships. This should not be a surprise to us because researchers have found that the greatest human healing takes place in attuned, predictable, safe relationships (Perry & Hambrick, 2008; Siegel, 2010).

I (TLO) believe it is important in this text to acknowledge the visionary work of Cynthia Chandler. Her work *Animal-Assisted Therapy in Counseling* was the first to outline the practical implementation of animal-assisted interventions in the counseling field. Now in its third edition (Chandler, 2017), Chandler has offered a theoretical framework for recognizing and processing relational moments of connectedness between humans and animals. Those moments of authentic, relational connection are critical to moving through human resistance and improving the self and relational awareness of the clients who seek counseling and psychotherapy for healing (Otting, 2016).

Editors' Commentary for Part I: U.S. and U.K

A consistent theme presented in the interviews for Part I (Chapters 1 through 4) is how interaction with animals can very quickly move a client to a deep emotional place that pushes past resistance and facilitates healing and development. The authenticity and immediacy of animal social behavior provides soothing nurturance and valuable reflection of a client's inner being. Clients often feel they can trust animals because they are intrinsically honest; animals rely on honesty and immediacy for survival. The more clients engage with an animal in therapy, the more likely it is that clients trust themselves in social relating. When socially engaging with an animal in a therapy environment, a client's fragile or damaged self becomes more available for tending and repairing. With an animal's presence, clients tend to take greater risks with self-exploration, altering attitude, and adjusting behaviors. Experiences and lessons from practicing social exercises with an animal can be generalized for more satisfying engagement with humans in the client's life.

Those interviewed for Chapters 1 through 4 all valued animals' natural way of being and interacting as gifts to humans. Humans who experience animals' nature in a therapy environment can be moved to primal places where emotional wounds lie. With assistance of a therapist to facilitate animal-assisted intervention, a client may explore emotional concerns more thoroughly and thus recover more quickly and deeply, as compared with interventions without human–animal interaction. Interviewees described how animal-assisted intervention is a complex form of therapy because of increased dynamics that occur when integrating an animal into the therapeutic milieu. Thus, it is very important that therapists have training and supervised experience when first incorporating into their practice animal-assisted interventions for emotional and mental health.

References

American Counseling Association. (n.d.). Animal-Assisted Therapy in Mental Health Interest Network. Retrieved October 2, 2017, from www.counseling.org/aca-community/aca-groups/interest-networks

Bekoff, M. (2007). *The emotional lives of animals: A leading scientist explores animal joy, sorrow, empathy – and why they matter.* Novato, CA: New World.

Chandler, C. K. (2017). *Animal-assisted therapy in counseling* (3rd ed.). New York, NY: Routledge.

Consortium for Animal-Assisted Therapy. (n.d.). Home page. Retrieved October 1, 2017, from www.coe.unt.edu/consortium-animal-assisted-therapy

Correa, J. E. (2005). *The dog's sense of smell.* Alabama Cooperative Extension System, Alabama A&M and Auburn Universities, document UNP-66. Retrieved October 6, 2017, from http://www.aces.edu/pubs/docs/U/UNP-0066/UNP-0066.pdf

Handlin, L., Hydbring-Sandberg, E., Nilsson, A., Ejdebäck, M., Jansson, A., & Uvnäs-Moberg, K. (2011). Short-term interaction between dogs and their owners: Effects on oxytocin, cortisol, insulin, and heart rate: An exploratory study. *Anthrozoös, 24*(3), 301–315.

HeartMath. (2006 Spring). New meaning to "horse sense." *A Change of Heart,* 5(1), 1, 4.

International Society for Anthrozoology. (n.d.). Home page. Retrieved October 6, 2017, from www.isaz.net/isaz/

Odendaal, J. S. J. (2000). Animal-assisted therapy – magic or medicine? *Journal of Psychosomatic Research, 49*(4), 275–280.

Odendaal, J. S., & Meintjes, R. A. (2003). Neurophysiological correlates of affiliative behavior between humans and dogs. *The Veterinary Journal, 165*(3), 296–301.

Olmert, M. D. (2009). *Made for each other: The biology of the human–animal bond.* Philadelphia, PA: Da Capo Press.

Otting, T. L. (2016). *Human-animal relational theory: A constructivist-grounded theory investigation* (Doctoral dissertation). University of North Texas. Retrieved October 1, 2017, from https://digital.library.unt.edu/ark:/67531/metadc955020/

Panksepp, J. (1998). *Affective neuroscience: The foundations of human and animal emotions.* New York, NY: Oxford University Press.

Panksepp, J. (2005). Affective consciousness: Core emotional feelings in animals and humans. *Consciousness and Cognition, 14,* 30–80. doi:10.1016/j.concog.2004.10.004

Perry, B. D., & Hambrick, E. P. (2008). The neurosequential model of therapeutics. *Reclaiming Children and Youth, 17*(3), 38.

Pet Partners. (n.d.). Home page. Retrieved October 5, 2017, from https://petpartners.org/

Siegel, D. J. (2010). *Mindsight: The new science of personal transformation.* New York, NY: Bantam.

Uvnäs-Moberg, K. (1998a). Antistress pattern induced by oxytocin. *News in Physiological Science, 13,* 22–26.

Uvnäs-Moberg, K. (1998b). Oxytocin may mediate the benefits of positive social interaction and emotions. *Psychoneuroendocrinology, 23*(8), 819–835. doi:10.1016/S0306-4530(98)00056-0

Uvnäs-Moberg, K., Arn, I., & Magnusson, D. (2005). The psychobiology of emotion: The role of the oxytocinergic system. *International Journal of Behavioral Medicine, 12*(2), 59–65.

Figure 4.1 Dr. Cynthia Chandler with her dog Jesse. Jesse works as a therapy dog with Dr. Chandler. Dr. Chandler is the author of the classic book *Animal-Assisted Therapy in Counseling* and the founder of human–animal relational theory. She is also coeditor of this book. Photo copyright of Cynthia Chandler (used with permission); photographer unknown.

Figure 4.2   Dr. Tiffany Otting is a practitioner and researcher of animal-assisted counseling and is coeditor of this book. She has a private practice in Georgetown, Texas. Photo copyright of Tiffany Otting (used with permission); photographer Julia Alexander.

Part II
Israel

5 Dr. Sarit Lev-Bendov, Inbar Barel, and Gal Hakim of Oranim Academic College

Israel is considered among the leaders in the world in the area of animal-assisted psychotherapy in terms of academic training and prevalence in clinical settings (Israeli Association of Animal-Assisted Psychotherapy, n.d.). Training is available at universities that offer certification programs, which require multiple courses in subjects on animal behavior and communication and the human–animal bond and supervised practice of psychotherapy and animal-assisted psychotherapy. Researchers and practitioners make significant contributions to the field of literature with publications in professional journals and books. For example, the edited work *Animal-Assisted Psychotherapy: Theory, Issues, and Practice* (Parish-Plass, 2013) presents ideas from several recognized leaders. We traveled to Israel to interview practitioners, instructors, supervisors, and researchers of animal-assisted psychotherapy (AAP). We discovered on our trip that a common format for providing AAP in Israel is the small zoo. A variety of animals, most being small in size, are kept in pens and cages in an area with space where a client can interact with them. For example, some of these animals might be birds, rats, Guinea pigs, rabbits, ferrets, chinchillas, snakes, and goats. Also, pet dogs that belong to the therapists are often incorporated into therapy.

We went to Oranim Academic College in Kiryat Tiv'on, Israel. Oranim is a teacher training college in northern Israel. The college was founded in 1951 by the United Kibbutz Movement. It was named after the small forest of pine trees in the area. We first visited with Dr. Sarit Lev-Bendov, psychologist and animal-assisted psychotherapist, who described the animal-assisted therapy training program that was started in 1999 at Oranim Academic College. Dr. Lev-Bendov is the former director of the animal-assisted therapy program at Oranim Academic College (see Figure 5.1). The interviews at Oranim Academic College took place on December 10, 2014.

Interview with Dr. Sarit Lev-Bendov

Cynthia: Thank you for joining us today.
Sarit: My pleasure.
Cynthia: Tell us about your program.

Sarit: It's a program designed to train people to become therapists, animal-assisted therapists. It's basically a three-year program taking students who already have a bachelor's degree, usually in psychology, social work, or education, and giving them the specific training needed to become an animal-assisted therapist. In our eyes, that means learning about our cotherapists, our animal helpers, and learning in quite a few courses in psychology and psychotherapy, specific courses and general courses, also, courses like group dynamic or courses that focus on themselves, learning how to be more aware of themselves as therapists. And maybe the other aspect would be the internship, which starts from basically day one with very close supervision, with both private and group supervision following through the whole training process.

Cynthia: So in Israel, the interest in becoming an animal-assisted psychotherapist is broad enough that you can actually dedicate a whole training program to that.

Sarit: Yeah, it's getting larger, I think, every year. I think the understanding of the animals' contribution to children's life and to people with specific needs, I think it's getting bigger every year. It's a small program though.

Next, I interviewed the current codirectors of the animal-assisted therapy program at Oranim Academic College. Inbar Barel is a psychologist who practices couples and family therapy and specializes in animal-assisted therapy (see Figure 5.2). Gal Hakim is a psychologist who also specializes in animal-assisted therapy (see Figure 5.3). They both practice, teach, and supervise AAP.

Interview with Inbar Barel and Gal Hakim

Cynthia: Would y'all mind describing for us your animal-assisted therapy training program here at Oranim College?

Inbar: You spoke with Sarit; she was the head of the program with me for many years.

Gal: We concentrate in this program on psychotherapy.

Inbar: The main courses are about animal-assisted therapy. Maybe we will introduce our dogs that are part of our life and our academic field and also our work. This is Shimi. I found Shimi in a canal near the road on a very rainy night. He was broken all over. He worked with me for one year. He's two years old.

Gal: This is Mobley. She's very, very shy. She has lived with us for a few years. She has a story similar to Shimi. She was found also in a canal. It takes her a lot of time to found a relationship with children or with people. I really like to work with her because she builds the relationship very slowly. She doesn't give herself away in a minute.

I think she brings something special to the sessions, the therapy sessions that I do. I work with her.

Inbar: Most of the people that we work with are having massive emotional problems. The client can identify with the animals, that they have a problem of their own. And they see the resilience of animals. I think the resilience of the animals gives a lot of hope to the clients. The fact that we are working with dogs that are not perfect, it's very important in all the courses.

Gal: I think with Mobley, some of the clients see she has just one eye, some don't. It takes them awhile. And some just can't go near her because she's so anxious. One child that I worked with, she told me, "She's disgusting. She's so bad. She's so needy. I can't be around her." I think she brings something very strong to the session, and sometimes I ask myself if it's good to bring her to this session or the other because the child that I was talking about, she couldn't bear her presence. She just couldn't see her. It was too much.

I think it's our preference to bring animals that are not perfect. But sometimes, it's too hard and it's a question, how much the clients can deal with, when it's good for them and when it's too much. I deal with this question a lot.

Inbar: I think it's really a magical field. I work many years in the animal-assisted field. I'm an animal-assisted therapist myself, and I see the student in the field. Every year I'm amazed about this field. It's really magical, and I think that in our time, we can see that the magic can be measured in research. Just this year, it's beginning to be measured. I'm really excited about it because there are so many things that we couldn't find words for this magic, the connection. Not just the animals themselves make the connection. You can see all the attachment patterns with the patient or the client connecting with the dogs. I think with dogs, more than other animals, because I work with other animals in my clinic, they [dogs] are very powerful; they [dogs] think about the attachment. You can see that there is a difference; it's really a different issue.

Cynthia: The dogs contribute additional dynamics, additional psycho-dynamics to the whole relationship. And it gives you additional information that you can work with.

Inbar: When I work with couples for example, they can speak about the dogs, and I can discover other things about the problem behavior. We can see the problems in the families and in the dynamic between the couples. It's much easier to speak about the dogs than to speak about themselves or about the problems in their relationship.

Cynthia: It enables them to talk about difficult issues.

Inbar: Through the dogs. Through the problem of the dogs. The dogs are like a part of the family, and it's very, very important. Because other animals that we work with, like for example, there's a rabbit here or rats; there also can be a shift of sorts [seen] like as part of the family, but not like dogs. Dogs are really very much like a part of the family. That's why in the psychotherapy, all the behaviors of the clients are like a member of the family. It can be a sister or a brother or a husband or a wife or siblings or part of themselves.

Cynthia: The dog is considered to be like a member of the family, so it's close enough to that whole idea of it's being a loving being, it gives and takes love, that the clients can associate with the animal. And at the same time, though, the dogs are just a little less threatening than looking at another human being. So your clients can identify with a dog like a family member but are not as threatened by a dog as a human. Why do you suppose people are less threatened by a dog in therapy than a human therapist?

Gal: I think dogs are special in this because in general our perception is to work with animals that make a connection. We work on attachment; we work through the relationship. That's our baseline in all sessions. It doesn't matter if it's a dog or a rat or a donkey. But we look for the animals that can make the attachment. We work on it. I think dogs are unique because dogs have very similar characteristics as a human being. I think that's why we can be with them in the potential space. With the dogs we can go in the space, like it's very close to reality, but not. They take us as close as it gets I think.

Inbar: Many of my clients are very emotionally damaged from the people who were supposed to love them, from the parents many times. So the start of the therapy is very hard because I'm a stranger to them. They are used to being afraid of people or to being very careful. If we talk about attachment and they're [clients] trying to make a connection, we can do it in a way with the dog that is a shortcut because they [dogs] break the ice and they [clients] accept them. Of course, many of them [clients] are like Boris Levinson [1969] said – many of them start with the dog or with the animals, and they give us a chance to reach for connection and make it easier for us to work with them in the therapeutic alliance. And then we can work with them much easier. I think the intimacy comes much faster, and the environment is different when you have animals in the room.

Gal: I think there are two more important things that we didn't talk about. One thing is the simple fact that the dog moves from object to subject. Our baseline is the intersubjectivity theory [Stolorow, 1994, 1995]. When we work, make progress in the therapy session, we think of how we can go from object to a subject. I think with dogs, you can do an amazing job with it because they're a real subject. You can't just project everything on it because he shows you, for example, right now, Mobley is shaking. You can't see it and not do something about it. So it really helps you to develop the intersubjective relationship. I think one of our things is the feeling for what I do with her hair. Inbar asked me before, "What does she eat because she really feels so nice." I think of going to regressive stages in therapy, to go to the autistic contiguous position [Thomas] Ogden [1989, 1993] talked about. So I think with dogs, you can really go there. You can go to the regression in session. You can do it with other animals, but I think with dogs, they really make a strong attachment with you. So I think [with dogs] the first attachment with the contact, the touch, the aesthetic is unique because it's in a relationship. It's not just to take and pat a rabbit and to take another one and to change between them. It's to make a relationship and to feel the energy that is special between us.

Inbar: They're also an emotional barometric. They [animals] feel us, and their behavior reflects our emotion and also the client's emotion. So it's a matter of projective identification. Sometimes, I think they [animals] know how to do projective identification.

Cynthia: The animals can feel and respond to us.

Inbar: They are feeling and responding. It's very, very important in the psychotherapy process because we can see the process and be a bit outside of these relationships. When it's just me and the client, I'm in the relationship. I can't move outside and see how to identify the process, but dogs show me that. And I can also be in the session but, at the same time, be outside of the session. It makes the therapeutic field. I think it's much more complicated on one hand, but it makes it easier to see the scene and to understand it, much more activity.

Cynthia: The animals seem to give you much more information that you can utilize.

Inbar: And it's not just the information. It's really the whole, because it's not just I can see and know how to deal with it. It's all the relationship in the room. It's a real reparation. And there is all the time a triadic process, or more than triadic. Another thing I think about is that, when we speak with students or when we read about animal-assisted therapy, most of the time we think about the projecting we do on animals, that each animal reflects ourselves in some way. But if I speak about dogs, I think dogs are much more than just a reflection because they're really a cotherapist in the room.

Cynthia: Each of you have talked about the importance of the relationship. How do you teach a student that? How do you teach them to understand and appreciate how the animal facilitates the therapeutic alliance, how you want to facilitate a relationship between the client and the animal because, in doing so, then the animal can reflect the emotions that are going on in the client, help bring those emotions to the surface, allow you, the human therapist, then to process those with the client. How do you help a student understand that?

Inbar: I think, first of all, we work with the student about themselves. They bring their own stories, their own childhood, about living with animals. I think, if we will check why people become animal-assisted therapists, we will figure it out that they've been rescued themselves with animals. I think this is the only way that they can become animal-assisted therapists, by looking at their background themselves. You must go through all the process yourself to feel it and to be able to recognize the wounded places in their heart before you can do it with somebody else.

Gal: I think most of our classes are not theoretic. It goes from theory to their life, to their experience, to their experience with dogs, with other people because we do the therapies for other people. I think many times people come to this field, that they are very hurt from other people and they connect to animals. Like Inbar said, they go through their wounded places in themselves, and they try to do therapy on themselves. I think that's the main thing. They do therapy on themselves, and they're required to go to therapy if they can't do it in here, like it's an additional thing that they go through. It's a very long journey for themselves.

Inbar: The student must go through the theory in classes and go to the field, and we are giving students many hours of supervision all the time. All the time supervised. It's very important for us. I think in our Oranim College specifically, we teach many, many hours of psychotherapy before the animals are in the frame. They must be therapeutic people before they know how to speak the language of animal therapy.

Cynthia: This is a very complex, advanced form of therapy.

Inbar: Yes, yes.

Gal: Yes.

Cynthia: Well, let's finish up with letting each of you speak about the value of animal-assisted therapy and anything else that you'd like to say.

Inbar: I think I was born to this field, really. When I was young, in the army, I trained dogs, but still in the army, I created a project for working with people and dogs.

Also, when I was very young, I thought all the time about the connection between people and animals. I grew up in a kibbutz, and I worked with people and animals. I can see that when I was older I tried to figure out how it was so natural for me to go to this field because I believe it and I see how it helps so many patients or clients when other traditional therapeutic fields failed. It's a really amazing field, and I think we must relate it in a very serious level because sometimes I feel that it's like a bomb that you can explode if you're not doing it right. Because people speak more easily and share their inside world with us because of the animals. And we have to be very careful, and we have to respect the defense mechanisms because the animal, well, because the animals make us a bit naked. I hope you understand. I think there is a bit of a paradox because, when we sit with animals in the room in the therapeutic session, the animals make us a bit naked, all of us. Myself, because this is my child [the dog] and also here is my client. We have to respect very much the defense mechanisms because otherwise it can be very dangerous if you are not professional and don't know how to do it very seriously.

Cynthia: It takes us to a very vulnerable place very quickly, both the therapist and the client. And you have to be very aware of that.

Inbar: Yes, and to study many years to do it right. I think it's not something simple that you can learn in one month or one year.

Gal: I think they take us to the very earlier steps without words. It's so strong. Before I went to study psychology, I wanted to do therapy with dogs, without any words. I imagined myself sitting without talking, not just to talk about, just to feel it. I think they bring out the most primitive feelings that we have. It's so strong. So I relate to Inbar, that we need to be very careful with it. Sometimes, it's stronger than words.

Cynthia: Thank you so much. I'm deeply moved by what you shared.

Inbar: Thank you.

Gal: Thank you very much.

Inbar: Thank you very much for coming to Israel.

Editors' Commentary for Chapter 5

The program at Oranim Academic College is a well-integrated training approach for the practice of AAP. Students are required to take courses in psychotherapy theory and practice alongside several courses on understanding and working with animals. They also receive much supervision in the practice of AAP. The instructors in this program are experienced practitioners and supervisors who serve as excellent resources for students' training and supervised practice. The comprehensive training model for AAP at Oranim Academic College in Israel is very admirable. In the U.S., training for professional application of animal-assisted therapy is available at only a few colleges and universities and is usually restricted to one or two instructional courses and some supervised practice. In the U.S. there are opportunities for training in professional applications of animal-assisted interventions also offered by a few private associations. Those of us involved with animal-assisted counseling and psychotherapy in the U.S. very much wish there were more colleges and universities that offered comprehensive education and training in this field.

References

Israeli Association of Animal-Assisted Psychotherapy. (n.d.). Home page. Retrieved August 1, 2017, from www.iaapsytherapy.org/index.php/english

Levinson, B. (1969). *Pet-oriented child psychotherapy.* Springfield, IL: Charles C. Thomas.

Ogden, T. (1989). *The primitive edge of experience.* Northvale, NJ: Jason Aronson.

Ogden, T. (1993). *The matrix of the mind: Object relations and the psychoanalytic dialogue.* Lanham, MD: Jason Aronson.

Parish-Plass, N. (Ed.). (2013). *Animal-assisted psychotherapy: Theory, issues, and practice.* West Lafayette, IN: Purdue University Press.

Stolorow, R. (1994). The nature and therapeutic action of psychoanalytic interpretation. In R. Stolorow, G. Atwood, & B. Brandchaft (Eds.), *The intersubjective perspective* (pp. 43–55). Northvale, NJ: Aronson.

Stolorow, R. D. (1995). An intersubjective view of self psychology. *Psychoanalytic Dialogues, 5,* 393–399.

Figure 5.1   Dr. Sarit Lev-Bendov is the former director of the animal-assisted therapy program at Oranim Academic College, Israel. Photo copyright of Dr. Sarit Lev-Bendov (used with permission); photographer Amit Bendov.

Figure 5.2 Inbar Barel is a psychologist and the codirector of the animal-assisted therapy program at Oranim Academic College, Israel. She is holding Shimi in her lap. Photo copyright of Inbar Barel (used with permission); photographer Gil Nehoshtan.

Figure 5.3 Gal Hakim is a psychologist and the codirector of the animal-assisted therapy program at Oranim Academic College, Israel. Photo copyright of Gal Hakim (used with permission); photographer Inbar Barel.

6 Dr. Michal Motro and Tamar Axelrad-Levy of David Yellin Academic College of Education, and Dr. Lauren Wolfsfeld of the Hebrew University of Jerusalem

We traveled to Jerusalem, where we visited with Dr. Michal Motro, the director of the Institute for Animal-Assisted Therapy and Education at David Yellin College (see Figure 6.1). Dr. Motro introduced us to the clinic area and described the training program. Then the assistant director of the Institute, Tamar Axelrad-Levy, gave us a tour of the practice clinic for animal-assisted psychotherapy at the Institute (see Figure 6.2). The clinic had a large room in which the walls were lined with a few pens and cages holding a variety of animals and there was a large open space in the middle for interacting with the animals. Small cameras and microphones were attached to the ceiling, which allowed recording of the therapy sessions. While at David Yellin College, I also interviewed Dr. Lauren Wolfsfeld of the Hebrew University of Jerusalem. The interviews with Dr. Michal Motro, Tamar Axelrad-Levy, and Dr. Lauren Wolfsfeld took place on December 15, 2014.

Interveiw with Dr. Michal Motro

Michal: We are here in the animal corner of the David Yellin Institute for Animal-Assisted Therapy and Education. This is the oldest institute in Israel. It is 17 years old, and there are almost 300 people that have graduated from this program and are now all over the place in mental institutes, in delinquency programs, in kids that need special help programs, and with the elderly. And really, there is a lot of work, and a lot of people are gaining from these programs.

What we can say is that now, in this institute, we are really aiming at academic research that will really help to provide results that will be valid in any kind of academic discussions so that people won't say that "This is a very intuitive field" or maybe "There is something, but it's not really serious; it was never checked thoroughly." So now, we are on the verge of real academic proof of the situations here.

What we can say is that we see, for more than 17 years, work with animals brings about things that are very difficult to bring in other situations. Being with an animal really brings out things from the patient and from the therapist that were not there before, in a very expressive way, because animals need food, they need touch, they may be sick, they may be very sick, and you really have to approach these things which are really part of normal human life. But you can see them from a little distance. It's not really a far distance because an animal is an animal, and it has some characteristics that we have. So this is the situation where aggression can come out and can be dealt with and all kind of things that are really part of our life, our relationship with parents, with siblings. And in this situation, when you see them in another living creature, you can really bring something out more freely than in a human context.

And I'll say it again. You can really build with it. You can bring it out easier than in a human context. So that's the main thing. And what I'm happy about is that, these days, you can see institutes in Israel that teach animal-assisted therapy, and really, most of them do it very well. And, really, it's all over. And this gives me a lot of hope and happiness. And we are aiming now more into the academic world, into research, and into supervision and creating the new genre of animal-assisted therapist that can really help, with a lot of reputation and very experienced, people that can help other therapists, animal-assisted therapists, in their development as therapists.

Interview with Tamar Axelrad-Levy

Tamar: We are sitting here with Amy, the rabbit, and this is the guinea pig, which doesn't have a name yet. Kids give it a name whenever they'd like to give it a name. It's a she, by the way. And I would like to say something about why we built this clinic the way you see it. First of all, we have animals which are very social and can come to people, and they are very soft and can endure different things that some patients want to do with them, although I have to emphasize that, when we work here, we protect the animals, and I might get to that later. So the animals here can deal with different levels of stress which the patients are putting them through during the therapy sessions. The idea of building the animal corner like that is that, having big cages, like you can see the cage of the chinchilla, and this is the cage of the parrots, and rabbits, and guinea pigs, that the patient can decide whether he wants to sit inside the cage with the therapist or take the animal outside and sit outside [the cage] or whether he wants to do any activity with the animal inside while the therapist is outside [the cage]; everything is okay while the patient is here. Another thing is this open cage, which you can look outside and inside, which you can sit inside and look and see the entire animal corner, and I find out that sometimes patients like to sit inside and talk about different issues while looking at the snake, at the rabbits, or at the chinchillas. Also, inside, you can see big cages, which small kids can go inside and hide inside, and also sit in there and feel like this is their home; we do a lot of games and playing while we are inside this open cage.

All of that is to give the child the chance to express his inner world the way he wants to do that. So the animals . . . and I will say something which I want to be careful, but . . . the animals should represent inner images of his world. Like in play therapy, the toys represent the child's inner world, but we must keep reminding ourselves as therapists that this is an animal and not a toy. So it is important to have different types of animals. So we have the chinchillas living as a family, and most of the time, you have a very nice relationship between the father, the mother, and the children, and you can see family, although recently, one of their [chinchilla] kids was rejected by his family. We still have this rejected [chinchilla] child here, and the kids who are coming here know the story of this rejected [chinchilla] child, and children who are dealing with these issues in their family are sometimes . . . For example, I have a patient who asked me, "How can we make the family accept this chinchilla again into his family?" So this is the kind of thing which happens here through the animals, and this is how it raises the inner issues of the child.

Another thing that we have, the snake. Shall I take him out for a second?

So the snake is also an important animal, although not everybody likes snakes.

It's a corn snake. It was raised here by Michal [Motro], from a very young age, and he is very soft and nice. And kids know that he is here inside, and they can decide to take the corn snake and be with the corn snake. And we don't know yet, in animal-assisted psychotherapy, but I found that sometimes, when kids come in agitated and they're dealing with some sort of impulse and inner subjects, who are dealing with sometimes violence and suppressed things, they choose to take the snake. And we work with the snake. We let him crawl here, and then there's discussions which come up, like "Is he a danger to the guinea pig? Is he a danger to me? Will I be able to protect the animals, or even to protect myself, the child? And how dangerous is it to be with a snake and to let him crawl here?" So we work very much with this animal, but this is not the first priority of the children. Most of the time, when they feel secure enough, they decide to take the snake and work with the snake. Out of that, we have hamsters and mice and gerbils, as well, and rats, which are in the other room. And they're also very important animals in the animal-assisted psychotherapy because each type of animal can represent another issue of the child's world.

Another thing which you can see here, we have the kitchen. The kitchen is very important because, sometimes, kids are dealing with very early issues around food and touch, so here they can prepare [food] for the animal. Of course, I don't enforce them to prepare this; it's their decision. And they can decide whether it's going to be a very nice, fine, salad or whether it's going to be throw the vegetables into the cage. They have different things on this big can for food.

And sometimes, children like to dig inside and work with the food and play with the food, and a whole long discussion is coming up about the necessity of food: about not having food, about the fact that I have too much food here for the animals, and "What about the kids? Do they have enough food?" or "They don't have enough food." So while playing with the food, we can speak about the symbolic issues of food, of nurturing, of not being nurtured well while they were infants, and so on.

We have also some other tools to calm the animals. And if they want to see how much the animal weighs, and so on, they can do that. Of course, everything is due to their willingness to do that, and we try to find "What is the meaning of this activity which the child is initiating in the therapy session?"

That's about how this animal corner works for having psycho-therapy treatments for young children. Okay, one more thing about the supervision program.

Thanks to the college here, we got some [funds] for two research projects. One research project is also funded by the state of Israel, by the Education Ministry. The first research is based on a pilot research which we did two years ago, and the subject of the research is "What comes up when children play with animals?" The motivation to do this research was the fact that, we're letting children play with animals, and we want to know what comes up from the inner world. But as far as I have found, and also Michal [Motro] and other people here in our program, we don't know how children really play with animals. We have some research done by people trying to find out what children think while they play with their animals, but nobody really filmed that and analyzed what happens when children play with animals. So based on what was found in our first research, this pilot research, we decided to extend this research. This time, we are going to let the children play here, and we are going to document that. After they play in two different sessions, we are going to interview the kids and ask them some basic questions about their experience while they were playing with the animal. The children will come to this very room tomorrow morning, and they will be able to choose any animal which they want to play with, and they will play with the animal for 40 minutes. If they would like to change animals, it's possible. We have four cameras which you can see in four corners, and we have the microphones which come from the ceiling. Everything is going to go in a closed TV cycle into a computer, where we're going to have these four cameras, and we are going to have the videos which we are going to analyze later. We have some other researchers who joined us in that project, and we are going to do it as a team, analyzing together, seeing what comes up from those videotapes and trying to find out what are the major things which come up while children play with animals.

A second research which we're going to do, it's going to be from my PhD. We are going to film here ten different patients, who are going to participate here in animal-assisted psychotherapy processes for one year – meaning 25 to 30 sessions. And we already got the approval for all those procedures, and the college very nicely gave me this animal corner to use it freely for this research because they want to support me in this research. and I have to really say that I appreciate it very much. That part is going to start in January, maybe the beginning of February, while we are going to talk to the parents of the children [and] talk to the children; they will know that we're going to tape everything here. Also, we're going to analyze those hours with my supervisor and other people and see what comes up in animal-assisted psychotherapy. That's what those two research [projects] are which we are going to do this year.

And the last thing, which is very, very important for me, is the program for supervision which we put all together here by the help of Dr. Lauren Wolfsfeld from the Hebrew University, the social work department. Lauren is an expert in supervision of social workers and has other expertise in people who work in emotional treatments. She brought the idea to Dr. Michal Motro, and we started this program with Dr. Ofra Kamar, who is the director of the art therapy department here. For one year, we were building the course about how we train therapists who want to supervise other people who want to be animal-assisted therapists. So we worked very hard on this program, and I will let Lauren explain how this program worked. I was dealing with the part of how we work here with the animals, and we did some exercises and activities with those students here while starting the supervision program., but if I have time, I will say that later. I will let Lauren explain how this program worked.

Dr. Lauren Wolfsfeld was present this day at the clinic of the Institute of Animal-Assisted Therapy and Education at David Yellin Academic College, and she agreed to be interviewed about the supervision program she helped to develop for therapists who practice animal-assisted psychotherapy. Dr. Wolfsfeld is head of the Fieldwork Division of the Paul Baerwald School of Social Work and Social Welfare of the Hebrew University of Jerusalem.

Interview with Dr. Lauren Wolfsfeld

Cynthia: Tell us your role in supporting animal-assisted psychotherapy.

Lauren: I'd like to share with you an experience that I had, really, a privilege that I had, to be part of something very exciting that we built here at the college [at David Yellin Academic College]. Around five years ago, Michal Motro called me, and we had a nice meeting on the phone. One of the things that was very apparent from her discussion with me was that there was an anomaly. There was a situation that was not clear, and that was that, although the field of animal-assisted psychotherapy was already, I don't know, at the time maybe 12 years old or 10 years old, there was no way that a person who trained in this wonderful, special, helpful area would be able to supervise and be acknowledged as someone with certification and supervision unless they were either a psychologist or a social worker. Now, I am a social worker, but I understand coming from a very, very traditional hundred-year-old profession that you have to work and find ways to make these new professions develop and grow.

What we did was we took a year and we sat together, Michal [Motro], myself, and Tamar [Axelrad-Levy], I believe, and we built a model that I have implemented in other areas as well, to take seasoned senior therapists in your field and to allow them to become certified through the college as supervisors in this area. The program is very simple. It is a two-year program that has several components. One component up front – it was a small group, so it was really very interactive and very interesting, but learning the theory of supervision and techniques of supervision. Then there was another component where they learned, these wonderful professionals, the state of the art, what was going on in the field of animal-assisted psychotherapy. The third part was group supervision on supervision, where the students in the course could discuss their supervisors. What I didn't say was, because this is a college that trains students in the area of animal-assisted psychotherapy, we had a whole bunch of students that could be our supervisees. Until that date, the supervision in the college was done on a group basis.

We offered to augment the supervision of their students using the students from the supervision course. and I have to say, I've been a social worker for many years, I've been dealing with supervision, and I'm the head of the supervision department at Hebrew University School of social work, but this was an innovative, exciting, new way to allow people who don't have to be a social worker to supervise people in this field. You don't have to be a psychologist. You have to be a wonderful professional who knows enough about the field of supervision, which is basically how to be a private tutor and teacher. That's what we learned for two years. We have probably 18 graduates, and now, we hope that they will gain the recognition that they need within the field itself to be recognized as full-fledged supervisors. This year we took a break, but hopefully, we will be able to continue and have a wonderful, rich pool of great professionals who can then bring the world further to the younger generations. That's what we did here.

Cynthia: Thank you for describing the development of the supervision program.

At this point, Tamar Axelrad-Levy joined in on the interview I was conducting with Dr. Lauren Wolfsfeld. While serving as the assistant director of the Institute for Animal-Assisted Psychotherapy and Education at David Yellin Academic College, Tamar was also a doctoral candidate at the Hebrew University of Jerusalem, under the guidance of Dr. Wolfsfeld.

Interview with Dr. Lauren Wolfsfeld and Tamar Axelrad-Levy

Cynthia: So you've each done a formal talk, and now is the chance to talk more freely about how you think animal-assisted therapy is an important field. Anything you haven't already said.

Lauren: You [to Tamar] do the animal-assisted psychotherapy. You come from more traditional social work, so maybe you can talk about what you see is happening.

Tamar: So Lauren is my supervisor, advisor for my PhD thesis, and started to work with me two years ago. And while we were sitting together and trying to understand what am I going to do in this research, we had a very, very interesting discussion. What is this animal issue which we bring into the clinic, into the psychotherapy situation? And I was very much challenged by Lauren's questions on why should we bring an animal into this process for children. How does it help? So I brought the different case studies to the session, and I was sitting with Lauren and saying, "Okay, let's look at that. Let's see what is going on here and what we want to research, what we want to look at." I think it was also, for me, very interesting to see how people who don't work with animals, slowly, slowly get to understand how animals can help children to express themselves.

Lauren: I think that one of the things that Tamar was helpful in teaching was that, unlike play therapy, where there is a symbolic represent-ation of the inner world of the child, here there's also a real inter-action. And I remember very specifically, we're talking about a case where a child was touching a ferret, through a sleeve. And we spoke about the fact that there is, besides the fact that the child might be projecting aggression and anger, the ferret could have bit the kid. And one of the amazingly interesting parts of using a live animal in an interaction is that there is truly an interaction. That was something that we're trying to incorporate into Tamar's doctoral thesis. What does that mean? That it's not only an internal representation but also a real-life interaction that can be built and that can be transcribed and can be transformed as the child learns to deal with issues within themselves.

Cynthia: So working with a human therapist has been beneficial, a very important part of the process, but a human therapist can be threatening still because they might remind the child of another human in the child's life that is scary. And working with a toy can be very beneficial, but the toy doesn't respond like a social being. So the animal is a nice intermediary. It's not as threatening as a human, but it is also a reactive social being. It's almost as if the animal's presence gives greater opportunity for both conscious and unconscious processes. The psychodynamics of therapy are actually enhanced. The opportunity to recognize and utilize those psychodynamics is enhanced with the presence of an animal, and a facilitator who is a human therapist, and the client.

Lauren: Exactly. One of the other things I think, Tamar, maybe you can talk about a little bit, is that we're intrigued by the fact that there is a dual loyalty of the therapist in wanting the child to have the most successful therapy experience but also, at the same time, having to be protective and caring for the animal. And that's something, that dichotomy, or that tension, is also something that is very clear and very strong.

Tamar: That is a core issue of animal-assisted psychotherapy, in terms of how we train these students and the people, because besides the subjectivity of the animals which comes into the session, by definition I think, the kids who are coming to this therapy have an inner world which is intensified by not really nice things. And we want to let them express it in the room. And my goal, and my duty as a therapist, is to let them express it well.

Now, if this was a toy, okay, "You can throw this toy." And I can relate to that, that you are angry and you want to express your anger, but I can't let the patient do any harm to the animal. But on the other side, I want to let him express his inner world. How do we do these two things together? I claim that a well-trained animal-assisted psychotherapist is sitting in between these two things, and he's moving his head to the animal and to the patient and saying, "What shall I do? What shall I do? How should I do this?" Let the patient express himself and protect the animal. And most of the people that I interviewed for my PhD, who have been working for many years in the field, say, "We are sometimes tired of [challenged by] this situation, to be in between and to make very quick decisions." Whether I'm going to protect the animal or how I am going to protect the animal and not educate the kid, saying, "No, no, no. You are not allowed to do this." Because this is not psychotherapy.

How can I channel the child into doing something that he will still be able to express his needs, and his word, and his inner world, but yet, the animal will be protected? And we have dozens and dozens of examples of that and how animal-assisted psychotherapists are dealing with those examples. And I think this is not solved yet, this issue.

Cynthia: Give us some examples of moving closer to that resolution.

Tamar: I'll say a remark, that I'm not talking about those sinister situations where we feel there is a danger to the life of the animal. That's cut clear; I stopped it and I said, "This is too dangerous for the animal." But now, I talk about the gray areas. Okay, one of my children [client] was very, very afraid of making changes to her body. This child was very much afraid of changing, and she did a haircut. And as I saw her coming into my clinic, I said, "Uh-oh. Today, my hairy guinea pig is going to deal with this haircut that she went through." And she took this beloved guinea pig, which she worked with, and she was starting to pet her, and she said, "Do you think we can give her a haircut?"

Now, the guinea pigs, sometimes they need haircuts. We can do that. This is something which we can do. So I said, "Let's start to give a haircut," and I spoke about the fact that she wants this guinea pig to feel as she felt when she went to do her own haircut. Sometimes guinea pigs need haircuts, as you saw their hair. So it's not something which is going to interfere with them. So I said . . . I told her that she wants to let her guinea pig feel what she felt while she went for this haircut, and she said, "Yes, she has to feel that." She started cutting hair, and I was very much checking that she is looking and not going to her head because she has her ears, which are very gentle, and her eyes. And I said, "You can do the haircut from here to the bottom." And she was listening to me, and I said, "Okay, she's listening to me. I can let her keep going with this activity." The guinea pig was quiet for a while, and she was cutting some pieces and collecting the hair outside, and we were talking while she was doing this haircut. We're talking about what the feeling of this guinea pig is now, and this reminds her of her feeling and why she has to feel that, as she felt while she was doing her haircut.

And at one point, the guinea pig starts to whistle. Small, small whistles like that, and I said, "Oh, maybe she is telling us something." So she said, "Well, she's telling us that she doesn't like it anymore." And that was the point I decided to bring the animal subjectivity into our discussion, saying that, maybe for her, that now, she has this very important thing that she feels like she has to continue and do this haircut. This is her need, but now her need is standing with another need of the animal, which is telling us, maybe she doesn't need it anymore. And we have two different needs in our room now, and it's very difficult to know to what need we are going to listen.

And she was listening to me, and then she said, "Well, Tamar, let me do another ten cuts with the scissors, and then I'll stop." I said okay. She did. The guinea pig kept whistling. And then, when she came to ten, she said, "One more! One more, Tamar!" I said, "Okay, one more." And then she put the scissors outside, and she was agitated. She wanted very much to continue, and I said, "I feel how much it's difficult for you now to recognize the guinea pig's needs because your needs are much stronger, and they're very precise . . . they're very present here in the room." But with that, she decided to listen to her [the guinea pig], and it's very difficult to listen to her [the guinea pig's] needs while you have your own needs. So this, I think, of the gray area, is an example of how we should deal with that. But I have to say that I'm very, very smart to say that now. I was standing there, and I was asking myself, "What am I doing? What am I doing?" I knew that she's going to do a haircut, almost making her bald. I knew it's going to get to that, but I was dealing with myself, inside myself. "Tamar, what is going to be the point that you are going to bring the subjectivity of the animal?" And the guinea pig helped me because she whistled. I don't know how this situation would have been with a rabbit, which doesn't usually do any noise to say that something goes wrong with him. Like Amy [the rabbit], she is so quiet. She would let her do it forever and ever, and I would have to raise her voice [be her voice]. In this case, the guinea pig helped me and raised her own voice.

But sometimes, I have to raise the voice of the animal [speak for the animal], and that's the most important issue of how we deal with that. And we sometimes, as different in play therapy, we live in a world of the child. We're taking from the inner world to meet the reality which is going on in the room. And we have to be gentle and soft and not attack the kid with that. And that's something which we should learn. I don't think I'm good in that yet. And I keep learning, myself, all the time how to do it, how to bring the subjectivity of the animal into those situations and knowing how I'm moving from one media, the inner world of the child, to the reality which is created here in the room. And the reality is also including me because some things that a child is doing is not good for me.

Cynthia: What you described is very complex, and a psychotherapist would need to be very aware of the child's needs and very aware of the animal's needs and utilize that awareness in facilitating the therapy, all the time succeeding in keeping the child safe, and the animal safe. So it's an advanced form of therapy. It's very complex, and you're making decisions as you go. It's not always clear exactly where you're going. You do have limits; you do have clear limits about safety. It is also very important that you be aware of animal behavior, for instance, so that you recognized when the guinea pig whistled that it was communicating some distress and discomfort. And you helped the client understand that.

Tamar: In a course of ethics which I teach here, our second year, I send my students to do a project. It's not only knowing the nature of this specific species, like rabbits and guinea pigs. It's knowing this specific animal which I'm working with. As I told you, Amy [the rabbit], I know her limits. I have to stand up for her limits, Amy the rabbit. The guinea pig, on the other hand, has its own limits. She knows when to tell the patient, "That's it. That's enough." So I send my students to watch their animals for 20 minutes, far away from the cage of the animal, and to learn how they behave, and then to approach the cage and see how the animal responds to them while they are near the cage. They have to write reports and to write and to see the differences on the behavior of the animal in those two situations and then, again, when they come with a client to the therapy session. So they have two to three different times that they report. The animal by her own, the animal with self, and the animal with a client. And I say to students, "This is very important for you to learn the nature of the animal. That's why you have to know the animal by heart." It's not just bringing in animals.

That's why it's small; this is a small collection of animals, so I know everyone by heart. I come every morning and say good morning to all the animals. I know who is hiding, who is going to come and climb on the cage, and who is going to sniff. And if he doesn't do that, I know that something is wrong. And I am going to check this animal. So before I get into my clinic sessions, I have at least half an hour, if not more than that. Here, it's more than that, to walk around the cages, look at each animal, and see how the animal feels today, whether I'm going to work with this animal or not. And if the animal is not well, I'm not letting the client work with her. And I will say, "I think this animal today's not well. We wouldn't let her work today. Let's choose another animal." This is another part of the reality.

Cynthia: When you're training students, how do you help them understand these complexities of animal-assisted psychotherapy?

Lauren: Because my training is in a different sphere, I left the delicate parts of the animals to the professionals here. And, that's why we added a state-of-the-art supervised training, and that's where these kinds of issues were discussed and learned.

However, I can say that just listening to my wonderful student here, two things come up from the world that I come from. One is, what do you call the child that's coming for therapy? You [to Cynthia] interchange "patient" with the word "client." And I think that it's really, really important, when you're talking about psychotherapy, to recognize that we've come a long way, baby, and that we're no longer so painfully psychodynamic.

And I think that we have to be very, very careful, from the world that I train, and that's one of the things that we did in our course, [discuss] "What do we call the person who comes to treatment?" We talked a lot about the modern theories and the postmodern theories, and that's the world that I could bring. It used to be, when I was a student many, many, many years ago, being eclectic was a way of saying you didn't really know much about anything. And now, being eclectic is a very, very respectful way of looking at people first and using our knowledge as a bridge to help better understand them. So that's one thing that we could put an emphasis on.

The second thing is that, in some ways, having a creature, having a living animal in the room, takes in a whole new area that's not so psychodynamically oriented, but it's more family oriented and allows that wonderful thing that's called "enactment." When you have a family in the room, you can do it in live time. You can say about a child, there's two systems of needs that are colliding in this world [of animal-assisted psychotherapy]. And it's teaching them something about themselves and their needs and being with them and being for them, but in a context of life. And I think that's something that is very interesting because here, we're still very psychodynamically oriented. But still, I don't know how it is in the United States, but here, we're very psychodynamically oriented in this field. And yet, we're enabling things that can't happen in that little world of one on one. And these other tensions were brought up in the course, and we talked about it extensively in trying to train people to think about what they do.

Cynthia: Any final thoughts to share about the value of animal-assisted psychotherapy?

Tamar: I think it's a great profession, which should be taught deeper and wider in the world. Also, the way in which we are doing it here in Israel, which, as far as I know, is not very well known in the world, needs to be expanded. While we go into thinking of these traditions, psychodynamic therapies, we're talking about the kid doing it slowly in his own pace and in his own way, and it takes time. And here, I think the animal enforces the reality and [helps the child] to deal with reality more often. And if there is a good therapist there, we can make it [accomplish it] in a short time, but with good results because you deal with all those different roles and the kid does these steps because the animal is there. And he loves the animal, and the animal is so approachable and bringing so many things to these sessions. So the kids usually are driven to do this change because of the presence of the animal, not only because of the therapist.

Cynthia: The animal helps bring the issues to the forefront much quicker.

Tamar: Yes, and so the issues can be dealt with much more quickly. We love the animals, and most of the kids love the animals. So I think they are more willing to deal with these issues than they would have done with [just] an adult in the room because the animals make it more simple, more precise. I can talk about the guinea pig which needs a haircut. It's much easier to talk about the guinea pig who was afraid of the haircut when she [the client] was afraid of that. While she [guinea pig] started whistling, it was because she was afraid. It's wonderful. So we discussed her feelings and the needs of both of them [client and animal] in one discussion. And that's what's fabulous in this profession, I think. You do both.

Cynthia: Do they associate you with the animal and like you quicker and faster because of your association with the animal? Have you ever considered that a possibility?

Tamar: I think there is a point in that, which I haven't yet figured out, but I think, yes. Part of what came up from the interviews, which I am doing now for my PhD, is that clients see their therapist as reliable, more than other people, because they take care of the animal and that they are very fine caregivers or they're a good enough mother to the animal. I think they see the therapist as a good enough therapist because they see how we take care of the animals.

Cynthia: And that piece of information allows them to trust you more, and also they can reveal more about themselves because of that.

Tamar: I think so. I hope, while I'm running with my PhD, I will be able to say something more about it, but it comes up from the interviews. This is one of the issues which is important, one of the components of this therapy.

Lauren: I would say that, after years of trying to understand what really helps, I'd say it was compassion. In traditional therapy, empathy is usually something that the therapist tries to show the client, but here [in animal-assisted psychotherapy], the child has an opportunity to translate empathy into compassion for another life. If we had one thing to teach kids, it would be how to really move out of themselves and see the other person. And that can happen in the room with the animal, and it can't happen if the animal is not there. It can't really happen with a doll, and it can't happen only with a dyad.

Cynthia: They can take that relational risk with the animal, and then that can be transferred to other humans. They relearn how to engage and trust with humans.

Lauren: Exactly. They can rehearse it.

Cynthia: Rehearse it in a safe place.

Lauren: Mm-hmm [affirmative].

Cynthia: Thank you so much. I really enjoyed visiting with you today.

Tamar: Thank you very much, to you.

Cynthia: And I appreciate you sharing all these wonderful things that you're doing in your program. Good luck in your research.

Tamar: Thank you.

Editors' Commentary for Chapter 6

Incorporation of a small zoo model for therapy is intriguing, and we could appreciate the therapeutic value of this model. The small zoo model involves a small number of a variety of animals present in the immediate therapy space. This arrangement allows a client to move from one animal to a different animal in the same therapy space. This model is not common in the U.S. However, some therapists in the U.S. have a therapy space where a variety of a few small animals are available for a client to interact with, such as guinea pigs, rabbits, or birds or an aquarium of fish.

David Yellin Academic College of Education, located in Jerusalem, has a comprehensive training and supervision program for animal-assisted psychotherapy. Students are required to take numerous courses in psychotherapy and courses on information about animals and working with animals. Furthermore, thanks to collaboration with Dr. Lauren Wolfsfeld from the Hebrew University of Jerusalem, Dr. Michal Motro and Tamar Axelrad-Levy of David Yellin College, and others, a program for training professional supervisors for animal-assisted psychotherapy has been developed. This provides consistency in training and important oversight for the field.

Figure 6.1   Dr. Michal Motro is the director of the Institute for Animal-Assisted Therapy and Education at David Yellin College, Jerusalem, Israel. Photo copyright of Dr. Michal Motro (used with permission); photographer unknown.

Figure 6.2 Tamar Axelrad-Levy is the assistant director of the Institute for Animal-Assisted Therapy and Education at David Yellin College, Jerusalem, Israel. Photo copyright of Tamar Axelrad-Levy (used with permission); photographer Tamar Axelrad-Levy.

7 Rabbi Eitan Eckstein and Efrat Maayan of the Retorno Jewish Center for Addictions

We traveled southwest from Jerusalem to the Retorno Jewish Center for Addictions. It is located very near Beit-Shemesh, Israel. Efrat Maayan described Retorno in the following way.

> It is a therapeutic community for detoxification: drugs, alcohol, gambling addiction. Many of our patients are amazing intelligent and talented people who, due to difficult life circumstances, undiagnosed learning disabilities, family problems, traumas and identity difficulties, have been sucked into a sad cycle of addiction, self-destruction, crime, and inability to manage life. We also have groups of American, Canadian, European and Australian Jews who come to this wonderful place to receive treatment and save their lives. The animal corner is an important and central place for them to give hope, belonging, healing, connection to themselves, experiences of success, rehabilitation of the ability to take responsibility and reconnect to life and love.
>
> (Mayaan, personal email communication, August 16, 2017)

At Retorno we first met briefly with Director Rabbi Eitan Eckstein, who provided a history of the program (see Figure 7.1). Then psychologist Efrat Maayan, a practitioner at Retorno, gave us a tour of the animal-assisted therapy area there, the small zoo. They had just built new pens for the animals that, in color and shape, looked very natural, much like very small versions of the sloping hills of the landscape surrounding the facility. The animal pens and cages surrounded a small yet spacious domed enclosure where a client could take an animal inside to interact with the animal. The room was cozy enough for individual therapy yet also large enough for small group therapy. The interviews with Rabbi Eitan Eckstein and Efrat Maayan took place on December 15, 2014.

Interview with Rabbi Eitan Eckstein

Eitan: My name is Eitan Eckstein. I am the CEO of Retorno, Israel. Retorno is the Spanish word for "return." It's called this because, 25 years ago, I began working with addicts in Mexico as a community rabbi. I came across the reality of kids, good kids, from the best families, doing drugs, alcohol, and getting lost in this wild world. I began working with addicts in Israel around 17 years ago, and we now have a few projects in the field of addiction treatment. We are doing a lot of work in addiction prevention and education. Thousands of students come here every year for our prevention programs, and thousands of soldiers. Professionals, teachers, and social workers come here to learn our special approach towards treating kids and adults with addiction.

We have two communities. One for youth, an in-patient program for teens ages 13 to 18. The other is for adults ages 17 and above. There are around 50 teenagers and 70 adults. We also have an outpatient program, not on campus but in a nearby facility. We work with many tools. One of the strongest tools in my opinion is the therapeutic petting zoo – treating people through animals. We also have a therapeutic horseback riding program. The zoo approach of treating through animals is led by our psychologist Efrat Maayan.

Teenagers who come here do so for a year and a half. This is a very long time! The connection between them and the animals is very special. First of all, they have responsibilities. They have to feed them and take care of their health. We have all kinds of animals, even animals with medical problems. The teenagers see that, even though the animals have problems, we keep on caring for them; we don't stop just because they have these problems. This is a very big message for the kids because the kids were also animals who were thrown out of their community, out of society. Many kids come here because of problems that they had within their families, emotionally, physically, or mentally. Over the years, we've found that working with or through animals is one of the strongest tools that we have.

Interview with Efrat Maayan

Efrat: I am a clinical psychologist and animal-assisted therapist for many years. I have worked with children and adults in all kinds of places in Israel. This place [here at Retorno] is the small zoo, a place for therapy with children and adults with addiction. [She reaches in an aviary and picks up a small green parrot and places it on her shoulder.] This is Donna, one of my best friends here. Donna, she's one of the best therapists. She has a sad story, has a great problem. She lost her husband two years ago, and she was really depressed after that. Because of this, she took out her feathers. This kind of behaving, plucking out feathers, is a sign she has stress. When her husband died, she was really depressed about it, and she started to take out the feathers. Now, I think, she can't stop it because there's been two years from when it happened until now. It's become like an addiction to hurt herself. When the people here in Retorno see her, they immediately feel the same because they also find themselves inside a circle of self-destructive behavior all the time. They cut their skin sometimes when they're really upset, and they try to go back again and again and again to their addiction and all of this harmful behaving around the addiction. I think this is the reason why they like her so much, and they feel the same like her. Also, Donna doesn't, she doesn't want to go to anyone immediately. You have to work at being very, very patient to become a friend of Donna. When at last she's ready to be with someone, it feels like it is a million dollars or something like this. I tell the girls here all the time that she teaches them "My body is just my territory. No one can touch me or come close to me if I don't want it." It's a very important lesson. All these girls here, most of them had a very, very cruel sex relationship with men and sometimes, inside a family, sex abuse. The study from her, this lesson, "I don't want to give my body to everyone that wants to touch me. I'm the only one to decide." [To the parrot, she says,] "Thank you, Donna. You're a great teacher."

[Then she moves to a rabbit pen.] These puppies [baby rabbits] were born a few days ago. The mother is one of the rabbits here. She took out her fur to put here to make them warm, and she built this beautiful nest for them. Now, when the girls saw this a few days ago, we had a meeting after that, and they spoke with tears about how they were jealous of these babies, how they want to have such a good mother like this wonderful rabbit, and how they want to recover themselves so to be able to be mothers one day to children like these small babies. Now, we wait until they open their eyes. We can't touch them until they open their eyes, and it's really important for these people to learn how to wait, how to be patient, not to do things the moment that they want to, like they did before: "I want a drug. I want to drink alcohol. I want to go out and do very cruel things, so I just do it." And through these wonderful animals, they learn how to hold themselves, more and more, to be patient.

Each time before we start a group meeting, we have a prayer for good. It's the prayer of AA [Alcoholics Anonymous]. So one of our kids here, he made his own prayer for the animals. It's really fantastic. He made it so beautiful. It says, "Oh, Lord, please give me the strength to wake up in the morning to feed the animals. Give me the peacefulness to get them, to love them, and to love myself and to give whatever I can give to them and the wisdom to make the work as you wish. Amen."

Cynthia: That's beautiful.

After our interview with Efrat, she showed us some more animals and facilities at Retorno. Then, on the same day, we drove to her private practice clinic a few miles away to see her small zoo of animals, which included a waterfall and koi pond. There, we continued the interview. Efrat Maayan also supervises students and teaches university courses on subjects related to animal-assisted psychotherapy (see Figure 7.2).

Cynthia: We are here again with Efrat Maayan at her private practice clinic. Tell us more about your work.

Efrat: So this is my heaven, I think. My own clinic for children and adults and youth. Usually the parents bring the children to have therapy in this area. For many parents, it's much easier to bring the child for therapy in this kind of fantastic area because there are so many animals and nature around. It's not strict, like to come to the office of clinical psychology. I work with people from five years old to 60 years old in this place, with many kinds of problems. Many children that come to this kind of therapy are suffering from ADHD and learning disabilities. They don't believe in themselves. Sometimes, they have problems at school or problems with friends. They think many wrong things about themselves, like "I'm stupid; I will never be able to succeed. I will never be able to have a good work or profession." Many of them are really smart kids, wonderful kids.

I think it's important to speak a little bit about the idea of making this space a clinic with the birds, goats, the ferret, the rabbit – these kind of animals. This [type of] area is really unique because we developed it in Israel. We call it the small zoo. It provides a mirror to the soul. In addition to the room inside, I decided to take my patients outside to a very large area like this. This outside zoo area is a "therapy room," all that you see here.

Cynthia: We are outside here with the animals, the koi pond, and the waterfall.

Efrat: Yes, and like the work we do with children inside, where we put in the room dolls and cars and soldiers and other toys and many things for creation, here [outside], we have goats. We have a ferret. We have rabbits. We have a guinea pig. The dogs, very energetic dogs. Cats. Inside, we have hamsters and birds, but not very many animals inside, not as many animals as this small zoo [here outside] but enough to maybe touch.

The most important part of us is inside our soul. And the animals here create the opportunity to mirror, to reflect for the clients that come here, to reflect many kinds of families. Like, for example, I have a family of goats. The male goat, you can see it from here. His name is Falcish. He is a real violent husband. When he wants food, he just rams his wife with his horns. This female, her name is Mishmish. She is a fantastic mother. She gives birth every year. In a while, maybe one month from now, she will have babies again, baby goats. It's wonderful to see. It's a very, very exciting moment. Sometimes, I can see the birth with the children. When she is breastfeeding the small goats, the child can identify with this small goat and project his own wish to be a baby again and to have this wonderful feeling of mother nursing you and touching you and hugging you. Last year, she had three babies. She fed just two of them. The small one, she is still here; her name is Kikha. She [the mother] didn't want to give her milk, not at all, and I had to feed her with a bottle. These are wonderful stories that can happen only in this kind of place because some of the children that come to animal-assisted therapy, they feel neglected. They feel maybe not neglected in the full way, but they feel that their parents don't give enough attention to them or feel like maybe they prefer my brother and not me. And through this kind of experience that happens in this kind of area, it happens all the time. They [the patient] can talk to me about their feelings, about their experience of "What does it mean to be a child in my family?"

Sometimes, they can never ever speak about this kind of experience in another way, just through this projection about the animals. So this is one kind of family. We have more kinds of families, like the rabbits that you saw before. That the mother really makes a beautiful nest and she protects them very, very softly. But after she gives her milk, once a day, maybe twice a day, no more; she goes out. All day she eats and runs around and is not touching the babies. So it's another kind of family.

The male chicken, we have chickens here, the male one, he stands and protects his family. He finds the food. When he finds the food, he calls his family to eat. But he is not really connected to his children. But the male rat inside, when he has babies, he sits on them and he warms the babies. So we can see many kinds of experience here and many kinds of families, many kinds of relationships between children and parents, between peers. Sometimes, jealousy. Sometimes, fighting. Sometimes, being together and liking each other.

Cynthia: This is reflected in some of the animals' natural behavior.

Efrat: Yes, but it reflects also the inner zoo inside our soul because we have so many parts inside our soul. And this place has many animals, but not too many. It's not too many. And in every cage, there is just two grown-ups, the male and female. And the babies, when they grow up, I give them to another place like this. So we don't make it very full and, you know, overflowed, like there is a name for every animal. And we can really feel like the animal is a best friend to us.

The ferret is a wonderful animal for therapy. They're like an ADHD child. They want to play around and they never stop. They never stay in one place. They are very curious. And they just try to go wherever they can't go. They make a lot of mess inside the room. So many children can really identify with them. This is Crimble. Crimble is a wonderful ferret. Now, because he's so wild, when a child holds him we have a leash. When a child holds him and can handle him, I say to the child, "If you can be the leader, the commander of this animal, you can be the officer or the commander of your inner feeling, your inner anger."

Many children come here because they can't control their anger, so we start to work about their anger through being a leader of the ferret. And then, when the anger comes to the child, I remind him, "You could do it for Crimble; you can do it for your own feeling." Also, you know when a child holds this kind of animal and feels his fur, his softness, it makes a wonderful path to the ancient part inside our heart. The parts that we grew up with before we had words.

Cynthia: The very primitive self.
Efrat: The very primitive self. Exactly, thank you.
Cynthia: How long have you been practicing animal-assisted therapy?
Efrat: I think, all my life actually. I grew up in the kibbutz, in the north of Israel. And in my place, there were a lot of animals around. And from the moment I remember myself, the animals were my best friend. I didn't have social problems. I was a very social child, but they would always be there, the animals. When I was sad, when I had lost my family, when I had a fight with friends, I went to the horses, to the dogs. They would always be there to speak to me. And when I was teenage, I had many problems with school. And in 11th grade, they just throw me away, and my rehabilitation was through taking responsibility about the animals in my kibbutz.

We had a zoo in the kibbutz, a small zoo, like in all the kibbutz at this time. It was a revolution for me because I was a very rebellious teenager. And from this place of rebellion, to not do what they tell me to do, I became responsible. Responsible about animals, about children, small children that come to work with me. And suddenly I saw what a great opportunity of healing there is in this area.

Now, after the army, I went to study psychology, and it was not comfortable for me to sit down in the chair and say "uh huh" all the time. During my practical, I discovered a book by Boris Levinson [1969]. There was no place to learn this wonderful field in Israel, but when I discovered this book, it was "Wow!" Someone invited me to think about what I dreamed about all my life, and then I started to connect or to bring animals to my practice.

And I built my first place in a resident treatment center for neglected children in Jerusalem. This was my first place like this. It was 20 years ago, in 1995.

Since then, I have developed this area and I teach this area, this unique part of animals, just the therapy of working with animals like this in a small zoo. I make lectures and teach and supervise people that study this.

Cynthia: How would you briefly explain to someone who is studying to do this, working in a therapeutic small zoo environment, how to pay attention to the animals' behavior and the clients' behavior, for what I call, therapeutic opportunities, to reflect upon something as an opportunity to enhance the healing. When you see something in the child, see something in the animal or an interaction, and you think, "Aha, that's a therapeutic opportunity," and when to reflect and how to reflect. How do you recognize those moments?

Efrat: I think it is experience, and sometimes, I feel it from my stomach. But sometimes, it's very, very easy to see it, like for example, I think about one of the teenagers that you saw before in the tunnel [back at Retorno], when he came close to Donna [the parrot]. And he was, you know, like "This is my right to take you, and I want to do whatever I want to do with you, and you owe me." Like this was his behavior. And she just bit him in the same moment. It was a great reflection for him: "Stop yourself. Behave yourself. Think about the other. You don't think about the other; you just think about yourself. Does she feel it is right for her to have a connection with you now?" So sometimes, it's really very, very easy. And sometimes, it's like "behind the ground," and you have to learn how to see the subtext. Some projection, or really like this, for example, the ferret. They have babies, and they have six babies. The female takes the babies downstairs during the day and brings them upstairs during the night. Now, one day I [was] standing there with a child [patient]. And the female took three of the babies upstairs to sleep with them, and she left the rest of them with the father. And he slept with the other three. So she [patient] said, "Why does she leave them with the father?" And then she thinks about it a little bit, and this is one of the techniques we use. We don't give the answer. We try to figure out what is the projection of the patient about the animals because they behave. They behave all the time. They make us think, right in front of our eyes. And she [patient] said, "Yeah, I know why she did it. She wanted to teach the father to be a good father and to be involved in taking care of his children." Now, this girl, her father was involved but just in a very violent way in her life. And since this moment, we opened a very wide field of connection between her and her father. Something that she couldn't speak about before.

Cynthia:	The natural animal behavior provided opportunity for her to project her own issues onto that behavior.
Efrat:	Yes.
Cynthia:	Which then allows for processing that.
Efrat:	Yes.
Cynthia:	Her realizing things in her mind that you're reinforcing, reencouraging.
Efrat:	Exactly.
Cynthia:	Giving her that space, that permission to do that.
Efrat:	I want to say something more about working with a child in a place like this. As a clinical psychologist, I am usually looking for the wall of feelings, yeah. To find complex feelings inside a soul, or in a relationship with parents, but in this place it is possible to make many types of therapy. Not just the projective therapy but also to touch the animal, to work with the animal. To clean the cage, for example. To build a nest maybe. To build a small house for a hamster or pot to feed the rabbits.
Cynthia:	A feeling of meaning and purpose and responsibility.
Efrat:	Yes, and success. It's very important. It's very important because many of these children have learning disabilities, and maybe even an orphaned child that feels self is less from the others because I don't have a father. And when he builds this kind of thing and he sees the animals are really happy and use it, it's giving a great feeling of success and confidence. Also, working with fears. It's a great place to work with fears. For example, just to climb on top of the cave here, the goat's cave. Maybe sometimes to even go inside the goat's place.
Cynthia:	To be with them.
Efrat:	Yes, and think, "Hey, I could get over this fear. So if I could get over this fear, maybe I will be able to get over the night fear or any kind of other fears."
Cynthia:	We only have a couple of minutes left. Is there anything else you'd like to say about therapeutic zoo?
Efrat:	Be careful because it's kind of an addiction.
Cynthia:	A positive addiction.
Efrat:	A wonderful addiction. This is my own treatment. It's really fantastic to wake up at six o'clock and come here to feed the goats. I can't think about anything else I could do that allows me to be able to take inside my heart all of the sufferings that I see around me [from patients]. But in another way, I can't think about anything else that will give me such a great gift to see the healing power inside of human beings, even the most neglected or the most wounded people that I can see around myself all the time.
Cynthia:	You see incredible healing happen here.
Efrat:	Yes, incredible healing and incredible inner powers of the soul.

Cynthia:	People can recapture their personal power.
Efrat:	Yes.
Cynthia:	Or personal strength.
Efrat:	Yes, that's it. Thank you so much.

Editors' Commentary for Chapter 7

Our time interacting with Efrat Maayan was a special honor and extraordinary experience. She is one of the earliest practitioners of animal-assisted psycho-therapy in Israel and is the founder of the small zoo therapy model in Israel. As we understand it, the philosophy behind the small zoo is to provide clients an atmosphere in which they can immerse themselves, that is, an environment much different from the rest of the clients' world. Within a therapy space filled with animals, clients can lower personal defenses and project issues and concerns onto their observations of and interactions with the animal beings.

Having practiced her model of therapeutic small zoo longer than anyone else in Israel, Efrat Maayan has developed her model further than the others we observed. Rather than strategically placing a number of animals in pens and cages around a perimeter inside a room, Efrat designed her primary therapy space to be outdoors, though there is also an inside place in case of bad weather. All of the animal dwellings have a natural-looking exterior similar to large rocks or boulders; they simulate the color and shape of the large, low hills in southern Israel. She has created this at Retorno, the addiction center where she practices, and also at her private practice clinic. At her private practice, she has also created a koi pond and waterfall.

Efrat believes the type of therapeutic setting she has created promotes a client's accessing very primitive emotions during therapy. Thus, with assistance of the psychotherapist, the small zoo could stimulate much healing and recovery for a client. Efrat also spoke of the therapy space she has created for her private practice as being beneficial to herself. We could definitely understand this because we found this space to be very calming and peaceful just in the short time we were there. We could imagine how worthwhile it would be for therapist and client to spend time in this space.

Reference

Levinson, B. (1969). *Pet-oriented child psychotherapy.* Springfield, IL: Charles C. Thomas.

Figure 7.1 Rabbi Eitan Eckstein is the executive officer (CEO) of the Retorno Jewish Center for Addictions. He is also the director of the therapeutic riding program of Retorno. Photo copyright of the Retorno Jewish Center for Addictions (used with permission); photographer unknown.

Figure 7.2 Efrat Maayan holding a ferret. She is a clinical psychologist and an animal-assisted therapist. She is the founder of the therapeutic small zoo model in Israel. Photo copyright of the Retorno Jewish Center for Addictions (used with permission); photographer Ilan Rozenfeld.

8 Nancy Parish-Plass, Private Practice

Nancy Parish-Plass was our host for our visit in Israel (see Figure 8.1). She welcomed us into her home on the kibbutz. She set up appointments for our interviews and chauffeured us back and forth. Additionally, she and her companion drove us to see many interesting and historical places of Israel and hosted us for some traditional meals. Nancy's generosity with her time gave us wonderful memories we shall always treasure. Nancy is the editor and a contributing author of the classic book *Animal-Assisted Psychotherapy: Theory, Issues, and Practice* (2013). The interview with Nancy Parish-Plass took place on December 16, 2014, at her private practice clinic at the kibbutz in northern Israel.

Interview with Nancy Parish-Plass

Cynthia: Please tell us about your training, practice, and other contributions to the field of animal-assisted psychotherapy.

Nancy: I'm an animal-assisted psychotherapist. I work in a shelter for children who have been taken out of the home by emergency court order. They live there and go to school there. Together, with my therapy work there with my animals, I also do some case managing there. I've worked in a number of facilities for the Welfare Department, mostly with at-risk children. I also have a private clinic on my kibbutz, which is right outside of Haifa. There I work with normative kids, but have discovered a number of children suffering abuse in the home even in that clinic.

I studied animal-assisted psychotherapy at a local program. It was a three-year program. I then went ahead and studied in an advanced program in psychotherapy. I studied for a masters in social work, specializing in children and youth, at the University of Haifa, and I am presently finishing up my thesis involving research in the area of therapeutic alliance and animal-assisted play therapy.

I am the founding and continuing chairperson of the Israeli Association of Animal-Assisted Psychotherapy [n.d.]. I'm also very involved on the international scene. What we're trying to do, both in my work in the international scene and here in Israel, is to try to raise the standards in academic training, the practical training, and the theory behind the work that people do in order to improve the field of animal-assisted psychotherapy [AAP]. We hope to gain respect for the field as a truly clinical therapy field to work with both children and adults, various populations, and in various settings. I happen to be working more in the direction of psychodynamic therapy, but there are a number of us working from various theoretical orientations. But we all work according to certain basic principles centering on the human–animal bond and how that can be used, leaning on classical clinical therapy principles. What we're trying to do, through the publishing that I and also others have done, is try to focus on theory building and understanding the mechanisms behind how AAP works. We try to understand how we can use the human–animal bond in order to expand the recognized psychotherapy principles, in order to really get into what's happening with the client and help them reach insight and change. I feel that, in Israel, we have a very special model. And so, in 2008, I published an article about my work with at-risk children, using that as a venue to explain our practice here in Israel of animal-assisted psychotherapy. I got such a wonderful response. So I said to myself, "Okay, an article is not enough." I gathered a number of my colleagues here, in Israel, and I edited a book in order to present the theories, issues, and practice of animal-assisted psychotherapy from our point of view. And this is just the beginning. I really do hope I was able to take Boris Levinson's book [1969] a few steps further. Boris Levinson really is, as far as I'm concerned, the grandfather of the field. I hope he would be proud of me. One purpose [of the book] was to supply more information about the field of AAP, and I very much hope that other people will use it as a basis for their practice, for more theory building, understanding more mechanisms, and as a basis for research. We're just at the beginning. I hope that the things that I've written, and I hope to keep writing, and what my colleagues are doing here in Israel and our connections on the international scene, will bring up the level [of the field] more and more.

I'm also a member of the editorial board of HABRI Central [Human-Animal Bond Research Institute, in Washington, DC], which is a repository and Internet hub trying to bring researchers, theoreticians, and others together for the purpose of using the human–animal bond in many different ways. I, of course, deal with therapy. Whatever I can do to help push the field of AAP forward, that's what I'll do.

Cynthia: Would you like to show us around your clinic?

Nancy: Okay. Here, I have my rats. Let's take a couple out. This is Pistachio. Each one has their own individual personality. Pistachio is a little bit, more shy than the others. Here, we have Choco. Choco is more of our little ambassador. She runs up to the kids a lot more. She's braver, she's more social, and she runs to her mommy. Her favorite place is underneath my hair. When I first get them, they love to lay underneath my hair for a good sleep. Here, we have Pepper, as in black pepper. Pepper is a little bit slower. Pepper has cancer, as you can see here. She's probably near the end of her life. She also has a little bit of head rolling here, if you can see her walk, but she can still get around and she's still a happy little rat. Very sweet, she's always been very sweet.

The whole idea of sickness and death is very important. It's reality. It's these children's reality. Children that I work with have loss, sickness, death, losing people, losing important things in life. I once had a little girl whose grandparents had died, and she had a very hard time dealing with it. She wouldn't talk about it to anyone. Very slowly, she started talking about the grandparents with me but wouldn't talk at all about losing them and how she felt. I had another rat, Casper, who had a lung disease, and she was slowly dying. The girl, she went through all the stages of [grief described by Elisabeth] Kübler-Ross [1969], of the denial, different ways of trying to deal with it. She said, "We should go onto the Internet and look for a solution there," and asked, "Why didn't you go to the vet?" When I said, "I did go to my vet," [she replied,] "Well, then he's not good enough. We have to take her somewhere else." Slowly, she was starting to come to terms with what was happening. We often fed her. All the animals love to eat cornflakes. What happened was Casper didn't want to eat anymore. She was getting near the end. The girl said, "My grandmother didn't want to eat very much near the end either." That's when she started talking about her grandmother and the whole process and how she felt and how difficult it was. We were able to work through Casper, who was dying, and we went through the whole process. Soon the rat died. But before, I told the girl that this was going to be the last time that Casper was going to come, and so she brought a little present. Actually, she brought a little toy rat so that, when I would leave Casper at home when I would bring the other rats to the following session, Casper wouldn't be alone in the cage, that she would have a little toy rat to be with. It was a little windup toy. I even kept it. I still have it at home. Then I was able to tell her about two or three weeks later that Casper did pass away, and we talked about it. What was interesting was that about a month later, her great-grandmother died, and her parents said that her whole attitude was different. It was so very, very different. She was also very close with her great-grandmother. It was a very close family. Working through the rat when she had not in any way been able to talk about what happened with her and her grandmother, her feelings, or her grandfather for that matter, helped her with the loss of her great-grandmother. Without these guys [the rats], I'm not sure that the change would have happened and certainly not at that level.

Here, in the room, you'll see later we have all the art materials, things that they [the patients] can cut out or use anything in any way that they need for the therapy. One little girl I have has a problem with her sisters. There's a lot of fighting between the two sisters, and she's scared. She loves her sister, but she's scared of her. A couple of months ago, I also had another rat, Milky, who was more of a vicious rat, something that is not usual with rats. I had to separate Pistachio out from Milky.

What she [the patient] used to do is, the rats used to try and get each other through the bars, and she [the patient] was very frightened for what might happen. She made this [small cardboard barrier], and she would put it here to separate between the two rats so that Milky couldn't hurt Pistachio. She was very worried, and she made it clear that she loved both rats. Sometime soon, she'll [probably] be able to get angry at Milky, who is trying to hurt Pistachio, but for now, that's where she is in the therapy. She loves both, but she has to separate them out because she can't let the older one hurt the younger one. That's how my patients are using the materials together with the rats to get at their own issues. The need for protection is important to this girl. The parents have a difficult time seeing the difficulty of the daughter. They're busy saying, "Oh, kids fight all the time. What's the big deal?" They're having a hard time, and I'm working with them right now, trying to get them to see the daughter's distress. It's very hard.

Here, around the room, we have all the various tools of play therapy. What I do in my practice is I combine two different modalities, animal-assisted psychotherapy with play therapy, which together you could call animal-assisted play therapy. I have the dollhouses. Here, I have a dollhouse over here and a dollhouse over there. Inside the dollhouse, I have figurines, furniture, and even a little toilet in there, all of which bring out content. I have all the games. I have Parcheesi here, regular cards, all sorts of board games, card games. I've got LEGO, weapons, a great Star Wars sword, handcuffs. I've got here tanks and soldiers. Bubbles. I've got the babushka doll. It could be a family or a mother swallowing her child; you never know.

I love this, all the little characters, the action figures, the monsters, whatever. Very importantly, I also have here a doctor's kit, and it includes a real stethoscope inside. Play animals. I've got all the different dolls here. A kitchen there. I've got my [real] dog, Mushu. I've got here balls, brushes for Mushu, hair bands, a leash, and other Mushu-related things. I guess this is the time to introduce Mushu. Say hello, Mushu. Mushu has a lot of hair, so the kids sometimes get nervous because they can't see her eyes, as it covers them. They might go ahead and make her a ponytail so they can see her eyes, if they're nervous about that, or not. She hates it and pulls off the hair band herself. We talk about whether or not she likes that they're doing things to her. This is Mushu's place right over here, on the beanbag. She loves to sit there. Sometimes, the kids like to share it with her. Sometimes, they push her off, or she'll try to push them off. Lots of very authentic interactions there.

Food has a very important place in AAP. Whenever you have animals, you have to have food. Here I have the cornflakes. All the animals love the cornflakes. Mushu loves the cornflakes; the kids love the cornflakes. They're allowed to do anything they want with them, as food. I've had kids sit there with water and make a real mishmash of it, whatever they like.

A lot of times, with all the toys, the kids combine the animals with the toys. We've got a rubber snake. Kids tend to know that snakes eat rats, so they might try to threaten the rats with the toy snake. There's a lot of openness here for children to express themselves, to express their fears, their aggression, and they do that a lot between the animals or between the toys and the animals.

By the way, about Mushu, usually for most of the children, she's the sense of warmth, of softness. I had a young adolescent who's already very deep into the criminal world. He was very, very controlling, very, very calculated. He had a great problem with emotional expression. It took me a long time till he could say the most difficult expression, "I don't know why. I don't know why I do what I do." It freaked him out, the fact that he wasn't in control, and he didn't know why. It scared him. He couldn't even actually talk about that fear, but this was the way he started to do so. It was the first time he opened up. Then he walked over to Mushu, this large kid, always controlling, very much into the criminal element, and he laid down next to Mushu in a fetal position, surrounding Mushu. He actually fell asleep for about 15 minutes. Then, when I said, "Well, we have to finish the session," he looked up to me, just looked up to me like that, and said, "Can't we be here for another hour? I need it." He could not depend on his mother. He was stronger than his mother. Since he was seven, he was in charge of his mother, who had many, many problems. This is the first time he was able just to lie down with somebody soft and warm.

I've had many children who also had very difficult family backgrounds, with a mother who was very rejecting or couldn't be depended upon. The children know that there's such a thing as a good mother, but they don't have one. They often can't accept the good mothering from another woman. It's too threatening. So I've had kids go up to Mushu and cuddle with Mushu, and try to almost climb into her, and say, "She's my mother. She's soft and warm, and she's my mother." That's the usual way that Mushu is seen. However, I had one child who said about Mushu, "She's got black hair like daddy. She's got tiger eyes like daddy." As you can see, she doesn't exactly have tiger eyes, but the client needed to project that onto somebody, and she then wanted to be in control. Her father, who was very physically abusive and mentally abusive, was very tyrannical at home. So she started tying up Mushu to the side, not letting Mushu have her food or water. The client was eating cornflakes, and Mushu wanted some too. So Mushu started barking. The little girl started screaming, saying, "I hate it when you yell at me like that. I hate it when you hit me like that. You're not my friend." So she was using Mushu in her own way that she needed, having nothing to do with Mushu's very soft, quiet personality and the way that she's usually used, but this was the way that she needed to use Mushu.

There was an interesting development with this client, something that we should be careful about in therapy. We should be aware of how the children perceive their own stories and the implications of the process. She eventually developed a phobia of dogs due to the scary story she herself made up about Mushu, using her own transference onto her. Her mother started telling me that she was scared of dogs in the street, where she hadn't been scared before. We work so much with the child's inner world that sometimes a child can get stuck there. The client was confused as to whether the story she made up about Mushu was real or not. She got lost between her inner world and outer reality. I usually like to say that Mushu is real, but at a safe distance, at a safe psychological distance. She's like a person, but she's not a person. She has emotions, but they're not a person's emotions. But the mix between fantasy and reality became too confusing for her, and she started being scared of all dogs, as if all dogs were her abusive father and were dangerous. So what I had to do was carry out a bit of an intervention and explain to her that Mushu was like her father, but wasn't really her father. At this point in therapy, she had Mushu on the other side of a wall in order to keep her father far away from her so she could play happily without feeling tense. Wanting to be with us, Mushu would get upset and bark. The client would shout out, "Stop screaming at me; you can't get to me anymore." In reality, her father was now in jail. I decided that we would go, and we would take a peek at Mushu. "Let's go see if Mushu is okay, because Mushu's not really Daddy." We went to check to see if Mushu was okay. Mushu was very happy we had come, and she then wagged her tail. I would then say, "Oh, Mushu's wagging her tail because she's happy to see us." And then I would say, "Okay, let's go back into the story. We're pretending again that Mushu is Daddy." By going back and forth, she was able to understand the difference between her inner world and the story she was creating and the reality. That was very important to her. Then her mother reported to me that she was no longer afraid of dogs outside of therapy either. This is something I think we therapists have to be aware of, especially in AAP, where there is even more chance for confusion. What we see as an opportunity where the animals are real, but not really human, could cause confusion. I think we always have to be aware of how that is affecting the child in therapy and their life in general.

Okay, see what we have here. I'll take them out so you can get a better view. We have some Siberian hamsters, Punch and Banana. Let's see where they're hiding right now. They hide a lot. Let's see; here they are. They're very sweet, usually, but they can bite. And the kid knows that from the very beginning. When they have babies, this is my dysfunctional, at-risk family, because in the real world, which here we get the real world coming into the fantasy world, the parents might fight, the father might eat the babies when they're born or could drive the mother crazy, and the mother will eat the babies. So what you have to do when the babies are born is always take the father out, put the father in a separate cage for about three weeks till the babies are old enough that the father is not likely to hurt them anymore.

I work with at-risk children, and so that brings out a lot of very familiar content to the children. I once worked in a shelter for battered women and their children, and it was interesting that one child looked at the father in another cage and said, "The poor father is all alone without his family." That's what she needed to talk about, that although the father had battered the mother, she loved the father very much. She knew that the father missed her, and she was working through the issues of why they were separated from the father, why she couldn't have the father. How did the father hamster feel, that he was all alone in a different home?

Okay, I think at this point, what I want to say is that as cute as the rats are, in nature, outside of this room, they eat hamsters.

I won't let it happen inside of this room. So what I have here in the room is sort of a microcosm of the child's world, where there might be an aggressor and a victim. The hamster is the potential victim, and the rats are the potential aggressor. You get some children who identify with the aggressor, and they'll take the rats and maybe bring the rats closer to the hamsters to see if the rats really will eat the hamsters or if I will let it happen. Of course, I do not let it happen. Some children will identify with the hamsters, and they'll do everything they can to protect the hamsters. I had one child totally cover the cage with note cards. What he said was, "I covered the whole cage so that the hamsters would feel comfortable and warm and safe inside because, you know, outside, there's a very dangerous world out there."

Now, I'd like to introduce my birds. Notice that here is a Star Wars figure. This one child found it a very threatening figure, so he would hang the figure from the bars [of the birds' cage] like that. He said it was somebody from the outside looking in, threatening the birds, saying the birds knew that there's this threat outside. Inside the cage, they were fine, they get along well, everything is fine inside the cage, but the birds always know that this figure is out there. Sometimes he would try to bang on the cage, and I had to stop him from doing that to protect the birds. We must always protect the animals. Then I would reflect on the birds, how they would feel, and he would talk about how the birds feel, having somebody threatening from the outside looking at them. You never know what this means for the client. With this child, it turns out it was because the mother was diagnosed with an illness that was not necessarily expressed as long as she received a weekly injection. However, the injection also caused her to be sick on that day, and the figure was like an illness that was outside and was threatening the family. For a long time, the parents refused to talk with their son about it, keeping it a secret from him. The parents did not want to let him know that the mother was diagnosed with this disease. Sensing the secret, he kept on talking about the threat, coming from the outside, on the family, but he didn't know what it was. Sharing with the parents their son's content and process, I was able to convince the parents that it was a very hard process; they had to talk to the child about what was happening. Finally, the parents did talk with the child about it, and this threatening figure was soon set aside. It was no longer an issue because he knew what was being talked about. This secret came out, and it was something that was openly talked about, and he didn't need the figure to threaten the birds anymore.

This is my cockatiel. His name is Nezeq, which in English means damage. He does a lot of damage. He loves to eat things. He can be very, very sweet. You can see right now, he loves being massaged and he can be very sweet. He can also be very obnoxious, very threatening. He's not being very threatening right now. He has many parts to him. He can be sweet, he can be threatening, he can be frightened, can be many, many different things. All his emotions are out there. They're very, very much out there in the open.

I had one child, I remember, who was in total denial of his very angry outbursts. He could even be dangerous towards other kids. Whenever anyone tried to talk to him at home or at school about his behavior, he would say, "I never get angry. I don't even know what you're talking about." One day, he was talking to me about Nezeq, and he said, "I know you love Nezeq very much, even though he can be a little bit biting and scary, but I think I can sometimes be like Nezeq too. I think I'm a very nice boy. I can be very cute. But sometimes people say I can get very, very angry. So I think I'm like Nezeq." That was the first time he was able to start talking with anyone about his angry outbursts and open to me about what happens, how he starts it. Apparently, he even goes through some sort of dissociation. He's not even sure that he remembers all of it. But he was able to start talking about it through Nezeq and then able to talk about it in a very direct way after that.

Here's Poofy. Poofy's a palm dove that was brought to me when he was two weeks old. I hand-fed him, and I've had him for five years now. He's going to his favorite place on top of the curtain rod. Sometimes, it drives kids crazy that he wants to be up there most of the time. The children spend a lot of time trying to convince him to come down. Some kids try to scare him into coming down, and so we talk about "Will he come down if he's scared?" or "Why is he up there in the first place?" They try to take the window and shake it back and forth. I do have to stop them. We talk about that animals have the right not to be frightened. I work with the kids' impulse control together with him. We talk about how to make him feel comfortable enough to come down to the floor. He will, with a lot of work. They have to be very patient. Not all the kids have the patience, but that's probably because it's not their issue. They're not interested enough. If the kids really need to work on that issue, then they will.

They work with the past stories of the animals. I have another cockatiel, Molly, who's at home right now, that I bring with me to the emergency shelter. One child was brought to me who, at seven, had sexually abused a younger sibling. I'm sure that he had very little awareness of what he had done, but rather his behavior came more out of high, high anxiety in a very neglectful house. When I do intakes, there are two questions that I always ask. One is,

"What's the history of animals in the family? Did you ever have any pets, and what pets did you have? Who's responsible? Who feeds them? What type of food do they get?" I ask how old the pets are. Often, there were pets that died. How did they die? What happened? What was the reaction? Frank Ascione [1993] describes a link between child abuse, wife battering, and animal abuse. So I get a lot of information from the answers to my questions about the family, the family dynamics, or abuse in the home. Many times, they will first talk about what happened to the animals and then talk about themselves.

This little boy, coming from a very neglectful home, said, "I used to have a bird just like Molly." A lot of these kids say, "Oh, I have a bird at home named Molly. I have a dog named Mushu." A lot of identification occurs in AAP. He said, "But she died because there wasn't any food. I told my mother for two weeks that there was no food, but she didn't go out and get food, so she died." That was giving me insight to what happened in the home. The neglect suffered, some of his feelings and how he felt about the neglect, and that someone could die because of neglect in the home. As I said earlier, this child had sexually abused a younger sibling. Nezeq, as you see, he likes being touched. Molly does not like being touched. So he then said, "I think I know why she doesn't like being touched because, when she was in the store before you bought her, somebody there touched her down below, you know where, and now she's scared of any touch at all." That was in the first couple of sessions, relating Molly to his home life and using what he felt about what was going on with her to express his family dynamics.

About 90 percent of the kids going through abuse never open up about their secret. The animals can be a way to create that first therapeutic alliance so that the therapy can happen. I had one child who had been in therapy before, and the therapist and the family said that the boy did not create any relationship with the therapy, for the most part stayed quiet, refusing to cooperate. He walked into my therapy room, in a school setting, and said, "I know that this is therapy." I answered, "You're right. It's therapy." I never try to pretend it's an activity or just a fun thing. This is therapy. The child has to know. He said, "And I'm not going to talk to you." I said, "Whatever. Whatever you want." He said, "Why? What am I supposed to do here?" I said, "Well, I've got the animals, and I've got the toys. I've got the art supplies. Whatever you want." Then he started playing with the animals, and he said, "Well, you're an animal person. Maybe you can tell me what's going on with my animals at home," and he started talking about his dog and was very upset. He had a dog that was about 15 or 16 years old.

He said, "My father used to love the dog, but now the dog is sick and a little bit smelly and doesn't look nice, so now he locks the dog outside. Is that good for the dog? Is the dog going to be okay?" He was very worried, and he was already seeing me as someone he could confide in about his worries, about the dog, but not yet about himself. Then, about another couple of weeks later, he told me he had some parakeets and they had babies. He was all excited. Some baby birds were born. Then he came to me about three weeks later, and said, "I don't know what happened. All of a sudden, I got up in the morning, and they were all dead, and I don't know why. Do you know why they would've died?" I was already starting to wonder about the father. I was getting very worried knowing about the link. So I went to the school psychologist and said, "I want to go to the Welfare Department." She said, "No, you're imagining it. This family, they're a wonderful family. It's a very, very upscale family. Both parents are professionals, highly esteemed professionals in their field." So I said, "Okay, I'll hang in there," as a beginning therapist with a little less confidence in myself.

Then he started talking to me about his little brother. His mother sometimes had to work late at night at the office. He explained that the father would sometimes lock the two-and-a-half-year-old little brother outside when he was crying because he couldn't stand the crying. The client said he would sit outside with his brother so he wouldn't be alone. I reflected on the work of Frank Ascione [1993] and his ideas about "the link," that animals and children share a common fate. Here, the dog and the little brother were sharing the common fate of being locked out of the house when they were bothering the father. Slowly, the child started opening up about being hit by the father, and all sorts of things were happening. This was all within about a two-month span. This kid, for a year and a half, did not open up to the school psychologist about anything happening in the home. The school psychologist said, "I think he's probably just projecting and transferring, and this is in his inner world."

There's a lot of denial about things actually happening. It's hard for adults to see this happening to children. It is a lot easier for them to just deny, even among mental health professionals, apparently. I told her that I was going to report the case to the Welfare Office. She said, "Wait a week, and I'll do a psych evaluation, and you'll see." She got permission from the parents for the psych evaluation. Because of the results of the evaluation, she called me up that night and said, "We're going to the Welfare in the morning." It really opened up a whole story of psychological, physical, and eventually we found out about sexual abuse going on in the home. Much later I asked the child, "Why did you open up to me?" He became very serious, and he said, "Because I saw the animals trusted you, so I thought I could trust you too." That was a sentence that I've heard in many different versions, from many different kids who have opened up their secrets to me. It's all about the special therapeutic alliance that happens in AAP. I really, truly believe that animal-assisted psychotherapy is a way that we can get to some of these kids.

Cynthia: Nancy, thank you for introducing us to the work you do and showing us all of the wonderful things in your practice and introducing us to each of your lovely animals. How do you go about explaining to the general public the value of animal-assisted therapy?

Nancy: Well, I think that, first of all, people have to know that animal-assisted psychotherapy really is therapy. Once they realize they want therapy for a child, or for themselves, people look for a type of therapy that they think might help them. Many people will go to therapist after therapist, type of therapy after type of therapy, so it's important that they understand "What can you get from animal-assisted psychotherapy that will be an added extra value?" What they have to understand is that it expands the possibilities; it expands the opportunities. It expands what content can come up, expands the type of expression of that content. It helps people connect to their inner world. It helps them connect to the therapist in a very different way. That way, they can get to their issues in a different way, ways that with other therapies, maybe they weren't able to.

I find a lot in my practice that parents think that they're bringing their kids to a fun activity. Again, they have to understand it is therapy. It's not just they're having fun so they're going to get better. That's not what it's all about. Many years ago, it was thought that play in itself was therapy. Research showed that you have to have that person there mediating between the child and the play of the child for therapy to occur. That's what happens in animal-assisted psychotherapy. There's a therapist present, mediating.

I admit that sometimes I do call the animals my cotherapists. They are there, and they do help me. But I am the therapist. I am the one who has been trained. And I'm the one who has studied, and I know that, with this particular problem, I need to do such and such intervention. And the animals are there to help me. They help me in many ways; they also help me when it's difficult.

Cynthia: One example of a therapist role is to emphasize different interactions that are spontaneously occurring between the child and the animal, to help stimulate issues to come to the surface and to help

Nancy: the child to understand the greater meaning behind an interaction that they're having.

Nancy: Exactly. That's a very important point. Those interactions bring up so much content; it brings up the whole life cycle. It brings up birth; it brings up sickness. It brings up death. It brings up rejection. It brings up loneliness. It brings up aggression. It brings up so many issues that are part of all our lives. But for some people, because of their life circumstances or maybe sometimes because of their organic makeup, these issues take on a very, especially strong place in who they are. Maybe the animals can bring these issues up, but the therapist must be there to point them out. If these issues are not recognized, and not given words to, then symptoms will come and go, and this process will create problematic reactions within the client. The client will not know what to do with the content, the reactions, that come up, or they may put it aside and say they're not important. The therapist is there as a witness, and reflects. And the child is not alone with all that is going on. Then what we see is a very important result, an acknowledgment. That's number one.

Secondly, there is mediation: "How do you feel when the animal does this?" or "How do you feel when you're worried about what's going to happen to the animal?" or "How do you feel when you saw these two animals interacting with each other in that way?" Not only acknowledging that this is an issue, but then acknowledging how the child feels about the issue, what the child's experience is, that's important. The child realizes "Well, this is important, and I'm not alone with it. Someone wants to hear me" and feels the acceptance of the therapist. Not all therapists can do this, but all therapists should. We must accept what the client's version is and then run with it. The versions may change, the reactions to what happened may change, because we're allowed to grow and develop, and that's what we want to happen within therapy. It is important to understand things from different points of view, different points in time, at different stages in therapy. That way, the client isn't there alone. I think that the idea of not being alone is really important. The client sees the fact that we're not going to let the animals be alone either, and they can identify with the animals. Even the fact that I can identify with the animal shows that I'm there for the animal and for the child together. It helps the client see me as much more authentic, much more caring.

Cynthia: Nancy, thank you very much for spending time with us today. I think that this has been very valuable and educational and others will benefit much from you introducing us to your animals and describing and explaining for us how you do animal-assisted psychotherapy and animal-assisted play therapy. I think your excitement and your enthusiasm is contagious, and I appreciate you sharing that with us today.

Nancy: Well, thank you, because I think it gives a stage in order to reach more kids. I think that AAP is especially effective with at-risk kids, especially the at-risk kids that have not yet been discovered or who are in therapy because of behavior problems. I think that AAP can help these kids open up about the maltreatment they are experiencing. If we can find more of those kids, and we have to find them, we could help them. Thank you.

Editors' Commentary for Chapter 8

Nancy Parish-Plass is dedicated to the fields of animal-assisted psychotherapy and animal-assisted play therapy. She practices these modalities, publishes her ideas, and promotes the work of her colleagues by including their ideas in a comprehensive, edited book. She helps many clients with emotional concerns, especially children. Furthermore, she cofounded and directs a professional association to promote animal-assisted psychotherapy in Israel. Additionally, she helps promote and preserve the work of practitioners and researchers across the globe. It is people like Nancy who move the field forward and pave the way for future generations.

Editors' Commentary for Part II: Israel

The comprehensive training and supervision programs for animal-assisted psychotherapy at the colleges in Israel are a very attractive idea. The numerous courses provide a sound basis for understanding animals and animal behavior, human–animal interaction, and a psychotherapeutic process that incorporates animals. The amount of supervision that is required of students provides much oversight as well as support for the students during the learning process. The focused approach of study to become an animal-assisted psychotherapist in Israel is currently unique in the world. Within this framework, the students pursue the primary goal to become an animal-assisted psychotherapist.

The U.S. model is very different. In the U.S., training in animal-assisted therapy is considered an adjunct to training in psychotherapy. The U.S. model is to obtain training in a psychotherapy field, such as counseling, psychology, social work, or marriage and family therapy, and then also obtain training in professional applications of animal-assisted therapy. The training for professional practice of animal-assisted therapy is difficult to find in the U.S. Today, only a few colleges or universities in the U.S. offer this type of professional training. So, students of psychotherapy in the U.S. struggle to find proper training and adequate supervision for professional application of animal-assisted therapy.

We really admire the model of training and supervision in Israel for animal-assisted psychotherapy. However, currently in Israel, there are no regulated licensure requirements to practice psychotherapy. In contrast, in the U.S. it is mandatory to have a government administered license or certification to practice in a field of psychotherapy or any mental health field. The mandatory credential required of practitioners in the U.S. helps to regulate standards and quality of practice.

We found the small zoo as therapy construct practiced by psychotherapists in Israel to be very intriguing. The idea of creating a therapeutic atmosphere within which child or adult clients can immerse themselves and reflect upon their inner worlds offers a highly therapeutic medium for growth and healing. As we understand the model, the variety of animals and animal families in the small zoo may tap into the more primitive emotional state of the client, thereby allowing deep emotional trauma or other emotional issues to come to the surface in the moment in the therapy space. This emotional openness allows for greater processing with a therapist that can move the client toward greater self- and other awareness and healing. This may facilitate faster and deeper recovery by the client than when therapy does not involve animals.

We use the word "client" here because in the U.S. where we practice, therapists more commonly refer to an individual in counseling or psychotherapy as a "client" regardless of theoretical approach. But in Israel, where the animal-assisted psychotherapy is based on a more traditional psychodynamic model, some therapists more often utilize the term "patient." This is based on the premise that the client is "ill" and the therapist is "treating" the patient for an emotional or mental illness. It reflects a hierarchical model of treatment with the therapist as expert at a level above the client in the hierarchy. In contrast, today in the U.S. most psychotherapists have moved away from a hierarchical model. They typically refer to the person being served as a "client" because the therapist and client partner to facilitate growth and healing for the client. The term "client" is indicative of someone participating in counseling or psychotherapy in almost an egalitarian manner. In the U.S., the term "client" is thought to be a more encouraging and empowering term to represent the role of a person receiving service.

We were pleased to hear how often psychotherapists in Israel referred to the importance of animal welfare and protecting the animals, such as dogs and various animals of the therapeutic small zoo. These therapists set limits on behaviors of clients so no physical harm comes to the animals with which the clients interact. While the physical safety of the animal was emphasized consistently by therapists we interviewed in Israel, it is our opinion that the emotional safety of the animal was not considered as much as it should have been in some instances. In a few cases described, there seemed to be some sacrifice of an animal's emotional welfare for the allowance of greater projections onto the animal by a client. These practices were described as attempts to present as much opportunity as possible for therapeutic projection. However, it is our opinion that sufficient opportunity for client projection can be provided while still preserving both emotional and physical welfare of an animal. We feel it is not appropriate to allow a client to act out projection with an animal to the degree it may do emotional or physical harm to the animal. It is also not appropriate modeling for social interaction with an animal. Furthermore, as was exemplified in a case presented to us, it could even do emotional harm to a client.

One of the reasons animal-assisted therapy is so effective is because clients often project with the animal. This brings important client issues and concerns to the surface so they are accessible for processing. When client projection is involved, there should always be careful preservation of animal emotional and physical welfare. Careful monitoring is required of a therapist regarding the type and intensity of client projections. And a therapist should intervene when it is determined that animal emotional or physical welfare may be compromised. Preservation of animal emotional and physical welfare when a client engages in projection includes well-timed therapist's interventions. These include (a) differentiation (i.e., explain that client feelings are important but the animal is not the source of the feelings); (b) limit setting (i.e., explain that a particular behavior with an animal is not allowed); and/or (c) redirection (i.e., encourage expression of those more intense client feelings with a nonliving object).

We agree with psychotherapists we interviewed in Israel that the occurrence of a client's projection during animal-assisted therapy can be used as a powerful tool for insight and healing. Nevertheless, we believe that, when animals are involved in therapy, therapeutic projection by a client can still occur and be used effectively without a therapist allowing projection by a client to be acted out or communicated to the extent that it may be harmful to the animal, either physically or emotionally. The animals are sentient beings in the therapy space; they have feelings that should be respected. The therapist can convey empathy and understanding for a client who is projecting in a session while also helping the client to differentiate between the client's inner world and the animals that are present. When working with a child who is projecting with very intense emotion onto an animal and the animal seems to be uncomfortable with this, the therapist should redirect the client and encourage projection of very intense emotions upon inanimate objects in the space, such as toys in the case of a child client. This is always a difficult thing to consider. Some of the psychotherapists in Israel spoke of this difficulty, that is, the dilemma of deciding how much to allow a client to act out intense projection onto an animal before differentiating and/or redirecting the client's projection. Differentiating an intense projection of a child or adult client involves valuing and reflecting the client's emotional expression while clarifying that the animal is not the source for the client's emotions. Differentiation can provide the client validation and support while encouraging conscious processing of the emotions being displayed. Redirecting an intense negative projection of a client away from an animal and toward inanimate objects allows the client freedom of expression while also protecting the animal.

Another concern we have about the animals in the small zoo therapy environment is that some of the animals were known to bite. Though clients were warned of the potential aggressive behavior of the animal, the clients were still allowed to interact with them. Also, some animals who were sick were presented for therapy. Thankfully, the clients were directed to limit or avoid interaction with some of the sick animals. The natural tendencies and state of health of the small zoo animals were presented for the purpose of symbolizing real-life situations – negative ones, such as aggression, neglect, illness, and death, and positive ones, such as parenting and nurturing. In the U.S., there is typically a different attitude about animals who are sick, aggressive, or anxious in that, most of the time, they are not included in therapy sessions.

The small zoo animals in Israel are considered symbolic representations of the natural cycle of life and of other things, pleasant or painful, that occur in life and family systems. This is one of the reasons it works so effectively. The concept of the therapeutic zoo in Israel is not just about having a variety of animals; it is about working with animals in natural ways. Thus, some animals who have issues are not excluded from participation and are in fact sometimes preferred. For example, Inbar Barel said, "The client can identify with the animals, that they have a problem of their own. And they see the resilience of animals. I think the resilience of the animals gives a lot of hope to the clients. The fact that we are working with dogs that are not perfect, it's very important in all the courses." And Gal Hakim expressed, "I think it's our preference to bring animals that are not perfect. But sometimes it's too hard and it's a question, how much the clients can deal with, when it's good for them and when it's too much. I deal with this question a lot." To allow for greater therapeutic opportunities for clients, animals of the small zoo that participate in therapy in Israel do not have to meet strict health or behavioral criteria.

Notably, we see that a constant awareness is required of a therapist to consider how an animal's participation with a client may be detrimental to either the animal or the client. The therapists of the therapeutic small zoo in Israel spoke of the need to be aware of both human and animal welfare, and the preparation programs also emphasized this important concept. The requirement of the therapist to be continuously aware of the behavior and needs of both human and animal participants adds to the complexity of involving animals in therapy. And when you have multiple animals in the same therapy environment, such as with the small zoo format, this becomes even more difficult to accomplish.

In some cases presented, some of the parameters established by therapists of Israel for the emotional and physical welfare of humans and animals were not satisfying to us. However, neither of us practice therapeutic small zoo, but both of us do practice canine-assisted and equine-assisted counseling. Based on our training in the U.S., a dog who participates in therapy must be well behaved, obedient, confident, sociable, not overly shy, not nervous or anxious, not aggressive, and in good emotional and physical health. It seems that the incorporation of pet dogs into therapy in Israel is still considered, in a way, almost like the small zoo. In other words, you take the animal as it naturally is, for the most part, and thus present natural opportunities for clients to recognize their own needs through the needs or behaviors of the animal.

The small zoo as therapy model in Israel seems to be very clinically effective. We are very thankful for the generosity of the therapists, researchers, instructors, and supervisors who took time to talk about and show us their work. However, we believe practitioners of the therapeutic small zoo in Israel could further develop their ideas regarding appropriate parameters for animals' participation in therapy and human–animal interaction. We are aware that our belief is based on our U.S. culture and training as well as our lack of experience with therapeutic zoo. Thus, we must be cautious about imposing our own cultural values and beliefs onto others. Additionally, we acknowledge there are emotional and mental health programs in the U.S. that incorporate as forms of animal-assisted intervention care for farm animals, wildlife rehabilitation, animal rescue, and socialization and training of dogs and cats for adoption. Supervised caring for animals, even when animals are sick or injured, is part of several intervention programs for emotional and mental health in the U.S. So there exist different ideologies regarding incorporating animals into therapy. One ideology requires that animals participating in therapy be healthy, friendly, and well behaved. Most programs with this ideology go so far as to require a handler and an animal pass a standardized team evaluation. This is the professional world within which we, the editors, work. And then there is another ideology that allows animals who are sick, not very friendly, and not well behaved to participate in therapy. A mutual and important consideration of both ideologies is that human and animal safety and welfare must be a priority at all times. The first ideology seems to satisfy this consideration more clearly than the second ideology. However, humans and animals can gain much benefit from each other during times of mutual suffering and recovery. So it seems important to support the existence of programs with the second ideology. It does seem more difficult for programs with the second ideology to resolve certain questions. For instance, what is the best thing to do for the human and for the animal during certain instances in therapy? When and how should limits be established for human–animal interactions and when should animals be excluded from participation in therapy to preserve safety and welfare?

Another issue we would like to discuss is how a clinician we interviewed in Israel referred to the effects of animal-assisted psychotherapy as "magical." While we believe the use of this term in the interview was intended only as a descriptive metaphor symbolizing the powerful effects of the modality, we are concerned that speaking in this manner interferes with gaining respect for animal-assisted therapy from medical and psychological communities. Research on neurobiology has provided evidence that no "magic" is involved with the effects of human–animal interaction in psychotherapy. In the U.S., and many places around the world, psychotherapists do not include the terms "magic" and "magical" in our vocabulary associated with animal-assisted therapy. The powerful effects of human–animal interaction in therapy are explained by scientific understanding of social interaction, social connection, and social relating. Scientific research has demonstrated the physiological mechanisms in humans and animals that explain the effects of human–animal interaction.

They include mirror neurons; the social response system, and accompanying hormones oxytocin, endorphins, and dopamine; the stress response system, and accompanying hormones adrenalin, aldosterone, and cortisol; and so forth (Handlin et al., 2011; Odendaal, 2000; Odendaal & Meintjes, 2003; Olmert, 2009; Panksepp, 1998, 2005; Uvnäs-Moberg, 1998a, 1998b; Uvnäs-Moberg, Arn, & Magusson, 2005). Referring to outcomes as "magical" detracts from the scientific credibility of human–animal interactions. Instead, we would be better served to present scientific reasoning for the efficacy of animal-assisted therapy. We must promote the legitimacy of animal-assisted intervention as a modality applied in the framework of social science. We were pleased to hear how those affiliated with universities in Israel were aspiring to continue to contribute to scientific literature on animal-assisted interventions with their own research endeavors.

References

Ascione, F. (1993). Children who are cruel to animals: A review of research and implications for developmental psychopathology. *Anthrozoös, 6*(4), 226–247.

Handlin, L., Hydbring-Sandberg, E., Nilsson, A., Ejdebäck, M., Jansson, A., & Uvnäs-Moberg, K. (2011). Short-term interaction between dogs and their owners: Effects on oxytocin, cortisol, insulin, and heart rate – an exploratory study. *Anthrozoös, 24*(3), 301–315.

Israeli Association of Animal-Assisted Psychotherapy. (n.d.). Home page. Retrieved October 5, 2017, from www.iaapsytherapy.org/index.php/about-iaaap

Kübler-Ross, E. (1969). *On death and dying.* New York, NY: Scribner.

Levinson, B. (1969). *Pet-oriented child psychotherapy.* Springfield, IL: Charles C. Thomas.

Odendaal, J. S. J. (2000). Animal-assisted therapy – magic or medicine? *Journal of Psychosomatic Research, 49*(4), 275–280.

Odendaal, J. S., & Meintjes, R. A. (2003). Neurophysiological correlates of affiliative behavior between humans and dogs. *The Veterinary Journal, 165*(3), 296–301.

Olmert, M. D. (2009). *Made for each other: The biology of the human–animal bond.* Philadelphia, PA: Da Capo Press.

Panksepp, J. (1998). *Affective neuroscience: The foundations of human and animal emotions.* New York, NY: Oxford University Press.

Panksepp, J. (2005). Affective consciousness: Core emotional feelings in animals and humans. *Consciousness and Cognition, 14,* 30–80.

Parish-Plass, N. (Ed.). (2013). *Animal-assisted psychotherapy: Theory, issues and practice.* West Lafayette, IN: Purdue University Press.

Uvnäs-Moberg, K. (1998a). Antistress pattern induced by oxytocin. *News in Physiological Science, 13,* 22–26.

Uvnäs-Moberg, K. (1998b). Oxytocin may mediate the benefits of positive social interaction and emotions. *Psychoneuroendocrinology, 23*(8), 819–835. doi:10.1016/S0306-4530(98)00056-0

Uvnäs-Moberg, K., Arn, I., & Magnusson, D. (2005). The psychobiology of emotion: The role of the oxytocinergic system. *International Journal of Behavioral Medicine, 12*(2), 59–65.

Figure 8.1 Nancy Parish-Plass is an animal-assisted psychotherapist and animal-assisted play therapist in Israel. Photo copyright of Nancy Parish-Plass (used with permission); photographer unknown.

Part III
India and Hong Kong

9 Minal Kavishwar of Animal Angels Foundation

We traveled to Pune and Mumbai, India, to interview Minal Kavishwar, who is a psychologist and founder of Animal Angels Foundation and Animal Angels Therapy Center in India. (see Figure 9.1). We also visited extensively with other staff, such as Akash Lonkar, who directs the program in Mumbai and is Minal's brother. Additionally, we observed the work of several therapists of Animal Angels Foundation. Minal Kavishwar and her brother, Akash Lonkar, drove us around to see many interesting and historical places in India and hosted us for several traditional meals, giving us wonderful experiences and memories.

Animal Angels Foundation is the only organization in Asia that is a member of the prestigious group IAHAIO (International Association of Human-Animal Interaction Organizations, n.d.). According to its website, Animal Angels Foundation is India's largest and only registered nonprofit organization that has introduced and developed the field and scope of human–animal interaction and animal-assisted interventions in India. They are a team of trained therapy dogs/pet parents, volunteers, and mental health professionals who have provided human–animal interaction–based programs since about the year 2003 (Animal Angels Foundation, n.d.). A primary goal of Animal Angels Foundation is to enhance the quality of human life through interaction with animals. Animal Angels Foundation members work with special needs children in schools and institutes. They also work in the psychiatric setting in hospitals and institutes for children. Additionally, the Animal Angels Foundation members are active in crisis and disaster response in India.

Minal Kavishwar was first in India to be registered as a handler–animal team with her dog through the Pet Partners organization (known at the time as Delta Society). I interviewed Minal Kavishwar in Pune, India, on March 15, 2015.

Interview with Minal Kavishwar

Cynthia: Minal, thank you for joining me for the interview today.
Minal: Thank you, Dr. Chandler, for this wonderful opportunity.
Cynthia: I'm excited for you to tell everyone about your program. When did it start? And all of the populations that you serve and how you serve them.

Minal: Okay, well, when somebody asks me how I ended up in this field, it's actually very strange to look back and just evaluate the journey of how I got to start working with animals. Academically, I'm a clinical psychologist, and because of my passion, I was learning canine behavior and animal behavior. It happened so that the lady from whom I was learning animal behavior got called to a school for mentally challenged children where they needed a dog. This was back in 2002. And until then I had absolutely no idea of this wonderful field called animal-assisted therapy. Since I was a mental health postgraduate, she said, "Why don't you join me and come to this place where we are trying to figure out how the dog will fit in the school." And that's when I realized that instead of just training the dog to be a pet in the school premises, the dog could be an emotional support to the children and provide them the kind of acceptance that they probably don't get in the society. That was the only thought I had, which pushed me to learn more about how dogs and humans could work together. And then I found out about this entire field called animal-assisted therapy. That's when I found out about you, and I contacted you and asked for more guidance in terms of how I could learn and how I could incorporate this in the work that I'm doing. And that's where it all started.

We got our first therapy dog, who was a Labrador. She was called down from Bangalore, and her name was Kutty. Kutty means "the little one" in one of the languages in India. So she literally was the last pup of the litter, the youngest one. So she was called Kutty, and the name stuck because for children, it was very easy to call out that name, Kutty. So she came down to the school, and I started working with her. For me, it was a new experience because I was working with a therapy dog for the first time, learning how to train a therapy dog and then how to work with the children as well. But it was a good experience to blend both of my passions – working with a human population as well as working with animals.

And I should say that working with Kutty was such a wonderful experience because I believe she taught me more through my relationship with her than I could learn through books or studies because she would show me instances of what an animal or what a dog could do or how a dog could break boundaries and reach out to children in a way that humans probably can't. Kutty recently passed away last year. She lived ten beautiful years of life, and for the ten years, she's been an integral part of the school. The school is called Jidd School for mentally challenged children in Thane. It's run by the Thane Municipal Corporation. The principal of the school, Shyamashree Bhosle, she adopted Kutty to be her own pet.

Initially, we had thoughts of having her stay in the school premises, but this worked out even better because then she had a family.

So Kutty would come to the school with the principal every day, be in the school premises throughout, work with the children, and then go back home. When she was in the school premises, our primary work was to work on the behavior problems that the children with mental disabilities had. When we spoke to teachers, we found out that the major issue was to be able to deal with these behavior issues, everything, including not being able to fit in a classroom setup, temper tantrums, stubbornness, not being able to express. So nonconformity, adolescent issues with mentally challenged children, that was another tricky area to work on. And we saw that, with Kutty present in the classroom setup, these issues were quite easy to handle for the teachers. And along with that, since they had many other therapies going on in the school as well, like physiotherapy and speech therapy, we could integrate that along with Kutty. We would encourage children who were noncommunicative to call out to Kutty, or they would do that spontaneously most of the time.

There are so many stories from Jidd School where a child who was labeled noncommunicative because he had never attempted to talk all of a sudden in a play session call out to Kutty. And that's the first time that teachers had ever heard him say a name or speak actual words. Then from there, they started working with him in a particular direction, and then he was able to start communicating in a better way. But just getting that first push, the first encouragement spontaneously to say something, was to Kutty. We had a lot of children who had associated disabilities, mental retardation with associated disabilities.

And we had similar cases with children who were paraplegic, waist down, who were bound to a wheelchair, some children who couldn't move waist down, and some children who used crutches or calipers. And in the class, if I would announce who's going to take Kutty for a walk, all the children would have their hands raised, irrespective of their ability at that point in time. That just showed the kind of motivation Kutty brought about in them.

And we had a lot of activities with the children where the children learned to leave their crutches and calipers on one side and try to hold the railing and walk the dog. To be able to forget their support equipment and try to take a step on their own, that was a huge thing for them. And Kutty would maintain her pace, be patient enough to let them walk one step at a time, and just give them a new hope in terms of mobility.

Cynthia: Your integration of Kutty into the work at the school was a new concept in India?

Minal: Yes, that was a very new concept, especially for a school setup for any kind of a mental health population. And that's where it all started. Till then, I, myself, was trying to find resources within India or guidance within India as to how should I proceed with this because I had a concept but I didn't know how to do it. But then I found out that there was no work done in India in the field of animal-assisted therapy before that. Yeah, sure, there have been visits but not in the technical realm of animal-assisted therapies.

Cynthia: No professional application?

Minal: No professional application, correct. So there were a lot of instances where dogs were taken to school to interact with children, but that doesn't really classify as therapy.

Cynthia: It was social interaction?

Minal: It was social interaction.

Cynthia: Visitation, not therapy with intended treatment and results?

Minal: Yes, also no documentation of such work and how it affected the different populations that the dogs interacted with. So, once I realized that this is what lacked in India, I decided to document whatever work I was doing because then, I thought, at least this is how I would take it further. So once I realized that there was a lack of documentation of any sort of work based on human–animal interaction in India, I decided that I'll start documenting whatever work I'm doing here. And it started with simple pre- and postmeasures. The group that I was working with, I just took three parameters: behavioral issues, motor control, and social interaction. And I just decided to measure these three things because, once you start getting into it, the field just expands in front of you. And then, at least for me, it was like I was at a loss for picking up on particular areas of observation because I saw multiple impacts of AAT [animal-assisted therapy]. But to narrow it down for documentation purpose, these are the three things that we decided to document first. That was probably the first documentation of effective animal-assisted therapy on mentally challenged children in an Indian setting. That helped me to convince the mental health faculty around me on the benefits of animal-assisted therapy because now, I had something to show them in terms of how the kids benefited out of this. And it took time.

There was a lot of resistance initially, even within the mental health community or the medical health community. Not many of them were aware of the scientific and the therapeutic use of animals in these kinds of settings. They just thought that "Yes, kids would feel good. Kids would feel happy. The patients would feel happy, but what is beyond that?" There's a structure to it; there are objectives, which we can achieve through this interaction. So getting this point out to the mental health community was essential. That is what I realized after three years of work because, after Jidd School, I started looking out for more similar projects that I could do. But then I found resistance.

Mrs. Bhosle was visionary enough to be able to help us run this program in her school [Jidd], but beyond that, it took time for us to find more avenues to implement this work. So the data that I had from Jidd School helped me convince, not just convince, but helped me show a direction in terms of this is what we can do for your kids. And then slowly, we did start finding other avenues of implementation.

But by the time I was doing Jidd project, I realized that, if I develop myself as a private practitioner, then yes, I would have a monopoly in the field because there's no one else doing this. But then, I would also be limiting the work and the outreach of my work because what I felt was that, even though I have grown up with animals around me, I never had a pet of my own. And I realized that many people in India love animals but they don't essentially have the privilege of having their own pet. So what do I do with people like these? Or this is one side to the story; the other side is that there are a lot of people who may not even afford therapy. So as a private practitioner, how many people or what kind of people were to come to me? And that is where the limitation was.

So then I decided this needs to be taken to a massive scale. In order for people to really realize the importance of animals in their lives, I need a bigger working ground. And that's when the concept of starting an organization or a social foundation came in, and I had more like-minded people and my friends and my teammates come along. We had volunteer pets, people who would volunteer their pets, for this work. And that's how we had a bigger team. Otherwise, then it would have been a limitation of me and my dog and my private practice and that would be it, but I wanted to take it further.

So it started with two dogs, Kutty and Goldie, and now, we have about 15 odd dogs in Pune and 20 odd dogs in Mumbai. And we are still planning to grow more in cities like Delhi and Bangalore. So, yes, the objective was to be able to reach out to a larger number of people, also, different socioeconomic groups, because, like I said, only a selected section of the society would be able to afford therapy or go to a counselor or a practitioner using animals in the practice. But there's a large number of people who cannot afford or wouldn't even know that they need to go to a therapist. So then I started focusing on how I could take my therapy animals and benefit them.

And that's where all these programs that we are currently working with came to be, like the Bal Kalyan Sanstha in Pune. It's a recreational center for children with disabilities. So most of the time children with disabilities don't get the same recreational opportunity like the other children. So this is a one-of-its-kind center in India where any child with any disability can come and access the facility. And we've been running the animal-assisted therapy program over there since 2007, and that is a place where schools all around Pune send their children at least once in 15 days. So that becomes a central place for us to reach out to multiple schools with multiple disabilities at the same time. We have, in rotation, about four to six dogs working there. And we have rabbits and fish who have now become a part of the program.

And again, when I see the program running, I feel good that the vision that I had to reach out to children who had probably never seen a dog before, be able to interact with a positive dog and benefit out of it through the motivation that a dog provides, to the spontaneous expression that a dog facilitates. So that's what makes me happy.

Cynthia: This is an award-winning program. You received an award actually from the United States. Your practice is in Pune, this beautiful place, but you were trained as a Pet Partner from the Delta Society, which that was its name many years ago; it is now called Pet Partners.

Minal: Right.

Cynthia: But you received the Delta Society [Pet Partners] Beyond Limits Award. And that was your work with Kutty?

Minal: Yeah, that was my work with Kutty. Me and Kutty as a team, we were the first registered Pet Partners team from India. And then we went on to receive the award for her work at Jidd School and her work with posttrauma for the 7/11 train blast victims [July 11, 2006, serial train bombings in Mumbai – a terrorist attack which killed 209 people and injured over 700].

Cynthia: Where do you go from here? What's your vision? You've accomplished a great deal, but you have ideas about where you want to go with this. What lays ahead? What is your dream to continue this?

Minal: There's a lot of work that needs to be done, and I think I've barely started. It has been ten years that I'm in this field here in India, and I've seen a tremendous shift in the attitude of people and in receptiveness towards therapy and towards animals. Also, a lot of interest from not just the mental and medical health communities, but also youngsters and students, pet owners, so there's been like a very positive shift in the past say four to five years. But I see that there's a lot more work that needs to be done for the field to be consolidated in India and also to create a base from where new students or new faculty would come and do more work in the field. So I think I'm in a position where I can, in whatever way I can, do at least the groundwork of preparing the society, preparing the culture, preparing formats of how we've done it till now so that people later can take it from there and grow the work. And I think my focus right now is in training individuals, professionals as well as students, in learning the therapy and using it in a professional way.

So thanks to you, I've now been able to incorporate your material into my practical training program of animal-assisted therapy. And I've seen good response in the amount of students that come and contact me for internships or for postgraduate studies in animal-assisted therapy. And it's just good to see more and more people getting involved in this.

Cynthia: I've met some of your delightful students. And I hear that you're helping people set up programs elsewhere, such as Dubai and possibly Singapore.

Minal: Yeah, and Sri Lanka. I had a recent request from an organization in Sri Lanka that is working in rescue and rehabilitation of animals. They wrote to me saying that they have a lot of rescued dogs and they would like me to come and train them and look at the possibility of training certain rescue dogs as therapy dogs so that they can also promote their rescue program in terms of how these dogs are really wonderful blessings for us.

Cynthia: I can see that you have this love for training. And you have an opportunity to share your ideas with professionals who want to practice animal-assisted therapy and enthusiastic students who want to learn about animal-assisted therapy. So if you wanted to send a message to students who have an interest in animal-assisted therapy, what is your philosophy, your ideas that you could enlighten them about the value of animal-assisted therapy and the importance of its practice in society?

Minal: Oh, that's really something to think about. If I look at it from how it's been for me, I think it's more about how you feel when you're with animals, what it makes you feel. For me at least, I know that I find my center, and I find a tremendous emotional calmness when I'm working with animals and that it's a mutual learning and constantly learning from the animals that I work with. I have a beautiful relationship with each and every animal that I have worked with, and that has helped me grow as a human.

And if students and practitioners, or anyone who wants to work with animals, look at it from this perspective, it's a great opportunity to just leave aside the professional angle and look at it from a very growth angle, growth as a human being, growth as a spiritual being, because I believe that there's a reason why we all are connected, including the animals that come into our life. And they just help us look for things beyond the professional aspect or

Cynthia:

Minal:

beyond practice and all the things we have created for us. They teach us to, like you have mentioned, they teach us to be genuine. And it's a mutual learning. So as students and professionals, if we can be as free as them in our relations, we can achieve much more.

Cynthia: Thank you for sharing those ideas. Is there anything else that you would like to share about your program or your ideas about animal-assisted therapy?

Minal: I think I would like to talk about the program we have set up in Dubai because for us, that has been a great opportunity to be able to help someone create a program similar to us. Like I know it's been a ten-year-long struggle, which is still going on, tackling different cultural challenges and practical issues. And to be able to replicate that in about three to four months for a setup like Dubai, which has even greater cultural challenges and weather challenges, but the thing is that the program has such great potential.

The program in Dubai is primarily an animal-assisted and a holistic treatment-based program. And I had a chance to select and work with a variety of animals who now work for the therapy program over there, including a cockatoo, a horse, rabbits, a goat as well, and two therapy dogs who were trained here in India by our team and then sent over to Dubai, and still, they're working there; it's been a year now, and they're working there quite successfully. So it's very good to be able to help others create such wonderful programs and be able to share that experience.

Cynthia: Well, thank you so much for taking your valuable time to share with us your beautiful program and helping people understand how animal-assisted therapy can be applied in India and so many other places. It is a growing field. It is expanding. And I appreciate how you emphasize in your program the value of that connection between humans and animals.

Minal: Thank you so much for giving me this opportunity to be able to connect with so many people abroad, all over the world. Thank you so much.

Editors' Commentary for Chapter 9

There is no doubt the services provided by Minal Kavishwar and her team at Animal Angels Foundation in Pune and Mumbai are pioneering work. They are the first to provide animal-assisted therapy services in India and the first there to offer training for aspiring animal-assisted therapists. The work in their communities is slowly helping to change views of the people of India toward dogs and breaking through cultural barriers of resistance around the idea of dogs having value for involvement in education and social services. Pet ownership is not as common in India as it is in the U.S. It is expensive to care for a dog in India. People have limited living space, and there are limited places to exercise a dog. Purebred dogs are preferred for ownership by the general population of India who can afford a dog. Large packs of stray dogs, mostly mixed breeds, bunch together under bridges or on corners of major intersections in the city, left to fend for themselves. These dogs are mostly not rescued or cared for and are a community nuisance. There are a few private rescue groups but no efforts that even come close to addressing the need for reducing the stray dog population or domesticating the dogs for adoption. Driving through Mumbai, we would come across a pack of up to 50 dogs on one corner, and this was common. Coming out of a restaurant one evening, we had a large stray dog come over and jump up on each of us, almost knocking one or the other of us down several times. It was starved for attention and food. We were told this is a common occurrence. This is how the stray dogs have learned to get their needs met. Some target people coming out of restaurants hoping for a handout of leftover food. My heart was deeply saddened by the state of these dogs, the terrible neglect.

The lack of availability of pet dogs, with appropriate temperament and behavior, is a barrier to providing animal-assisted therapy in India. Animal Angels Foundation incorporates both purebred and mixed-breed dogs, but the prejudicial attitude of the general population toward mixed-breed dogs, that they are all dirty and ill-behaved, makes it hard to gain acceptance of a therapy dog that is not a purebred. Even purebred dogs are viewed by much of the general population as not belonging in schools, hospitals, or service agencies.

Traffic in Mumbai is another barrier to owning a dog as well as performing animal-assisted therapy. The traffic is very, very intense – you have to experience it to fully understand the huge amount of chaotic congestion. Minal jokingly confirmed our whimsical observation that traffic signs and lights, as well as marked lanes on the roads, are treated by many drivers as merely suggestions and not as regulations. So the preferred mode of personal transportation in India is the motorcycle, which is not convenient for the transportation of a dog. We were told that parents in India encourage their children to buy a motorcycle and discourage them from buying a car because the motorcycle is viewed as a safer and more convenient form of transportation. Also, dogs are not allowed in taxis, rickshaws, or trains. In fact, we were told a dog would not fit on a train without being squashed because the trains pack so full of people – we chose not to partake in the train ride experience. So to provide animal-assisted therapy for the few schools, hospitals, and service agencies that will allow it, the Animal Angels Foundation staff have to accomplish much planning. First, they have to find a pet owner who is willing to loan out their pet for a couple of hours on certain days. Then a representative from Animal Angels Foundation assesses the dog for its appropriateness for therapy. Next, a therapist spends time with the dog to befriend it. Once familiarity has been achieved with the dog, the therapist becomes a handler–animal team with that pet. For the days of service provision, the therapist must arrange for use of a car and coordinate pickup of the dog from the pet's owner in time to make it to the service site, then provide animal-assisted therapy to the designated service user, and finally, get the dog back home through heavily congested traffic. To extend so much effort, Animal Angels Foundation staff must work together and expend much energy. This requires great commitment to the provision of animal-assisted therapy service, but team members told us that it was very much worth it for the opportunity to work with dogs to provide services to those in need.

Despite all of the obstacles and inconveniences of providing animal-assisted therapy, the Animal Angels Foundation model seems to be working. There are directors of some schools, hospitals, and agencies who are open to the idea of dogs' involvement in service provision. Child and adult service users are attracted to learn more about these dogs that are allowed into these facilities. Their curiosity and willingness to engage with the dogs and handlers provide opportunities for service provision. Successes with adults and children in these facilities have provided much positive publicity for Animal Angels Foundation. So gradually, the idea of animal-assisted therapy is beginning to change in India, and the training program developed and provided by Minal Kavishwar is attracting people from across India and other countries in Asia to learn how to provide animal-assisted therapy.

Though animal-assisted therapy is relatively new in India, we thought it important to include this interview in our book to showcase the important pioneering work of Minal Kavishwar and her organization, Animal Angels Foundation. We also wanted to demonstrate how the idea of using animal-assisted interventions as a service for humans with emotional and mental health issues and disabilities is spreading throughout the world.

References

Animal Angels Foundation. (n.d.). Home page. Retrieved October 4, 2017, from, http://animalangels.org.in/

International Association of Human-Animal Interaction Organizations. (n.d.). Home page. Retrieved October 4, 2017, from http://iahaio.org/

Figure 9.1 Minal Kavishwar is a psychologist and the founder of the Animal Angels Foundation and Animal Angels Therapy Center in India. Photo copyright of Minal Kavishwar (used with permission); photographer unknown.

10 Dr. William Fan of the Hong Kong Animal Therapy Foundation, Dr. Paul Wong and Dr. Rose Yu of the University of Hong Kong, and Steven Lai and Fanny Leung of the Chinese Evangelical Zion Church

I (CKC) was invited to Hong Kong by Dr. Paul Wong to make presentations at the Animal-Assisted Therapy Conference sponsored by the Department of Social Work and Social Administration of the University of Hong Kong. I presented a preconference seminar and a keynote address and participated in a panel discussion with Dr. William Fan and Dr. Paul Wong. Additionally, I copresented a postconference workshop with the assistance of Tiffany Otting. During our stay, we were able to interview professionals who practice animal-assisted therapy in Hong Kong. There is very little ongoing, formal training programs in Hong Kong for professional application of animal-assisted interventions. Practitioners of animal-assisted interventions in Hong Kong have mostly obtained their training from experts in other countries. They then share information with each other. However, as interest in animal-assisted interventions increases in Hong Kong, existing experts there are assuming more responsibility for training professionals in that region who wish to incorporate this modality in service of clients.

Animal-assisted interventions is in its very early stages of development in this region of the world. Thus, the work that is being done is certainly pioneering. The household pet is not nearly as common in Hong Kong as it is in the U.S. mostly, because much of the housing consists of small apartments, mostly in tall buildings, where pet dogs or cats are not permitted. Also, the primary mode of transportation is the metro system or a taxi, neither of which allow dogs. A personal car is not common. These inconveniences make it somewhat difficult for the animal-assisted therapists who practice in Hong Kong. Additionally, the idea of a dog or cat for therapy is very new to Hong Kong culture. Though the application of animal-assisted interventions in Hong Kong is in its early stages of development, it was interesting to learn about the various services.

A key figure in the field of animal-assisted interventions for emotional and mental health in Hong Kong is Dr. William Fan. I was very fortunate to be able to interview him. He is one of the first in his country to consider human–animal interaction as a form of therapy for the elderly and the mentally or emotionally disabled. He is also a leading advocate for animal welfare in Hong Kong. The interview with Dr. William Fan took place on June 3, 2015.

Interview with Dr. William Fan

Cynthia: Dr. William Fan is a psychiatrist and president of the Hong Kong Animal Therapy Foundation. Thank you for joining us today, Dr. Fan.

William: It's nice to meet you.

Cynthia: Tell me about the work that you do in animal-assisted therapy, the history behind that, and how it has evolved.

William: It all started about ten years ago. I and my wife have an organization for the welfare of stray cats. And then with all the welfare works, the idea came that why shouldn't I be putting my professional experience and skills into the animal welfare. We started thinking about whether we can apply some animal-assisted therapy in some of the population. Actually, the first program we started is a program called Elderly and Cat Scheme. The idea is to support some elderly citizens. Some of them may be living alone. We support them in both the resources, including the vet fees and the expenses for living with the cats, and then also other help such as getting the cat sent to their homes by our volunteers with the aim to support them to adopt a cat. You see, when you are trying to adopt older and adult cats, it might be quite difficult. We think that, if we can support the elderly, then the cat will have a home, and then the elderly will have a life companion. So we create a kind of balanced situation. As an animal welfare organization, we have some cases which are quite impressive. People get much healthier, and they are more engaged and lively after they adopt a cat. A merit of the program is that we keep visiting them because we have to check on how they are getting on with the cats. One barrier an elderly citizen would consider for adopting a cat is whether in the future their health or their situation might change and then they may not be able to take care of the cat anymore. That would make them hesitate. We guarantee that if they are unable to take care of the cat in the future, we will take the cat back and look for another adoption for that cat. We give the elderly a kind of reassurance.

Another good thing about sending volunteers to visit them is that they get to be a friend with our volunteer. The volunteers would come along and work with the elderly, and then we'd talk with them and then they would share their common interests in the animal. It's getting to be very successful.

Then we think that, if we can promote the idea of AAT [animal-assisted therapy] more to the Hong Kong public, that maybe more animals would be helping people. Then they would indirectly enhance the image of animals among the citizens. It's kind of indirectly promoting animal welfare too. Back in 2005, we had been giving some talks to students at City University. At that time, we promoted mostly the concept of the Elderly and Cat Scheme. That was how we started off back in 2005.

Cynthia: How successful has the program been in your viewpoint?

William: Far from very satisfactory. In Hong Kong, many of the elderly are quite hesitant in adopting a cat because [restrictive residence] policies are not very supportive. Even in some private residences, they would not allow the residents to keep the animal at home. That would be a main drawback. Despite all our promotion, I think the number of elderly and cat adoptions are still not very optimal.

Cynthia: Because of the barriers? The housing barriers, the hesitancy of the elderly to adopt a cat?

William: Yes, and then because we need to have local volunteers who come in contact with the elderly. If elderly people adopt a cat from us, we need to send our volunteer to keep up the contact. But the ideal situation actually would be collaborating with an elderly service so that people who come into contact on a daily basis would inform us if the elderly person fell sick and was hospitalized. Then we would know that we need to take back the cat. That's how we planned the scheme to be working, but it's not easy to engage a collaborating agency in this way. That is actually the main barrier. We need to collaborate with some other elderly service to make it successful. Up to now, we are only doing sporadic cases.

Cynthia: But in those cases, you have seen it making quite a difference in the lives of some elderly persons.

William: Yes, actually, one interesting thing is that you invite them to become an advocate for our program. They would do interviews, sometimes appear on television programs. One of the elderly we pointed at, her grandson, her grandchildren, actually became much more warm with her after seeing her appearing on the TV program. They were only visiting her once in a month or so. But since she's become so famous, that actually induced a kind of intimacy between her and the grandchildren.

Cynthia: She became a celebrity to her own grandchildren.

William: Yes. They probably think it was actually very impressive. That elderly woman, actually she was feeding some stray cat around this residence. She lived, at that time, in a kind of elderly unit where they share a kitchen but have their own apartment. She'd been feeding this stray cat for some time. Then she came to us and said,

"Well, okay, I really want to help that cat." We wrote a letter to the warden in her unit promising that we'll take care of the cat if anytime in the future she cannot take care of the cat herself. Then they allowed her to take the cat into her unit. She would live there with that cat. And then she became our advocate. She enjoys telling how more positive things can happen to you if you can live with a cat. Actually, because not only does she have a companion but actually it helps her to relieve her concern about this stray cat.

Cynthia: It helped her anxiety because she really wanted to help the cat.

William: Actually, the mechanical term, it empowers her that she feels that she can do something for the cat.

Cynthia: It gave her a sense of meaning and purpose.

William: Yes, and then the cat became a focus for her in real life.

Cynthia: Is there anything else that you would like people to understand about your program and how effective you think it has been?

William: I have been promoting AAT in different media, and I've been giving talks to different university students and hoping more people would buy into this idea. Then in 2010, I was approached by Social Welfare and Social Services. They have some funding for doing some AAT for socially withdrawn youth. I was invited to provide some supervision and consultation for them. Then at that time, we really engaged in a more structured program for AAT. It's a social service with focus for the socially withdrawn youth. What they've been doing is, they would have some case manager visiting the case, building up rapport and a relationship with the clients, and hopefully they would support them, then provide some vocational training, and then some coaching for getting a job or returning to school. Pretty much, they're social workers. For that program, the initial idea is to have some pet grooming training for them so that they would be able to consider whether they would be interested in doing something about animal grooming and so on. Then what we did, we introduced a dog we rescued on the street. The dog became a therapeutic dog in the center. Actually, the dog lived six days in the center and only returned to us on Sunday and public holidays. I think it's a breakthrough because that service was housed in a public estate and probably would have forbidden the dog to live there but for the AAT program. We engaged the district office of the social work department, and we got more high profile. We had a press conference, asked the media to come in to cover the program and report on how this dog would be very instrumental in helping socially withdrawn youth. Then Paul Wong did research on that program.

Cynthia: Dr. Paul Wong of the University Hong Kong?

William: Yes.

Cynthia: They went and researched the social services program with the youth and the residential therapy dog?

William: Yes. The results showed that taking care of the dog in the center actually was the most important point about having the therapy take effect. Because the socially withdrawn youth, they were responsible for taking care of the therapy dog, and then they would be taking him out for walks, giving him food, cleaning him up, and more important, when there were visitors to the center or newcomers, then that service user will be responsible for introducing the therapy dog to the newcomer and visitors. This was their duty, and that gave them a chance to communicate with strangers, presenting the dog and the role for the therapy dog in the center. I think that is an important issue, when you think that you have something greater than yourself, you have to do it for the therapy dog. They would not shy off from telling people, and then of course, they would have some material [instruction] and some role-play [practice] before they do that. Then gradually, they build up their confidence. So many of these socially withdrawn youth have the problem of very low self-esteem or a social anxiety, withdrawal and avoidance of social context. With this program, by introducing the therapy dog and by caring for the therapy dog, they improve and can overcome many of their obstacles. That explains why the AAT program worked very well for this group.

Cynthia: It became worthwhile for them to overcome their anxiety because they wanted to do something for the dog?

William: Yes.

Cynthia: By feeling like they were doing something for the dog, by taking care of it, introducing it to new people in the center, they became empowered themselves.

William: Yes.

Cynthia: Because they were socially withdrawn, but then became more socially interactive, more socially confident.

William: Yeah, because actually, they would be oversensitive to others who have comments or a response, so [before, they] actually avoided social situations. Some of them have actually been housebound for several years, so it's quite a breakthrough if they can talk to strangers. As you said, you are not so aware of yourself; you're thinking of how to present the dog, the therapy dog, to strangers. Then actually you wouldn't be so anxious. With success of course, the social worker will be giving them positive reinforcement; they would be giving compliments to them. Not all the service users are given the honor of taking care of the therapy dog. Actually, you have to build a relationship with the dog, and then the dog will trust you. And then you learn how to give small commands and then get the cooperation of the therapy dog. Then you know how to interact with other people, and then you must be responsible. After all this, then you would become the care [person] for the therapy dog. It's really an honor and an achievement just becoming appointed as the care [person].

Cynthia: And they're motivated to really work on the skills they need to gain because they want to become the caregiver of the animal.

William: Yes. I think the important thing is that, because of the interest of taking care of the dog, it's named Fat-fat, they all are made to go through several challenges. Once they achieve one step, they gain more confidence. So actually, far before they advance to the stage of talking to strangers, they have all these small steps of advances in which, all the time, is bringing up their confidence.

Cynthia: Well, thank you very much for joining us today, and I really enjoyed hearing about the work that you do: the welfare work with the cats and placing them with the elderly, and helping to bring the stray dog into the residential unit with the socially withdrawn individuals, and the tremendous progress that has been made there. It sounds like some wonderful programs.

William: Yes, nice to meet you. And we hope that we can do more for AAT here.

Cynthia: That would be great.

William: Thank you.

I interviewed Dr. Paul Wong (Wong, Wai-Ching) (Wong et al., 2015), who performed pioneering research that established clinical efficacy for the residential therapy dog program developed by Dr. Fan at the Social Welfare and Social Services. Dr. Paul Wong is an associate professor in the Department of Social Work and Social Administration at the University of Hong Kong (see Figure 10.2). We also interviewed Dr. Rose Yu (Yu, Wai Man), who at the time of our interview, was a doctoral student performing pioneering research on animal-assisted therapy. She was advised by Dr. Paul Wong. Since our interview, Rose has successfully completed her doctoral studies (Yu, 2017). The interview with Dr. Paul Wong and Dr. Rose Yu took place on June 5, 2015.

Interview with Dr. Paul Wong and Dr. Rose Yu

Cynthia: Dr. Wong, introduce yourself, and we'll have Rose do the same.

Paul: Sure. Thank you for the invitation to participate in this interview. I am a clinical psychologist by training, and I am assistant professor at the Department of Social Work and Social Administration at the University of Hong Kong.

Rose: My name is Rose Yu and my background is in social work, and I'm now working as a senior research assistant in the department.

Cynthia: You're at the University of Hong Kong?

Rose: Yes.

Cynthia: Okay. And as you know, this interview is to share with other people around the world things that are happening here in Hong Kong that are related to animal-assisted therapy. I know as researchers, you're very interested in furthering the field of animal-assisted therapy in Hong Kong. So tell me how you're involved in the activities of animal-assisted therapy here?

Paul: Maybe Rose start first?

Rose: Well, my involvement I think comes from my experience, first of all. I started to have animals as companions when I was very young, but I didn't have the great feelings for it. At that time, usually, if in a traditional Chinese or Hong Kong Chinese family, sometimes they took a puppy back home for a certain function, such as a guide dog, or protection against theft, or something like that. So we didn't actually develop a very strong bond with the dog at that time. And then when I grew older, I just felt like I like them. I like to see them, but I haven't had one who lived with me. Not until I am more than ten years old actually. At more than ten years old, I started to have my own companion animal, and then my relationship and my bonding started to actually develop at that time. I had both dogs and cats at that time. It's my personal feeling that I have gained a lot from the relationship myself as well. And at that time at my work, my supervisor was asking me was I interested to further my study, and I told him that as long as I found something I'm interested in. Then I don't know why, but just suddenly one day, I thought, "Well, maybe this is a topic that can sustain me through the study." Animal-assisted therapy, at that time, I knew very little about it. I just got interested in animals, just got interested in why I'm interested in them. That's about it as well. Once I start to talk about animals, I tend to be long-winded. Sorry.

Paul: Well, I had my first dog in 1993, and that was on the Gold Coast. I had a really big dog. I had a Rottweiler. He was 75 kilograms when he was four years old. Then that was the time I started to like dogs. I really love dogs, especially big dogs. Then I came back to Hong Kong, and then I lived with my current wife. She had four little dogs from the same family. The last one died in 2009. That was the exact year that my son was born, so it was a really tough time for me, for my wife, not so much for my son. He was too young. Then I thought, "I want to do something for the animals in Hong Kong."

Then in 2010, I first met Rose. and I found out that she was interested about doing something with animals too, so I told her my story. Then, probably not until 2011 or 2012, she came to me and said, well, she met someone who is using AAT. That was the first time I had heard about AAT in Hong Kong, so that's how we started to work together.

Cynthia:	And you're a PhD candidate, and Dr. Wong is your major professor.
Rose:	Cosupervisor.
Cynthia:	Cosupervisor, okay. And he supervises your research efforts, and both of you do research program evaluation of animal-assisted therapy programs.
Rose:	Yes. I got accepted by the graduate school, and I got stuck because at that time, there was actually very little or, as far as I know, no AAT program in Hong Kong, except, of course, Animals Asia, but they do visits, not therapy. They do AAA [animal-assisted activities]. So I was very frustrated. Actually, no one knows what AAT is. And then one day, I noticed from the newspaper that one of the youth centers in Hong Kong, actually it's the Zion Center started to work with animals, to work with animals in helping the client. So I initiated a contact and said, "Well, can I come and talk? I want to do some study."
Cynthia:	You wanted to go talk to them.
Rose:	Yes, because I know very little about research. I'm not confident, and I know that Paul is interested so I said, "Well, Paul, help me to do proper research." So that started our working together as a team and then started work with other projects as well.
Cynthia:	What did you find about their program at Zion?
Paul:	Well, the major project that they did since 2011, I think, their major target was to help what they call socially withdrawn youth. There was a term in Japanese called hikikomori [means pulling inward or acute social withdrawal]. It's a really recent phenomenon that young people at the age of 15, they start losing interest in going to school. They start losing interest in going out. They start losing interest in finding jobs. So they just seclude themselves in their homes and play with the Internet and play video games and whatnot. It can last for months to years. So this is a really interesting phenomenon in Asia, especially a bit more wealthy Asian societies. So then I look at the literature. I couldn't find any intervention that could help these kind of people. There are some in Japan. They actually build housing; there are housing areas for a bunch of young people that like to seclude themselves, and they have different apartments in the same area. The rationale was if they put similar youth together in the same building, then hopefully, they might talk to each other, but there are no evaluations, no scientific study on that at all. So because of that too, I'm so interested in that particular type of client and the intervention that they do. So we did an evaluation with similar youth here in Hong Kong.
	The unemployment rate, as guessed, was really high before they do the intervention. Ninety percent of them were unemployed before they start the AAT intervention, and after that, probably about 12 months afterward, the unemployment rate dropped

almost 85 to 90 percent to like 30-something. So even though the sample size wasn't that large, there was 69.

Rose: For the first phase, those who consented and completed the pre- and postassessment was only 56.

Paul: Yeah, 56 people. And even though the sample size wasn't that big, it's really encouraging because 50 percent of reduction in unemployment rate is really amazing.

Cynthia: So certainly, by those standards, it's quite a successful program.

Paul: It is.

Rose: It is, yes. And also because I also attended some of the prep sessions and talked to some of the young people, and what I found is actually, some of the young people, who really are quite withdrawn, they do not have eye contact with you. They seem to, when you talk to them, they just lower their head and said very little when I first met them. And then eventually, they started to come out because at that time, they started to have the onset of interaction with the dog Fat-fat. So Fat-fat was always around, so that helped a lot. I can actually see the young people start to build up their confidence and let people assist them in learning because they take responsibility, take care of Fat-fat in the center.

They also use other approaches as well. In part one is multi-intervention model. So apart from having the resident dog and using the resident dog as therapy adjunct, they also have this pet-warming training. They train the young people in how to take care of cats so the cats can be adopted by elderly and then to take care of the residential dog. Actually, it is a formal training we're funding from Hong Kong. In Hong Kong, there's a statutory board that provide funding, formal training for young people on various job skills, so that is part of it. And also, there is group activities with the handlers, together with them, and talking with the young people in the group. So it's a multi-intervention model. But anyway, what I observed is, all this and the young people talking about how they build up their confidence because before that, people told them "You couldn't even take care of yourself." Now, they feel that they can take care of Fat-fat, and he feels very good about it. So in that sense, I can observe, and then from our pre- and postresearch findings, I can also see that especially, as I mentioned, the self-esteem aspect, there's a lot of changes in them.

Cynthia: That's wonderful news to hear. Your department here at your university has provided enough interest in animal-assisted therapy that you've had a wonderful conference here this week, and you've brought in different speakers. They've presented on the work that they're doing in animal-assisted therapy. It tells me that you have an interest in furthering that. How much animal-assisted therapy is actually occurring here in Hong Kong, what types of animal-assisted therapy and who is doing that?

Paul: Well, we had a one-day conference and a one-day workshop. During the conference, there were five, I think, if I'm not wrong; there were five organizations. They came and presented about their work. Some of them were AAT, animal-assisted therapy. Some were animal-assisted activities. We had the Animals Asia. We have the Mongrel Club. We had the Zion presentation by Steven Lai and Fanny Leung. And then we had the Hong Kong Hong Chi Center. They generally help the people with autism, physical disabilities. And then we have the Hong Kong Institute of Animal-Assisted Therapy; they were using AAT to help people with autism as well.

Cynthia: Since animal-assisted therapy is fairly new in Hong Kong and it's not very commonplace, what is your perspective of how well it is being received? And is there much resistance?

Rose: My feeling is that, yes, it is very young, I feel, in Hong Kong. And people who practice it actually are trying to explore how to go forward, what are the skills that can be used, etcetera. And it's well-received in a small group of professionals, but it's not mainstream because in the mainstream, there's bound to be a lot of resistance, I'm sure. Of those who practice animal-assisted therapies, most of them are small organizations. For big organizations, they are more bureaucratic, and it's more difficult because they think more technically. And you have to have a therapy animal going into the facilities, which in itself in Hong Kong, sometimes it's not easy. And then also because living with a companion animal is still not very common in Hong Kong, both limited by space and limited by a lot of the housing. In both private and public housing, there are policies of not allowing animals.

A lot of people look at AAT with caution. In terms of like a person, maybe they don't feel the animal will be able to help. I think the common feeling about animals is that they have to depend on humans for their well-being and survival, which of course is true in a way, but I think a lot of people in Hong Kong see the animal like an object, as something of a plaything.

Cynthia: Instead of a friend or a family member or a companion, as a sort of distant object that has to take my time away from other things.

Rose: Or an object that's like a wonderful handbag.

Cynthia: A handbag?

Rose: Yes. A pretty little thing that you can show off to your friends.

Cynthia: As opposed to a living being that you can have a relationship with.

Rose: Yes, but I'm very happy that I think we have more people having interest, developing interest in using AAT in their professional practice, which I think is very positive because it's not just people who love animals. They want to work with the animal professionally and trying to understand, trying to come to workshops, go for trainings themselves, to learn more about it. I feel that there is more and more professional people in Hong Kong becoming interested in it.

Cynthia: And that was reflected, I think, in the conference attendance. There were a lot of individuals there that are practicing and some that were not practicing but were very curious and interested in possibly practicing, and they came to learn more about it. That's very promising for the field here, I think.

Paul: It is, and I want to add something on top of Rose's comments. We have a lot of socioenvironmental difficulties when we talk about AAT. I remember when I was maybe still five. That was like in the 1970s or 80s. People keep saying, if when you become rich, you live in Western-style houses just like the high-rise building, and then you possess purebreds, which is a really common thinking, as a symbol of wealth. So that was very common since I was born and probably until even now, maybe. So that's why some people see having a purebred as a possession like a handbag. Then we have mongrels; those are the dogs that they adopt and are being put in a construction site and then look after the security. And then when the site is closed, then they leave the dogs there.

Cynthia: Just abandon them, the dogs. They don't understand or appreciate these mongrels, these mixed breeds.

Paul: Right. So that's how quite a fair amount of Hong Kong people still see purebreds and mongrels, like that. And when we talk about mongrels and using mongrels as AAT partners, people are so skeptical. People are scared that mongrels are dirty, they have germs, they are . . .

Rose: They're unpredictable. They will bite.

Paul: They're aggressive and not normal. Those are the most difficult and the major obstacles that we have to change or to break through, the mentality of the local people of how they see different types of dogs, regardless of whether it's AAA or AAT or even animal-assisted education. If you bring a small purebred to a school, it might be more welcome than bringing a whole bunch of mongrels to the school.

Cynthia: Because of the cultural bias against the mixed breeds, that is, these mongrels.

Paul: Yeah. That's one of the things I think is very hard to break through.

Cynthia: What are some other difficulties for people who want the field of animal-assisted therapy to grow in Hong Kong? Are there other barriers that you also think might be there?

Paul: Definitely funding because Hong Kong doesn't have a lot of expenditure in our GDP [gross domestic product] for health care.

We have a really small amount of GDP compared with other wealthy societies. We have the small amount of GDP for health care, and this is even more true for the so-called mental health or psychological health. So with a small amount of funding available, this kind of funding will probably distribute to other more advanced types of therapy or interventions that have advocates, for example, cognitive behavioral therapy. Whenever there's a new intervention or new modality that comes along, people are skeptical. But the point is we have a really small amount of pot [money] from the government and I don't think the government is willing nor is happy to fund innovative research.

And then we have to rely on private funders, funding from private people, and it's getting harder and harder because the private funders or the private funding, they're probably influenced by the mentality of the government. They look for evidence. If you don't have evidence, they'd rather not fund it.

Cynthia: And that's one of the reasons you're so interested in the research and the program evaluation, to try to build up the evidence here in Hong Kong of why these programs are effective. Then that also may help you eventually convince someone to give more funding.

Paul: Absolutely. So Rose and I talk about this; we really want to help not just the client. We want to help the animals too, so it's not just the clients. And if we don't help by building up the evidence on that, there might be animals still in the streets. They are not adopted. They are not helping other people. So as a researcher too, that's how we can contribute. Myself, I don't practice AAT. I don't think I have the skills. I don't think I have the ability yet, but I can contribute immediately as a researcher. So that's how we got involved.

Rose: I want to add on what Paul said about difficulties of developing AAT in Hong Kong, and another thing, of course, is training. For me, especially at the beginning, I found it very difficult to identify what is a typical training for me because we do not have many people who know about AAT in Hong Kong. I think now it is better. People are more aware of what training resources are available, maybe not in Hong Kong locally.

And also another thing which I think would be a barrier in developing AAT in Hong Kong is there are not a lot of therapists who may be interested in AAT, or they do not have their own therapy animal. I think that could be a barrier, if every time you have to borrow someone else's animal; it takes a lot of arrangement, especially in Hong Kong. Not a lot of people have their own private cars. Hong Kong is not a suitable place to drive your private car, and animals cannot go on public transport. So just physically making arrangement to get the borrowed therapy animal to the place where you work is difficult. So I think this is another barrier that we have to deal with in developing AAT in Hong Kong as well.

Cynthia: You're both invested in this. You see the potential of how it can help people, how it can help the dogs. So what are your hopes and dreams for the development of animal-assisted therapy in Hong Kong?

Paul: I wish that we can build up the evidence for AAT as an evidence-based practice for helping people in need, especially among Asians. This is what I think and I hope that we can do.

Rose: I share with Paul, and also as more like a dream that, by showing evidence that AAT actually helps human life, we give the animal their proper honor and value in the world we live in. My dream is that through this kind of work that we do that bit by bit if we'll build up evidence. People realize that the beings on Earth actually share the same environment. So that's my dream.

Cynthia: Animals are something to be honored. They're much more than an object. They're a being.

Rose: Yes.

Cynthia: A lovely being that can nurture and love. All right, I want to give you the final word. Any last thoughts on your mind that you would like to share with the rest of the world about animal-assisted therapy in Hong Kong?

Paul: There are many obstacles because of the unique situation in Hong Kong, and I'm very happy that we had the conference. We have you with us, and you met a lot of people who are interested about AAT. And this group of people, if we work hard, we work together, we can make such a really difficult place to practice AAT as one of the easiest places to practice AAT in the world.

Hong Kong is a small place. I always call Hong Kong a public laboratory. If we test out something in a particular region or area in Hong Kong, that would affect at least 600,000 people because we have 7 million people total in Hong Kong. If we have one particular district and make it really user-friendly, environment-friendly, animal-friendly, we can act out our dream about doing AAT, and then we can use that as the showcase for the whole world. That if something changes mentally, sociologically, politically, environmentally, then 600,000 in one district, at least, will benefit from it.

Cynthia: So, Rose, what would you like to say, final thoughts to the rest of the world about animal-assisted therapy in Hong Kong, where you'd like to see it grow?

Rose: I haven't really thought about that, like long-term vision. What I want to say is, my belief is, that AAT is just one means, one of the means to let us understand or to let us see the life of every being needs our respect. AAT is a means for us to understand living things around us better and show respect to other beings who share the world with us.

Cynthia: Well, thank you so much. I appreciate that you've taken some time to be with us today. You've had a very busy weekend. You've worked very hard bringing together people for the conference over the past three days, and this was a nice culminating event for us. I appreciate the opportunity to come to Hong Kong and meet with you and visit with you and share this time with you. It's been very valuable for me and for my graduate assistant, Tiffany Otting. We're honored to be here.

Paul: Thank you very much.

Rose: Thank you very much, and thank you for coming.

Dr. Wong and Rose Yu were both involved in researching the efficacy of the animal-assisted intervention (AAI) service at the Chinese Evangelical Zion Church (n.d.) – a program directed by Steven Lai and Fanny Leung. Steven and Fanny had presented at the Animal-Assisted Therapy Conference that was sponsored by the University of Hong Kong. I interviewed with Steven Lai and Fanny Leung on June 5, 2015.

Interview with Steven Lai and Fanny Leung

Cynthia: I understand that animal-assisted interventions are practiced at the Chinese Evangelical Zion Church. Please share what you do, the population that you work with, and how you incorporate animal-assisted therapy in helping the population that you work with, the kind of animals, and the type of activities.

Steven: We have two programs to use AAT to serve people. One of the programs, the name is Regain Momentum program, and the service target is hidden youth in Hong Kong. This is one of the programs that we run by using casework and also AAT to help them. And another program is the Touch program, where we use AAT to help elderly people in our society. And the details, maybe Fanny can talk more about.

Fanny: Because the socially withdrawn youth are usually so shy or afraid to connect with people, we use an animal to make a connection with them. We may make a home visit, and we would counsel the youth together with the animal, with the participation of an animal. We would have some animal activities, AAT activities, such as pet grooming, skill training, and some thought gathering. The youth can participate in those activities; in other words, they are connecting with other people as well.

Cynthia: And the animals. Are they limited to dogs, or are there other types of species that participate?

Fanny: Most of our animals are dogs because dogs are more sociable. We have two cats in our center also, as some of our youth are more keen on cats than dogs. They would be afraid of a dog but love a cat.

Steven: In Hong Kong, cats and dogs are the most available animals or pets that we have. There is no other kind of animal that can be accepted in a domestic unit. Some people like goldfish or turtles, but they are not very suitable for our intervention means. So we use dogs and cats. Most people know dogs and cats, and they have a familiar impression about them. So that's what we use to provide our AAT.

Cynthia: The culture of Hong Kong is familiar with dogs and cats, and so it's accepted to have them integrated into a social services program. You say that the youth, when they spend time with the animals, petting the animals, grooming the animals, they're also engaging with other humans. So the animals serve as a catalyst for practicing social skills. How effective do you think it's working?

Steven: We've done the research, two research projects. Hong Kong youth help us to do two research projects. The research shows that our intervention has a positive change.

Fanny: Yes, mainly three things: low self-esteem, social anxiety, and perceived employability. And the outcomes are very inspiring and remarkable.

Cynthia: That's great. We heard that University of Hong Kong researchers assisted you by coming in and doing a formal program evaluation and they have found statistically significant changes in the withdrawn youth who interact with the therapy dogs in these three areas of social anxiety, self-esteem, and perceived employability.

Okay, tell me about the other program. You said that there is work with the elderly?

Fanny: Yes. We launched a one-year AAT project with the elderly in Wong Tai Sin. Wong Tai Sin in Hong Kong is the district having the highest population of elderly. We want to use our animal and our youth also as volunteers to visit them and to give them joy because they are all living by themselves and they feel lonely and depressed. So we want to give them joy and give them some warmth from the youth and the animal.

Cynthia: The youth that visit the elderly with the animals, are those the same youth that are in your withdrawn youth program?

Fanny: Yes, some of them are. We want them to get more improvement by helping others, to go from one being helped to one who can help.

Cynthia: I can see how you would get the increased scores in the self-esteem and perceived capability, or employability, because they can see how they can make a difference in other people's lives. So it's nice how you've merged the two programs, helping the elderly feel less lonely and helping the youth practice their social skills at the same time by sharing the animals with the elderly.

Fanny: Yeah, and it is very interesting, as the youth also told me that they will be speechless when they visit the elderly without the animal. But if there is an animal with them that they are very familiar with, like Fat-fat, our therapy dog, they feel so secure and so confident in introducing the dog.

Cynthia: So they actually tell you that, if they didn't have the dog there and they were asked to visit with an elderly person, they wouldn't be able to do it. They would be speechless; they couldn't find the words.

Fanny: Yeah.

Cynthia: But having the dog there, they have the confidence. So the dog is serving as a social bridge, providing them with that self-esteem, that confidence, that perceived capability to socially engage.

Fanny: And also, responsibility because they promised to visit the elderly and they don't want to disappoint them. So even if there is a day with heavy raining, they feel like they still need to take the therapy dog to the home visit with the elder. They may think of not going, but then they think the elder will be disappointed, will be unhappy, and then they try.

Steven: Keep their promise.

Fanny: They are very fast to take the dog to the home, to the elder's home. But all of them are wet.

Steven: That's the reason that we think, we believe, that AAT is useful to people. Our aim is to serve hidden youth, and we think that we show that there is something meaningful for animal to help people. Then we start another program to help elderly, still by using animal, AAT, to help them. We want to know more about how far AAT can go to help people.

Cynthia: One of your animals is a dog named Fat-fat? What breed, or is it a mixed breed?

Steven: Hard to say.

Fanny: I'm not sure.

Steven: We have to tell this little dog's story first, okay? He's abandoned before, so we just check his species by looking how he looks. We believe it is Pug.

Steven: Yeah, and it is maybe a little bit crossbreeding, right?

Fanny: We're not sure.

Cynthia: The dog has found a home serving in this program.

Steven: Yes, yes.

Cynthia: Do you have any other dogs serving in your program?

Steven: We have many dog organizations. They help us too.

Fanny: Dog partners.

Steven: Dog partners. They provide the handler and their dogs that help us.

Fanny: And we have also recruited some pet owners and their dogs.

Steven: In the local area.

Fanny: Yes.

Cynthia: So you rely a lot on volunteers?

Steven: Mm-hmm (affirmative).

Fanny: Yeah.

Cynthia: Pet owners who will bring their dogs and pet handlers who provide the dogs to come in.

Cynthia: Well, it sounds like you feel you've had a great deal of success in helping the withdrawn youth develop social skills and confidence, a sense of responsibility, and lower anxiety and have assisted the elderly to not feel so lonely. And all of this is because they get an opportunity to spend time with the dogs, grooming the dogs, sharing the friendliness of the dogs. Is there anything else that you would like to share about your program that would help people understand how good you feel about your program, why you think it's important, and why it works? Any final comments?

Fanny: I think AAT gives us a unique and exciting way of serving our youth, which we haven't thought of before. We have worked on these two projects for four years. So our teams have been very excited in doing them, but at the same time, there is some frustration because there are some limitations in bringing a pet. You need to coordinate so many things, not only just your client, but the animal and the pet owners. So yes, we also need much support from our organizations and our clients to work on this continuously.

Cynthia: It's sometimes very difficult to manage having the dogs available, having the pet owners take the time to bring the dogs in.

Fanny: Yes.

Cynthia: It is a challenge to have volunteers available to help the youth interact with the dogs. It's a great deal to manage because you rely so much on outside support.

Steven: Yes.

Cynthia: That can be very frustrating. It's worth it. It's worthwhile, but it's hard to keep it going.

Steven: It means this can be a very chaotic situation, okay. But it's not a large problem. We just keep going. It's good.

Cynthia: It's worthwhile. It's worth keeping going. It's worth the frustration. And I love the name of your withdrawn youth program, which is Regain Momentum. You have seen that this does give the youth momentum, not only in the short term, but it has a long-term impact.

           What has been some of the long-term benefits for these withdrawn youth who have participated in the program? Do you see that it carries over to maybe getting employment or being

able to socially interact? Is there any long-term benefits that come
from it?

Fanny: I see there is a kind of feeling of belongingness to our organization.
Whatever or whenever they are frustrated or failed in their job or
any relationships, they will come back. Compared to the work
without the dog, they may just get stuck in their home and then
can't seek any help. But because of the dog, they have built up
their relationship here. So whenever they are depressed and
unhappy, they will think, "There is a dog here," and they will come
back.

Cynthia: They have a place they can reach out to, to go back to and get help
for their depression so they don't feel like they can't ever go back
if they struggle.

Fanny: Yes. Even when a social worker is not here anymore, they changed
their job or quit, they, the social worker, will come back also,
because the dog is still here.

Cynthia: That must feel good, to know that it is a place that is so meaningful
to social workers and service users that they come back and visit
the dog from time to time. Sometimes when they're struggling in
life or maybe just because they miss the dog and want to visit with
the dog.

Fanny: Yes. Just miss the dog is okay.

Steven: I think the dog is one reason that they come back easily. Because
it is hard for Chinese people to say, "I have problem" or "Can you
get me help?" I don't know, maybe in Western world it's easier to
get counseling, to get therapy.

Fanny: Here it is a stigmatization.

Steven: But in Chinese people, even if they think, "Oh, I come to see social
worker. Oh, okay, I get help." Most of them get okay and then get
out, but if they have problem again, it's even harder for them to
get back for help. But in our center, where we have dogs and cats,
it just seems normal to get back. They feel, "Okay, I say hi to the
dogs. Who cares? At the same time, I can see the social workers."
We have check-ins. We communicate about their recent situation,
"Oh, what's up and down?" We can easily chat together and find
out information, or maybe we can start over. We can start again,
and it is an alternative way for us to keep in touch, an alternative
way for them to show us they are okay or they are not okay.

Cynthia: That's very powerful. What you're saying is that it's very typical
for the culture that people don't reach out to the resources. Even
if they do reach out to the resources one time, they're not likely to
repeat it, and that's too bad because they're limiting themselves
to resources that could be very helpful. The presence of the dog
and the cat gives them an excuse though. It gives them a motivation
to get back if they need to and use a resource that can be very

helpful to them. Because in their mind, they're like, "Oh, I'm just going to go visit the dog or the cat." But they also know they probably need to go back because they are depressed, because they're anxious. It helps them get over their own barrier, maybe a cultural barrier. They can take advantage of a resource that they might not be willing to do if it didn't have an opportunity to visit with a dog or a cat. That's very powerful, isn't it?

Fanny: Mm-hmm [affirmative].

Steven: It's good.

Cynthia: Very, very powerful. So you would say you're pretty happy with your work?

Fanny: It's also very hard.

Steven: It's hard, but it's worth it to do it. And we seem to have proved that we have some steps that are good, effective.

Fanny: There are lot of things we need to learn also.

Steven: Yeah.

Fanny: Especially therapy skills, how to do the interventions. Our team also has some frustration. "Am I doing AAT, or am I a social worker?"

Steven: "Am I a farmer? To train dogs?"

Fanny: "What I am doing?"

Cynthia: "What am I?"

Fanny: Yes. "What am I? What I am doing now? Is it really what I need to do?" Sometimes, when there are so many dog activities, they question, "Am I still a social worker?"

Steven: We have to explain to the public, and we explain to the client, "Oh, what we are doing, that is a social work element." Something like that. We are not just pet grooming or just coming with a dog.

Cynthia: You have to educate the public about the benefits of spending time with an animal. You say they might just say, "Why are you teaching my child to groom a dog?" You have to explain it's because it makes them feel better. Their self-esteem goes up. So you have to explain that it actually has emotional benefits that help them and give them social practice skills that they so desperately need. Constantly explaining can be tiring at times but very useful to educate the public about how beneficial the animals can be.

Steven: Yes.

Fanny: Yeah.

Steven: Honestly, we are so excited when we claim to the public that we use AAT to help youth and elderly because we think of it as work. Not from only our viewpoint but also by client feedback. It's good. I mean, in different parts of the world there's AAT. In Hong Kong, there's AAT. We know how to make it work in Hong Kong. It is happening, and it is really important.

Cynthia:	You say sometimes you ask yourself, "How do I define myself?" I think, because you're doing so many different activities with the dogs. But the bottom line, what I hear you saying is, the outcome is there. You see that it helps the people that you serve. It helps the youth. It helps the elderly. Even the researchers who have come in to measure your program and evaluate it are saying, "Yes, we see that there are measurable effects that are happening." You have to assume that you are being therapeutic if people are getting better. And if you are being therapeutic because people are getting better in the ways that they need to, with social skills and decreased loneliness and decreased anxiety, that does make you a social worker. That does make you a therapist, and you've incorporated the animals to assist you. That makes you an animal-assisted therapist also.

So good work. I attended the conference here, and I was very impressed with the program when you presented it at the conference today. I'm very excited that you agreed to be a part of this interview because I wanted you to share your program with the rest of the world about what was happening here in Hong Kong. Because wouldn't you say animal-assisted therapy is not very common here? It's new and it's not very common, and it seems to me that your program is one of the few programs that exist and also that is therapeutic, because it's run by social workers, and it's very effective. I think, in my opinion, your program really stands out there as an exceptional program. Would you agree with that?

Steven:	Yes. It is really an exceptional program that proves AAT and social work can combine together.
Fanny:	Yeah.
Cynthia:	Do you feel that in some ways, even though it's not perfect and you have your frustrations, that you can be a model to encourage other programs similar to yours to develop?
Steven:	Yes.
Fanny:	Yes. I think it somehow is a pilot.
Steven:	Yeah, pilot.
Fanny:	In Hong Kong, no other program or organization is doing AAT in this structure.
Steven:	And in such depth.
Fanny:	And on this scale, so we are kind of a pilot. We are happy to see other organizations that are also doing AAT in their own style.
Steven:	In Hong Kong, there's some limitation of social service development or social therapeutic service development because all our money, funding, comes from the government. They have strict guidelines or general practice of how to provide social service. We had a really harsh time to finish all the designed work. It is really challenging.

Fanny:	You start from zero, nearly.
Steven:	Yeah, to start from zero and to bring up another new intervention. At the very beginning, we just read books.
Fanny:	We also learn from some distant courses.
Steven:	From the very beginning, just the ideas. Then try to work out something.
Fanny:	Yes, the pilot of the pilot.
Steven:	After we read books and we apply for funding, we make a good start. Then we try learning by doing. But we have to learn more, to study via a distant program from different places, such as your university, and where there be gatherings of people, social workers, with the same ideas. Then we get the animals and live with them and train them. Then we have the confidence, and we have information about how to apply our skill. And then we try to use our experiences to help our clients. It is a process that we have to get through. It is very true that before that, no such organization have such kind of . . .
Fanny:	Guts.
Steven:	Guts, yeah, to plan it. We planned it on an organizational scale. We apply for funding, and then we get dogs and cats and all the equipment. Before that we just have pet grooming from tutor to come here, just case by case. After that, we build up all the things that we need from a social worker perspective to make it work. Then we show that it is a success. Other organizations will be able to learn more from our local experience and not just by books or distant learning. They can know what we do is good here in Hong Kong, and then they can try to modify and make it in their own style. Our program is just like a . . .
Fanny:	Spark.
Steven:	Yeah, a spark.
Cynthia:	That's a great journey. You had to learn from scratch, from pretty much nothing except reading books and some distant training. You had to figure out what this meant for the population you want to serve. Getting the dogs, experimenting, practicing, and wondering, "Did that work? Okay, let's do that. Did that not work? Okay, let's not do that." You did all the trial-and-error learning, and it took courage and perseverance and strength. You paved the way, and you found a way to make it work, to have successes. Now, you've accomplished that and proven that it's successful so people who may come after you and create new programs won't have all of the hardships, as many hardships, as you were willing to go through with your guts and your courage. Because you found out what worked and now they can learn from your successes.

    I really appreciate your efforts, and I think other people will appreciate that very much too. Because you didn't know it was going to work. You just hoped it would, and it did, and you proved it, and now you have a wonderful model for people to follow after. It has a chance to grow at a much faster rate. Thank you for your efforts. It's wonderful. And thank you for participating in the interview here today.

Fanny: Thank you.

Steven: Thank you.

Editors' Commentary for Chapter 10

There are many challenges to integrating animal-assisted interventions into social services in Hong Kong. Hong Kong is among the most densely populated countries in the world with the smallest average living space (Yu, 2017). Thus, pet ownership is among the lowest in the world. Most public and many private housing units do not allow pets. Space for walking or exercising a dog is greatly limited. Personal car ownership is inconvenient, and public transportation prohibits pets. Given that animal-assisted intervention most commonly involves work with domesticated pets, limited pet ownership directly results in reduced availability of qualified therapy animals (Yu, 2017). Because of many environmental and cultural barriers, it is remarkable that animal-assisted intervention is gradually gaining in popularity among social and educational service providers in Hong Kong.

People we interviewed for this chapter represent some of the earliest practitioners and researchers in Hong Kong of animal-assisted interventions for emotional and mental health. Dr. Fan, with his dual concern for animal and human welfare, developed ways for humans and animals to support and care for one another. Steven Lai and Fanny Leung of the Chinese Evangelical Zion Church integrated animals into a program that assisted the elderly and also withdrawn youth to reengage with society in meaningful ways. Dr. Wong and Rose Yu provided credibility for the work at Zion Church with research that reflected significant clinical efficacy for animal-assisted interventions applied within the framework of a social service program. Animal-assisted therapy is a relatively novel approach to social services in Hong Kong. The individuals in this chapter collaborated to provide scientific evidence that animal-assisted interventions are a viable form of therapy for this culture (Yu, 2017). It was their expressed hope that their practice and research will attract the publicity and financial resources needed to continue their work and to open doors for additional animal-assisted social services in Hong Kong.

References

Chinese Evangelical Zion Church. (n.d.). Home page. Retrieved October 3, 2017, from www.hkzion.org.hk/

Wong, P. W., Li, T. M., Chan, M., Law, Y. W., Chau, M., Cheng, C., Fu, K. W., . . . Yip, P. S. (2015). The prevalence and correlates of severe social withdrawal (hikikomori) in Hong Kong: A cross-sectional telephone-based survey study. *International Journal of Social Psychology, 51*(4), 330–342. doi:10.1177/0020764014543711

Yu, W. M. (2017). *Examining the environmental and cultural factors in human-animal interaction in Hong Kong: A mixed methods study* (Doctoral dissertation). University of Hong Kong.

Figure 10.1   Dr. William Fan is a psychiatrist and the president of the Hong Kong Animal Therapy Foundation. Photo copyright of Dr. William Fan (used with permission); photographer unknown.

Figure 10.2 Dr. Wong, Wai-Ching Paul is an associate professor in the Department of Social Work and Social Administration at the University of Hong Kong. Photo copyright of Dr. Paul Wong (used with permission); photographer unknown.

Figure 10.3 Yu, Wai Man Rose. At the time of our interview, she was a researcher of animal-assisted therapy and a doctoral student in the Department of Social Work and Social Administration at the University of Hong Kong; she has since completed her doctoral studies. Photo copyright of Rose Yu (used with permission); photographer unknown.

Figure 10.4 Steven Lai of the Chinese Evangelical Zion Church. He incorporates animal-assisted interventions to aid youth and the elderly in Hong Kong. Photo copyright of Steven Lai (used with permission); photographer unknown.

Figure 10.5 Fanny Leung of the Chinese Evangelical Zion Church. She incorporates animal-assisted interventions to aid youth and the elderly in Hong Kong. Photo copyright of Fanny Leung (used with permission); photographer unknown.

11 Yuen, Sin Nga Gloria; Ng, Chu Kong Morgan; Leung, San Wan Gloria; and Wong, Lo Ming of the Society of Rehabilitation and Crime Prevention

We traveled through the city of Hong Kong to a building that housed the Society for Rehabilitation and Crime Prevention (n.d.). There, I interviewed four staff members (see Figure 11.1). The interview took place on June 6, 2015.

Interview with Yuen, Sin Nga Gloria; Ng, Chu Kong Morgan; Leung, San Wan Gloria; and Wong, Lo Ming

Cynthia: We have a number of staff persons to visit with today who are in some way related to their animal-assisted therapy program. Let's have each of you go around and introduce yourself, your name and your job title and what your role is.

Gloria Yuen: I'm Gloria Yuen. I'm the senior manager of the society, and I'm working on some programs related to employment for the ex-offenders.

Lo Ming: Hi, I'm Ms. Wong Lo Ming, supervisor of the Society, and I'm doing community mental health work in the community. I do home visits, staff management, and much administrative work.

Gloria Leung: Hello, I am Gloria. I'm a nurse at the Society of Rehabilitation and Crime Prevention in Hong Kong.

Morgan: Hello, I'm Morgan, also from SRCP, a senior manager. My main responsibility is to oversee the community mental health service. Also, I am responsible for the professional development and quarantine management of mental health services.

Cynthia: I understand that you have an involvement with animal-assisted therapy as it is provided for some of the individuals that you serve. Please describe your animal-assisted therapy program.

Lo Ming: It dates back to 2012. At the very beginning, we were concerned about some of the service users; they are quite passive. We don't know how to better engage with them. So we began our work with the dog we obtained from the Society for Abandoned Animals. We began working with the dog, a resident dog, with our users who came here and then doing home visits with the resident dog. Then in 2014, we started working with three cats.

Cynthia: Let's learn a little bit of the background about your society.

Gloria Yuen: Yes, our society was formed over 57 years ago. We are working with ex-offenders and mentally ill patients. We know that there is much evidence to prove that animals can help assist ex-offenders to rehabilitate and reintegrate back into society. They can help people to connect with other people. In Hong Kong, it's quite difficult to start programs related to working with animals because there are many security reasons; people are still afraid of dogs. We have to work through many difficulties. But luckily, in 2012, we came across some agencies that have therapy dogs. They helped us pioneer some programs. So our team, they were working with the mentally ill patients and also those suspected mentally ill people in the community; they started the program and they are the pioneers to do that.

Lo Ming: Because we are community mental health professionals, the service users we work with, they are mental health challenged or suspected mentally ill. For some of them, they are quite difficult for us to engage well. So the very first question I keep asking myself, "Is there any other alternative intervention or any approach to better engage the persons?" So we have great encounters with the Society for Abandoned Animals. We call it SAA; it's an animal NGO [nongovernmental organization]. And they are so great; they are actually very respectful animal rights activists. And they are very committed and passionate to be working with us. So we start home visits with the abandoned dogs, and we also begin with some interests classes because we want to gather some more center members to together, those that share similar interests. So SAA, they helped us to start with some sharing sessions, introducing the mission of SAA, like loving animals, respect life, no killing, and no abandonment. We did not have very much education in animal knowledge, so we started with educational programs for our staff.

Cynthia: So you're working in cooperation with the SAA, which is an animal shelter for abandoned animals, a service and a shelter. And they provide the animals, but they also help provide animal education programs for your staff and the people that you serve.

Lo Ming: Yeah, exactly. So they also organize some grooming classes and also invite certain members to come together doing volunteer work in the center, in their shelter. So our clients, they are kind of passive, but once they are connected with the animals, they will come out with our workers, with our staff. And during the volunteer work, they are so happy with the animals. So this is one of the things we try to do. For the home visits with the dogs, we are trying to identify some of the service users who are living alone or some of our elderly center members; they are living alone and they are suffering from early stage dementia. And also, some of the service users, they are having physical disability, so they show interest in meeting with not only social workers but animals. So kind of reconnect with the community and reconnect with themselves again because they felt nobody miss him or her or they are too sick to go out. So they are looking forward to having animals visit them. These are things we are trying to do in the past three years.

Morgan: But I think, regarding the visiting program, I want to add some words on the program. I think in addition to the benefits to our service users to be visited, also I think it is very good for the abandoned animals because the visiting program enhances the opportunity for the abandoned dog to have contact with many people. So I think it will help them to be adopted by other people in the future.

Cynthia: A good socialization opportunity for the animal.

Morgan: And also, you know, our service users are people with mental illness. They always deny they have mental illness, so how can we engage our service users?

Cynthia: It doesn't seem so much like mental illness treatment when you're visiting with a dog, right?

Morgan: Yeah.

Cynthia: So it takes the social stigma or the discomfort with the idea of having a mental illness out of the picture, so they're less resistant to the treatment. They see it as an opportunity to spend time with the animal while you know it's also your doorway to provide treatment.

Morgan: It's also a kind of a normalization. We just talked to our service users and explained that we have a visiting program, would you mind to join us? They don't talk about the mental illness, just talk about the visiting program. Then the people with suspected mental health, they will come with us and go to visit. I remember one story in which a lady who had suspected mental health, in fact later she was diagnosed with schizophrenia. But in the very beginning, she denied that she had any problem. So we invited her to join our volunteer program to pay a visit to other members. I think after two or three home visits, she finally told our social worker that she had something

Cynthia:

she wants to share with our social worker; it is her mental problem. So we can engage our clients better in the program.

Cynthia: She felt safe and comfortable enough to talk about her mental illness after she had been involved in the animal-assisted therapy for a while. You were able to get her out of her home, out visiting with other people, engaged in social contact, in touch with social workers. She began to trust, and then she could get past her denial and get the help she needed, additional help.

Morgan: But honestly speaking, at that time, we did not know about animal therapy.

Lo Ming: We have no idea of the animals.

Cynthia: You were doing this without realizing that it was a form of therapy.

Lo Ming: Yeah, because other service users, they shared similar experiences. One woman, she didn't want to meet me, but I invited her to join the volunteer work, home visits with pets; she was so excited. After one or two times, she became even more opened up to me. She was diagnosed with depression, but she told me she showed very great interest in joining our animal group to relieve her stress. So for these past three years, our animal group interest classes helped her a lot. She asked me, "Don't stop me from joining this program." She is enjoying the program very much.

Cynthia: So you have a number of different services that you offer. You collaborate with the SAA; this shelter provides animals and training for staff. The animals get a chance to get out to meet and greet and get socialization, so it's good for the animal and may increase the animal's chances for adoption. And then the people that you serve, they can learn about animal care and animal education. They learn pet grooming and get to visit with the animals. They can volunteer with pet visitation at the shelter and with home visits for the isolated. They may not realize that it is treatment, and you may not want some of them to realize that it is treatment.

Lo Ming: It is a bridge between our work and our service users. It's a very great thing.

Cynthia: You have service users who some of them have severe mental illness, such as major depression or schizophrenia. You're helping them get reengaged with society through working with the animals, and an important part of the treatment is that sense of meaningfulness and purpose and self-confidence that they can gain from then giving back, serving other people. It's so powerful that they say, "Don't make me stop doing this."

Lo Ming:	Yeah, exactly.
Cynthia:	So not only are they motivated to participate in their mental health treatment because the dogs are involved, but they don't want to stop. So it is a powerful, potent motivational program.
	I understand that there is a cultural resistance in Hong Kong to mental health treatment. And I think this is true of people in all countries. But there are some countries where there is stronger resistance, and that includes Hong Kong. There's a cultural resistance to mental health treatment, to the idea of having a mental illness; it's pretty strong in this culture historically. So you need to find really powerful ways to help people feel like this is acceptable and it doesn't make them look bad with their family or with society, so this looks like fun dog visitation, but you know there's also opportunity for treatment. So you're able to reach people you would not otherwise be able to reach.
Morgan:	That's what I think, but also I would like to share with you another story about therapy cats. We have another program, the live-in animal program, started I think last year. I think Gloria [Leung] can speak in Cantonese about this, and then one of us can translate.
Gloria Leung:	[Translated from Cantonese by Lo Ming] Yeah, we started our work with live-in kittens. So the live-in kittens attract more center members to come to our center and take care of them.
Cynthia:	So you have cats that live in the residential center?
Lo Ming:	Three of them, yes.
Cynthia:	And you have people who you serve then volunteer to come and take care of them, feed them and so forth? What are the cats' names?
Lo Ming:	In Chinese, Long Long, Qing Qing, Fong Fong.
Gloria Yuen:	Yes, everyone comes to the center to say hi to the cats. Long Long is the elder brother, and Qing Qing is the younger sister, and Fong Fong is the youngest brother.
Cynthia:	Do you find that people come to the center more often because they get a chance to visit with the cats?
Gloria Yuen:	Yeah, and take care of the cats.
Cynthia:	And while they're here, while they're coming to visit the cats and take care of the cats, how do they benefit from the program? The cats get them here. What else can help them while they're here? I think it is therapeutic to spend time with the cats, but can they also get access to other services or education or treatment support while they're here, or do they just take care of the cats?

Gloria Leung:	[Translated from Cantonese by Lo Ming] Okay, so through taking care of the kitties, their daily lifestyle, they'll be more responsible, becoming caregiver.
Cynthia:	So the caregiving is really the treatment. Giving care to the cats translates into them taking better care of themselves, self-care and also learning to care for others.
Lo Ming:	Yeah, and education. So with live-in kitties, those service users can have more opportunities to connect with different people, meet many new friends in the center.
Cynthia:	Because the cats bring people here, and so then it becomes sort of a social group; people get to know each other, make connections and . . .
Gloria Yuen:	It also creates topics to share.
Cynthia:	They all come together and talk about the cats.
Gloria Yuen:	Yeah, about what happened to the cats.
Lo Ming:	We have an album of all the kitties, photos from the very first time they came into our center to recent, when they have grown up. All the pictures and the thoughts for the kitties, the service users wrote them down into an album.
Cynthia:	The cats living here and people coming here to see and care for the cats and feeling good about sharing stories about the cats creates a valuable support system. It becomes another type of extended family with shared interests, and the shared interests are the cats.
Morgan:	But I think it also provides some therapeutic effect on the individual surface; for example, I'm going to share with you that nowadays we have service users, ladies with schizophrenia and also Asperger's. The ladies are very passive and not willing to share, to communicate. So Gloria [Leung] has designed a program, an individual program for the ladies. The ladies go to our center every day to take care of the cats and also communicate with the cats and play with the cats.
Lo Ming:	Talk to the cats.
Morgan:	And I think the effect is wonderful as evidenced by the effect on the ladies.
Gloria Yuen:	With our members, certain suffer from schizophrenia and Asperger's. But they'll take care of the cats, they'll learn from the cats to adapt to a new environment. Maybe when a cat first comes to our center, it's more anxious. But now, the cat is well adapted to the environment.
Cynthia:	Individuals such as with Asperger's or schizophrenia, they tend to be isolated; they lack social skills. So they're motivated to come and be with these cats, and with the cats, they practice the very things that they need to do. They get out of the house, they come and be social, they talk to the cats, and they

practice speaking. So they learn these skills. They develop these skills, and it translates to some degree, with them being able to communicate with other people better and fewer behavioral problems. And it would be very difficult to teach them these kind of skills at all or as quickly or as fast because it would be hard to get them to come to the center if there were no animals.

Gloria Yuen: We have more and more smiling [around the center].

Lo Ming: One client, she will laugh now when we make a joke. She can laugh now, which I'd never seen her do before a year ago. And now, whenever she feels sick, she will tell us she's sick, but she didn't before. But now she will come over to us and say, "I'm sick, very much pain." It's a very wonderful sign, lots of changes in her, that's wonderful. Whenever a visitor comes to our center, we will ask her to come out and introduce a kitty with the album, with the pictures. And she would try, and she could make it. She is very different.

Cynthia: So she could barely do it in the beginning, and now she is much more vocal.

Morgan: Another story that I want to share with you is that one of our service users is also a lady with schizophrenia. After being discharged from the hospital, she was unemployed and idle at home, doing nothing. But she knows that we have the kittens in the center, we have a live-in animal program. So the lady comes to our center, but she did not take care of the cats; instead, she was responsible to make a Facebook page for the three cats. So every day she'll come to the center and take photos and upload all the photos to Facebook so that all the other interested parties know the development, the situation of the cats. After, I think, several months later, development showed up in her because she was busy, she had a very good schedule every day, she came to our center. So has a very good life pattern. And later on, she joined our employment service, the service under the supervision of Gloria [Yuen].

Lo Ming: Because normally people suffering from schizophrenia, they may be resistant to face a job interview or even be employed. They would rather do other things or be idle at home. But we see the changes from the lady; she opened up herself, she tried to do the things she is interested in, and she tried to not be so resistant to talk with us about what she wants to do. So I think this is quite a miracle that she tried to open up herself for different choices in front of her. In the past, she would not choose it; she would try to do the things she used to be. But now, with a more regular pattern of life, she can do a job steadily, and she can go to work punctually; she can stably earn money for herself, take care of herself.

Gloria Yuen: Now, in the open job market. From us, she received supportive employment services, lots of training and learning how to do job interviews. And now she is in the open job market, doing clerical work.

Cynthia: And this might not have happened if the animal-assisted therapy program wasn't available, because she didn't show any interest. But when the animals became available, became a part of the program, she showed interest in the animals by spending time with them; she learned all these skills. And now she is employed, in the open job market; that's a complete change in her quality of life, going from isolated to engaging in society and having a job. Very powerful.

Morgan: I think it's very wonderful for the animal program. Because I think that not only those participating directly in AAT [animal-assisted therapy] would be benefited but also other people, for example, as mentioned earlier, the lady who was not directly doing the AAT but instead took photos of the kitties and uploaded them to Facebook and created a Facebook page. That is how she benefited.

Cynthia: And other people got to read the Facebook, so she was contributing to society in a way that she knew would benefit other people who could learn about the program.

Gloria Yuen: She feels rewarded because people will say something and give feedback on Facebook.

Cynthia: They would post comments and that sort of thing.

Lo Ming: And also, I think it benefits the staff ourselves. Morgan, you can share about the team, what the impact is on the team.

Morgan: There's also a wonderful story. At the beginning, not all our staff welcomed the kittens. Some have hesitation, and also some had animal phobia.

Lo Ming: Allergy too.

Morgan: But I think gradually, I found that the whole atmosphere has been changed because every day in the morning, I have noticed that our staff in the morning go to visit our cats and greet them and say hello and say good morning, and then they go back to their work. So eventually, all the staff has built up a very good relationship with the cats, and also I think they already have some therapeutic effect on our staff because we are professionals conducting community mental services. It's a very tough job; every day we deal with suicidal persons and very emotional persons, so staff are always frustrated, always tired and burned out. But now they spend their time, when they are frustrated, they can talk to the cats.

Lo Ming:	Kitty morning talk.
Gloria Yuen:	I guess I'm always the very first one to go back to the office, so I got used to talking with them, the three kitties every morning. Sometimes, I will do storytelling because I just try to keep myself so quiet, sitting on the chairs so that they will come up. Because if you're too rushed to go into the room, they will be very scared, so I would like to sit quietly and wait for them to come up and then do storytelling. And they love it and walk around me and lick me, that sort of thing.
Cynthia:	Your desire to have them come up to you, you have to calm yourself, which is something you know you're supposed to do anyway, but you're not motivated to do it. But you're motivated to calm yourself and center yourself because you want to spend time with the cats, which is good for you. And they come up, and you have all this interaction. I really find it interesting that even the staff who were resistant at first to you bringing the kitty cats in, because of phobias and allergies and just not understanding potential benefits, even they have come to not only accept it but participate in it and benefit and enjoy the cats and look forward to the cats.

And I think what you said, Morgan, that this is a very difficult job, working with a very difficult population with some pretty serious disorders sometimes. And it's very stressful for you, it's hard. You want to help make peoples' lives better, and for many reasons, there are barriers and obstacles and it's stressful. And it's nice to have the kitty cats to be able to go and pet and relax and calm down and get your own "therapy" because the concept of burning out because of too much stress. Maybe this will help prevent you from burning out too much or feeling too much anxiety yourself. It's still going to be there, but I hear you saying the cats really help with that. Being able to go to the office and pet a cat really helps.

Gloria Yuen:	Actually, I'm kind of a dog person, but since they have come into my center, kitties Long Long, Qing Qing, and Fong Fong, I feel very great to learn about animal behavior because I'm not very familiar with kitties and their behavior. But now I learnt a little bit more; that is very great.
Cynthia:	Broadened your own horizons, did they? You thought you were just a dog person, but now you're also a little bit of a cat person too.

I really appreciate the time that you've spent with us today. I loved hearing about your program, the fact that you're reaching people that need this help so much and that might not otherwise respond were it not for the animals. As we draw to a close here today, I would like to go around and let each one of you have what I call the last word and just speak about anything else that you think is important to understand about the animal-assisted therapy work that you do.

Gloria Yuen: I believe in the therapeutic effect of the animals. It may not be easy to start a program to work with animals; you come across difficulties, especially when you're working in a team. Other people may disagree with you, and you have to work things out. You may need to start with a simple program, like some visiting-with-animals program and some animal knowledge education program. People can get a chance to interact with the animals, learn about them. It may seem like a very little thing, but at the end, you can accumulate experience, and people will join in and then you have a collaborative effort to do a lot.

Cynthia: It can be tough at the beginning. But you pull together, start simple with small steps, then build from there.

Lo Ming: Here, I would like to give thanks for the animals of the world. It's so true; they are just like a bridge between our mental health social work and our service users. Not only that, but I think animals are wonderful creatures that help us to reconnect to ourselves, help us in the sense of being more responsible and attending to self-care. But also they help us reconnect with the community. And I really want to say thanks to the animals of the world.

Cynthia: Well said.

Gloria Leung: I'm so happy to see a change in our members with their connecting to animals.

Morgan: I think that the therapeutic effect of AAT occurs not only for individuals but also on the community, and also for the animals themselves. We have mentioned earlier that our program involves the abandoned dogs. The dogs, I believe, they also benefit from our program, and I personally also learned a lot from the AAT, for example, the life education, because before, I don't know about the concept of animal rights. In the past, if I had wanted to start an animals program, I would have bought some animals. But nowadays, I will not. We will keep animals from the organization that adopted abandoned animals. So I think the effect is not just on the personal level but also in the community and on the life education level.

Cynthia: Thank you so much for joining us here today for the interview. I look forward to sharing your program with the rest of the world.

Lo Ming: Thank you so much.

Editors' Commentary for Chapter 11

These individuals at Society of Rehabilitation and Crime Prevention are dedicated to the worthwhile purpose of utilizing animal-assisted interventions to rehabilitate both humans and animals. Staff offer programs on animal welfare, animal education, animal care, and dog grooming that benefit both humans and animals that are in need. There is collaboration with a shelter for abandoned animals to help neglected animals become accepted and valued by society. Clients participate in activities with animals and gain valuable social experience and skills. This increases their opportunity to be employed and become self-supporting. The staff have successfully demonstrated how humans and animals can work together for mutual social benefit. This animal-assisted intervention program reflects the power of compassion for living beings, both humans and animals.

Reference

Society of Rehabilitation and Crime Prevention. (n.d.). Retrieved October 4, 2017, from www.sracp.org.hk/en/index.html

Figure 11.1   Staff members of the Society of Rehabilitation and Crime Prevention (SRCP), Hong Kong. From left to right: Yuen, Sin Nga Gloria (senior manager); Leung, San Wan Gloria (nurse); Wong, Lo Ming (supervisor); and Ng, Chu Kong Morgan (senior manager). Photo copyright of SRCP; photographer unknown.

12 Yim, Yat Kēuah; Angie Yu; Lily Tang; and Lau, Yin Fei Joyce of the Hong Chi Association

We interviewed four staff members of the Hong Chi Association (n.d.). This took place immediately after the interview with the staff of the Society of Rehabilitation and Crime Prevention in Hong Kong. We simply walked to a different floor of the same building. The interview with the staff of the Hong Chi Association (see Figure 12.1) took place on June 6, 2015.

Interview with Yim, Yat Kēuah; Angie Yu; Lily Tang; and Lau, Yin Fei Joyce

Cynthia: Thank you all very much for joining us today for the interview. Would each of you introduce yourself, your name and your job title?

Mr. Yim: I'm Mr. Yim, service supervisor of Hong Chi Association.

Angie: My name is Angie Yu. I'm a clinical psychologist at Hong Chi Association.

Lily: I'm Lily Tang. I'm a clinical psychologist of Hong Chi Association.

Joyce: I'm Joyce Lau. I'm a social worker for Hong Chi Association.

Cynthia: Tell us about Hong Chi Association.

Mr. Yim: Okay, let me introduce my association. Our association, named Hong Chi Association, was set up in 1965, and now we are the largest organization in Hong Kong mainly serving the people who have intellectual disabilities. We operate in over 80 centers, projects, hospitals for mental disabilities in different grades and different levels. We are first to introduce animal-assisted therapies, since 2013. I think Hong Chi Association is the first to try this service for those with intellectual disabilities. May I have the pleasure to first introduce Lily, who is the project director in charge of this program?

Lily: Okay, I would like to talk about our animals as therapy in the Hong Chi Association. It's mainly in our rural areas of Hong Kong and an integrated complex in which there are different kinds of services, such as Health Hostel for the people with intellectual disability, and also the Activity Center. We work with two types of animals.

Actually, there are other types of animals; we also have the fish. But mainly, we have two types of animals, they are the cats; we have two cats, and we also have three turtles [these are very large land tortoises that live outside]. It's difficult for a hostel in Hong Kong to have animals. Most of the hostels are located in the public housing estate in Hong Kong, where it is from very difficult to impossible for people to keep animals, such as dogs. And so this is a new try for us to keep animals in our complex and in this program. Our service user, which are people with intellectual disability and also people with autism, are responsible for taking care of the animals, including the cats and the turtles.

Because they are people with intellectual disability, they usually have difficulty managing their mood, and they may easily throw tantrums over us, and they may have sometimes, difficulties in relating with other people. They are weak in social skills, and so we introduced this project in which they have the chance to take care of the animal. Also, the animal serves as an agent to reach out to other people for socialization. I will pass you on to Joyce, our social worker, to introduce the activities included in our animal-assisted therapy.

Joyce: There are three service users with mild intellectual disability living in a hostel. They live with the two pets, including two cats, Kaka and Longlok, and they become the parents for them. All of them have the experience of keeping pets in their family. Daily, they need to feed the cats, clean the cat litter, and play with them. After that, we organize animal ambassador training. The trainers include a social worker from this hostel and a volunteer from the Hong Kong Animal Therapy Foundation. The training content, we teach them about animal behaviors, skills in taking care of and getting along with the animal.

After the training, we let them have the opportunity to share about how to take care of the cats and express their feeling about living with cats. Also, they organize the drawing competition and making toy competition for our service user. This can help our service user to understand more about our cats. This is a great chance to let them have a chance to communicate and interact together and let our service user to become happy and have a fulfilled hostel life. Our service user also can become confident and have a greater life satisfaction from playing with cats.

Angie: Now, we will pass on to Mr. Yim, who will talk a little bit about the turtles that's involved in our program.

Mr. Yim: In fact, we have three turtles in our complex. We have African tortoises, from Africa. An old man helps us to build shelter and facility for the turtles; he works for the building. Also, we have our trainee, our service user who helps build houses for the tortoise;

he is an autistic service user. He has very serious behavioral problems before, but after the trainings, he became involved in the activities and share in the daily list [of duties for] a tortoise, such as cleaning the tortoise house, feeding the tortoise, and becoming the tortoise's father. The tortoises walk around our complex and eat the flowers. The service users do things for the tortoises, wash the vegetables, and so forth.

Cynthia: You said the individuals involved in the service were autistic?

Mr. Yim: Yes.

Lily: Yes, in that particular program.

Cynthia: With that program, they're autistic, and they care for the turtles, they clean up, they prepare their food, clean their pens, build their houses. Does that increase their interaction with other people?

Mr. Yim: Yes.

Cynthia: What are some of the outcomes, the benefits of the individuals with autism, caring for and spending time with the turtles?

Mr. Yim: Autistic persons usually don't interact with others; they usually have some behavioral problems, such as aggressive behavior and destroy many materials in our complex. We feel it is very difficult to serve these groups with autism with serious behavioral problems. After we introduced the animal-assisted therapies for the autistic service user, I realized that there is a great change in the behaviors. Before, they did not interact with people and made no eye contact and haven't any facial expression. But after they are involved in this program, I realized that actually they have changed. First of all, they have more interaction with the instructor. They have eye contact with the tortoise very much, and we see a change of facial expression; they smile. I have never seen them smile since I have been working in the complex, more than ten years; they never smile in more than ten years. But when they see the tortoise, they smile. This is very wonderful and very encouraging that we started the program.

We also introduced this program to the elderly service users because, in Chinese, tortoise is a lucky animal, represents long life and happiness. So elderly persons are a fan of tortoise, and they can easily make friends together. And the motion of tortoise is very slow, just like our service user. They can walk together and build a friendship. I observe our service user has had a great change, with much better effectiveness.

Cynthia: That's pretty amazing that it brings out emotional expression; they smile and they interact. They start to socially engage because the turtle is a bridge to help them come outside of themselves and become more aware of their environment and they interact with the environment. It's very powerful.

Lily: Yeah, actually, we discovered different kinds of service users really need different animals. The service user with intellectual disability, maybe they're younger and they can take care of the cats, which is more active. But for our other service users, such as the elderly people and also people with autism, maybe they're more suitable to work with turtles, the tortoises.

Mr. Yim: We have plans to find out what type of service user is suitable for which type of animals while they are involved in the animal-assisted therapies, and we are planning to do research for this. Angie will do our research planning.

Angie: I am really happy that I actually joined Hong Chi Association because I actually just came back from the United States and hearing all the things that they do involving animals is so wonderful because I know we don't have a lot here in Hong Kong. Our new plan is going to be having different groups of people; we're actually going to do more of a pilot first because we want to see what kind of our trainees would be fitting best with different animals. We're going to be involving individuals and groups. We'll be using turtles and cats, and we're going to see the effectiveness of different types of groups. We're in the planning of that.

Especially after your workshop [she is referring to the training I did at the conference at the University of Hong Kong], we have thought about three more one-on-one animal things. That's why I came up with the individual idea, and hopefully, that's going to be a good thing to actually look at, the interaction and not just only looking at the outcome of it and see what we can find out and it's going to be really exciting to do.

Cynthia: Is there anything else that you can think of that you would like to share to help people understand your program or the benefits of your program, how important you think it is.

Angie: I'll start a little bit because I'm actually involved a little bit back in the States. I have a lot of colleagues that have their few dogs and go around, and I see the effectiveness of it. And when I'm doing therapy on my own, there are times I wished that I had a dog or a cat with me to do that because I can see the changes that come of it. Coming here and seeing what they do here, they use turtles. Because I study diversity back in the United States, so I know the importance of matching the client and the service, and I see it here. Turtles work for Asians, Chinese, because of their belief in the animal. I think this is something that we should keep in mind, not just dogs. Dogs might be good for a lot of populations but may not fit into, sometimes, the Asian population because they're afraid of dogs and they don't think it's effective. But having some kind of animal, like turtles, that they can easily get engaged with is something I think Hong Chi Association is doing really well.

Cynthia:	Each one of you, please share a final thought, sort of the last word of what you want to share with others, to help them understand the important work that you're doing.
Lily:	I guess what is most important for a successful animal-assisted therapy program is to find some staff who really love and care about the animals because they will need to understand animal behavior, which is very important. And they will need to know what type of activities are suitable for our clients and also the animals.
Joyce:	I think that before starting AAT [animal-assisted therapy], the staff need to prepare well to practice the AAT. Also, we teach service users how to take care of the cats. At first, they need to learn a lot. They sometimes feel that it is a burden to them. But we encourage them because we found that, when they took care of the cats, they have more chance to communicate and they can interact with more people. After that we have found that they have become more mature. They can speak confidently and behave better. So that's why we encourage them so that they love cats and love practicing AAT. We're just very excited to keep going on this AAT program.
Cynthia:	When you encourage the service user to keep attending to the animals, they start to really experience the benefits; they gain social skills. So you have to be patient with them, keep encouraging them until they start to realize for themselves the benefits they are gaining from the interaction.
Joyce:	Yes.
Mr. Yim:	I think when we apply the animal-assisted therapy, we cannot treat the animal as an object to meet needs. We should see them as our friends. We should consider their welfare and should not let them work overtime, just like us. This is very important because the therapist should love animals. That is the first condition for being a therapist for running animal-assisted therapies.
Cynthia:	It's a wonderful message. First and foremost, we must value, love, care for, nurture the animals, as an appreciation for the way they help us in our healing process and not just use them or exploit them. By honoring the animals, loving them, taking care of them, that makes us better people too, more humane people.
Mr. Yim:	Yes.
Cynthia:	Thank you so much for joining us for the interview today, I enjoyed hearing about your program.
Angie:	Thank you.
Lily:	Thank you.
Mr. Yim:	Thank you.
Joyce:	Thank you very much.

Editors' Commentary for Chapter 12

The staff of the Hong Chi Association serve the needs of those with intellectual disability and developmental disorders. They have found that incorporation of cats and tortoises into their services has produced great benefits for the clients they serve. From interaction with animals, clients are more social and have fewer behavior problems. Clients have an opportunity to care for the animals and socially engage with the animals and socialize more with people because of the animals. Caring for the animals and interacting with the animals also provide clients interesting and stimulating activities. The Hong Chi Association has found a creative and effective medium for serving their clients through incorporation of animal-assisted interventions.

Reference

Hong Chi Association. (n.d.). About. Retrieved October 6, 2017, from www.hongchi. org.hk/en_about_intro.asp

Figure 12.1 Hong Chi Association, Hong Kong. From left to right: Yim, Yat Kēuah (service supervisor); Angie Yu (clinical psychologist); Lily Tang (clinical psychologist); and Lau, Yin Fei Joyce (social worker). Photo copyright of Cynthia Chandler (used with permission); photographer Tiffany Otting.

13 Eddie Lee of the Hong Kong Institute of Animal Assisted Intervention

I interviewed Eddie Lee, founder and director of the Hong Kong Institute of Animal Assisted Intervention (n.d.) on June 7, 2015. He had just presented at the Animal-Assisted Therapy Conference sponsored by the University of Hong Kong.

Interview with Eddie Lee

Cynthia: Thank you for joining us today, Mr. Lee. I appreciate it very much.

Eddie: Thank you, thank you.

Cynthia: Tell us about your program, please.

Eddie: Okay. We are promoting animal welfare and also animal-assisted therapy in Hong Kong. But in our mind, Hong Kong people have not too well accepted what is animal-assisted therapy, though it is in Hong Kong for many years already. We think that, by promoting the better status of animals, we will also help with promoting AAT [animal-assisted therapy] in Hong Kong because people will have less reluctance to animals going to visit their organization, such as social civic center or the hospitals or daycare centers.

Cynthia: So by including education on animal welfare, that helps people feel more comfortable with animals and perhaps be more receptive of animal-assisted therapy services. Describe your program for us, the people involved, the animals involved, and more about the populations that you serve.

Eddie: At this moment, we have around 20 animal facilitators to provide the AAT service; we call them animal ambassadors. We have a board consisting of a veterinary surgeon, a dog trainer, and those who already learned about AAT before. We have assessment exams for them [the potential animal ambassadors] to pass in order to do the service. We will go do different kinds of services, including AAA [animal-assisted activity], AAE [animal-assisted education], and also AAT, to different venues in Hong Kong.

For those educational programs, not AAT, usually we will communicate with the schools or college beforehand to find out what their aims are. We may sometimes include some environmental protection ideas or animal welfare information. I myself am an environmentalist, so I wish to include or incorporate these ideas because the environment is tightly connected with animals. So we can merge the ideas altogether and promote them to the students because they are our future. This is included in our educational campaigns.

For two services, we will contact the service center and see what their aim is, wish is, to have animals inside their program, maybe some assistance for physical improvement, or some social skills improvement, or assistance with emotional or psychosocial issues. And we'll design program plans or some activities together with some professional psychiatrist helping us to assess whether the activities are useful or not, every time.

Cynthia: I really find that intriguing, the aspect of when you're involved in animal-assisted education at the schools or the colleges. Then when you bring the animals in, you include the part about the ecosystem, the environment, and how we need to take care of our animals and our earth because we can't live without one another. And at the same time, teaching about the benefits of animals, and I would imagine caring for animals. Is that a part of the animal-assisted program, the welfare part?

Eddie: Yes, sure, because nowadays, we are very concerned about animal fur or even vegetarianism because we are a society, a very free society, and we respect those who are vegetarian or nonvegetarian. So we will just mention about what is the benefit of being vegetarian to the human health and also to the environment because vegetarian sometimes is a very high demand on organic issues. So organic issues are also very helpful to our environment. And related to the animal welfare issue, it means we kill less animals. But we just mention some information for the students to think about for themselves.

Cynthia: You give them something to think about, introspect about. You have animal ambassadors to the social services agencies. It sounds like you network with various social service agencies who have populations that could be served by visits from the animal or interaction with an animal.

Eddie: We have different styles of services. Maybe I give some examples. For some sensation touch, maybe sometimes design some games. Maybe we have five to six animal ambassadors visiting their institute, and then virtually, we have the client look and describe vocabulary of describing the animals, so maybe the fur, the texture, the size, the color. And then after, we may play some game. Maybe you say cloth to cover their client's eyes or the animals, covered animals, and then they will describe what the animal is feeling.

So different kinds of games. Maybe they describe the animals to other members and try to guess which animal ambassador is behind the cloth, and then this kind of communication can encourage their vocabulary skills and also their sensory touch and also their intercommunication. We found this is very enjoyable for them, and also they will continue discussing about these kinds of activities. Even after we left for a few days, already teachers tell us that they are still explaining how happy they are on that day after even a week.

Cynthia: How long have you been providing these services? How long has your organization been in existence?

Eddie: Our organization was officially established in 2014, just last year only. But before that, I have some background preparation. Before I set up this HKIAAI, I served in the Hong Kong Guide Dog Association. From very young days, I actually wish to be a vet, but in Hong Kong there is no veterinary course. It is very, very expensive to study overseas, and I am not well off enough. So I continued my pathway on biology course science and also environmental science. But I have an opportunity by serving in the Hong Kong Guide Dog Association. They started up around 2011, and I joined at the very beginning. So I learned that with those special function guide dogs, who were trained to provide assistance for the visually impaired, that I can also treat with their interaction. The guide dogs help people improve their social skills and communication and open up their mind also.

I've observed about the society, the Chinese society, people may not like visually impaired people much. Sometimes, maybe they hate them because Chinese society is very funny this way.

Cynthia: There is a prejudice against disabilities.

Eddie: More than that because the tradition is the visually impaired will use the white cane. And in some traditional minds of Chinese people, if you are able person, if you are touched by the cane, you will have bad luck. I think this may not happen in Western country, but in Chinese society, they will think of this. Many people from earlier generation, they have in mind that visually impaired people are not good, "I cannot come into contact with them." I even experienced this bias myself because, when I served in the Guide Dogs Association, I learned [about visual disability] by covering my eyes. I learned from many hours of how to live without eyesight. And I've learned to walk along the road just in the city with covered eyes. And once a grandmother yell at me, "Don't walk my way; I'm walking around this road. You please walk aside." It's real obvious when I just cover my eyes.

Cynthia: So even though it was obvious that you were pretending to be a blind person so you could be more sensitive to the needs of those who are visually impaired, you still had people who weren't sensitive to your needs or your welfare and were even offensive.

Eddie: Even if there was a teacher there teaching me. So in their mind, there were some people blocking their way that was not convenient to them. So I would feel bad if I were really a visually impaired person. I would feel really bad even if my future was without eyesight for just a moment. But they have a lifetime that way, so I can feel how they feel, so bad. So the Guide Dog Service also opened up my mind on the animal and human bond because the guide dogs also make the society open up themselves to have contact with persons who are visually impaired because they ask, "How lovely your guide dogs is. May I touch him/touch her?" So the guide dogs open up a way to communicate with the visually impaired. And also the educational campaign. We also educated at different centers about what visually impaired is, and we could very obviously see that society is changing. After a few years of service, we found the society is more accepting of the visually impaired people and also accept the Guide Dog Service in Hong Kong.

Cynthia: And you think the presence of the service dog helped make a cultural revolution, moving in the direction of being more sensitive and caring?

Eddie: It helped a lot, and now people will more accept big dogs walking around a city. This is important because Hong Kong public transportation does not allow animals.

Cynthia: So as I understand it, your work with the Guide Dog Association really helped prepare you for your work in the animal-assisted intervention program that you do now. It helped you learn about the human–animal bond and being sensitive to the needs of those who are disabled and very aware of the cultural barriers that need to be overcome. And you've also discussed some of the difficulties of transporting animals. Also, your animal ambassadors and some of the agencies that you serve don't always have their own therapy animals that they can work with. So they rely on you to bring those animals in. You and your staff, you bring in the animals and handlers and the social workers can make suggestions for treatment goals and direct and guide your work. You provide the handler teams and the animal teams to provide animal-assisted interventions. You make arrangements for the transportation. And you take care of a lot of those details that the social service agency and the social worker might not be able to take care of themselves. Your agency takes care of that, the animals, the handlers, the transportation of the animals to the facility. So you provide a tremendous service to these various social service agencies.

Eddie: Yes, it is quite beneficial to have some individual organization that can arrange like contract services for them, can help them do the service. So the social workers can determine their needs and tell us, and then have them meet with us. We prefer having a first inter-action or warm-up session. On that session, we will not have any specific design. Just like how the members react and also feel like how we can cooperate in the future, see what the real need is. So we will usually design just one interaction before the real program starts.

Cynthia: Sort of a meeting and a greeting and a getting used to the animals before you actually start work on treatment goals, which are for later sessions.

Eddie: Even before the design of what to treat.

Cynthia: Is there anything else that you would like to say to help people understand the importance and the value of the work that you do?

Eddie: I think purpose and education are very important. So nowadays, we are very lucky compared with many years ago. Nowadays, we have many social media, such as Facebook, something like that. We can promote many ideas via that channel. And in Hong Kong, many people are surfing Facebook. We can promote ideas or the activities, and we can see the "likes" in the Facebook gradually increasing from the very beginning. When we started up, every post we had only like 50 or 60 "likes." But nowadays, sometimes several hundred. And for some very big event, sometimes even more than a 1,000 "likes." So in Hong Kong, that is good enough for a general organization. So we grab this chance to use this kind of social media to promote. And people can leave a message for us or ask questions anytime on Facebook, and we can reply to them. And also we will take a chance to educate them. Sometimes, we will post something that is very informative, just like "What is AAT?" or "How to become animal ambassadors," or "How to help," or other issues. Because many people may think what we do is animal therapy, therapy for the animal. So sometimes, we receive a call, "Can you help my dog? He's getting bad in society," or even asking for help for the dog's depression. So we will explain to them, "We can refer you to some specialist, but we are helping people."

So at this moment, at the very beginning of our service, this the first one to two years, we are still promoting and using trials on the design of the program. We are learning together with profes-sionals. So we will start up the real research maybe later this year because we have several, about ten, more series of design and we have already designed some content with them and how to measure [effects], and considering which measurements are more reliable or efficient so we'll have more studies in the coming years.

Cynthia: Thank you for joining us today, Mr. Lee. The services that you're providing for the social service agencies of Hong Kong and the educational facilities are valuable and worthwhile. I think it's important for others to hear what you're doing here in Hong Kong.

Editors' Commentary on Chapter 13

Eddie Lee and the staff of the Hong Kong Institute of Animal Assisted Intervention serve two primary missions: one, to raise the level of understanding and acceptance in Hong Kong society regarding animal welfare and the environment and, two, to assist in the provision of animal-assisted interventions for agencies who do not have their own animal-assisted teams. Their services require a great deal of coordination between their institute and the facilities they serve out in the community. Much preparatory planning is needed to match interventions with the clientele.

As acceptance of animal-assisted interventions for educational and emotional and mental health purposes in Hong Kong increases, the number of requests for this type of service also rises. Yet relatively few professionals in Hong Kong have the knowledge, training, or animals to provide animal-assisted interventions. The work of Mr. Lee and his staff is extremely important in this regard.

Reference

Hong Kong Institute of Animal Assisted Intervention. (n.d.). Facebook page. Retrieved October 6, 2017, from www.facebook.com/HKIAAI/

Figure 13.1 Eddie Lee is the founder and director of the Hong Kong Institute of Animal-Assisted Intervention. Photo copyright of Eddie Lee (used with permission); photographer William Li.

14 Debbie Ngai of the Hong Kong Animal Assisted Therapy Association

For the final interview in Hong Kong, I spoke with Debbie Ngai. She is founder and director of the Hong Kong Animal Assisted Therapy Association (n.d.). She had just presented her work at the Animal Assisted Therapy Conference at the University of Hong Kong. The interview took place on June 7, 2015.

Interview with Debbie Ngai

Cynthia: Debbie, thanks for joining us today.

Debbie: It's my pleasure to be here.

Cynthia: Tell us all about your program.

Debbie: Our program started, I think, seven years ago. It is aimed to provide professional animal-assisted therapy in Hong Kong for the people who are in need. And with our rationale and our belief, we believe the animal is an angel from heaven, so we want to let people and the society understand and realize how great they are. So we take a means of animal-assisted therapy to let that happen. We do a certain sort of training to train professionals because we believe being professional in animal-assisted therapy is very important. Then, second, we train up animal handlers because we believe handlers should be trained to protect and advocate for companion animals when doing animal-assisted therapies. They have to be familiar with the emotions, the stress of the animals that comes across during interventions. They have to know how to present a friendly attitude or understanding to our service user. And we do have assessment for therapy dogs. We want to carefully assess the therapy dog to qualify them to be a therapy dog to provide professional service for the clients. All these things combine together, animal-assisted therapies, handler and dog teams, and we carry out a good plan or good intervention for people in need. So we can achieve more sufficient therapy for the special needs students or teenagers, whoever the service user is in the society.

Cynthia:	I really like that you give so much attention to making sure the animal has the right type of attitude, training, and to make sure that the handlers understand how to read animal communication and advocate for the animals' welfare. All of this facilitates getting the animals involved with other people to maximize the benefits. Tell me about some of the populations that you serve, the people that you help.
Debbie:	For this year and for past years, we served, I think, about 80 to 90 marginal youths in an at-risk program. And then we served about, I think, 50 to 60 special needs students with conditions such as ADHD, autism, dyslexia.
Cynthia:	That's a lot of people that you served. When you bring animal handlers and animals to serve these people, what kind of activities do they engage in that you find are therapeutic or helpful in some way?
Debbie:	For the students with ADHD, the teenagers, we help them have higher control of their impulsive behavior because this is the first difficulty they come in with in their daily life. So we train for this, and then we help them have better emotional control by understanding the emotion of animals and how the animals deal with their stress. And then the animals serve as a mirror on how they react to their stress when they have emotions. This is for ADHD students. And for autism students, we found that we spend more time thinking about how to enhance their speech motivation and organization. We found it is very sufficient to use AAT, animal-assisted therapy, with them because they like to look at the animal, they talk to the animals. But without the animal they didn't have the interest. So we use this intervention to enhance their speech and their organization. I started a reading-to-dog program in my center. Just like with the autism children, they have to read the book to the dogs, and we teach him how to speak in an organized way, make sure that the dogs or the people understand what they are talking about. And with teenagers, we sometimes use dog training. We teach them how to train the dogs to enhance their self-confidence, their coordination with their body gestures and their minds. They have to stand still; they have to pronounce clearly. They have to stand up with confidence so the dog can understand their commands. And we do this intervention for the teenager with drug abuse or deviant behaviors. We use experiential learning. We ask them to do the pet grooming and the dog training, and we brought them to the dog center to practice. And then we observe how the dog reacted to them, and that will tell them what's happening here. Maybe the dog's behavior reflects something is off, and we inquire, "What's the problem, why do you hesitate, why are you showing a different side of yourself?"

Cynthia: You are serving a lot of different populations and engaging in a variety of therapeutic activities. You are able to reach individuals with needs and help them in ways that you might not otherwise be able to if they were not so motivated to spend time with the animal.

Debbie: Yes.

Cynthia: Such as reading to the dog, practicing the speech therapy. You mention that it was very difficult for them to look at a person or practice speech therapy. They didn't want to do it, but they were very motivated to do that with the dog.

Debbie: Sometimes, they think having traditional trainings or traditional therapy is to suffer. They think, "I have a problem; that's why I have to go to the therapist. I have to do the training session." But with dogs involved, they think differently, "I'm just having a playful time with the dogs." And they're feeling very relaxed. I think for the student with special needs, most importantly they are not feeling labeled, to participate in these things. They are very, "Okay, today I go to play with the dogs. I'm the reader to the dog. So I'm a little teacher; they're my students." I think this kind of relationship really helps to enhance their self-identity, that they are not a patient, not someone who has impairments.

Cynthia: And that seems to be very important. If it was just, "Oh no, I'm a patient; there's something wrong with me," then there's some dread, a sense of dread or suffering with having to go get treatment. But it doesn't seem like that at all with the dogs. It's playtime, it's recreation time, it's entertainment time for them. They have motivation to attend their training and treatment sessions. They're learning the things they need to learn. That difference of attitude probably makes them more open and receptive to learning.

Debbie: Yes, and they're very proud, "Today I go to AAT!" They are very proud to their friends, to their parents. And by having this, we integrate the therapeutic elements into our activities. Even the parents view this as more comfortable because, when children have special needs in Hong Kong they just think as a patient, "There is something wrong with me; I am someone with sickness, mental sickness." So sometimes the parents and the children, teenagers, suffer really a lot. I think with the aid of the animal here, they don't think like this.

Cynthia: So how successful do you think your program has been in the eyes of the people, the parents, maybe even the children themselves?

Debbie: Sometimes, most of the times, the parents were amazed because in their lives, unexpectedly, they have a child with autism. The parents never experience love or care from the child. They believe, "Okay, my child doesn't have the ability to love. My child doesn't know how to attend to another's needs." But when they see their child with the dogs, they realize, "Oh, he can." The dogs open up their possibilities.

Cynthia: So they see their children in a very different way.

Debbie: Yes, that's important.

Cynthia: So the parents gain a new perspective on their children. They've almost given up on their children's capacity to care or love because they don't see that. But the children are able to demonstrate care and love towards the animals, and the parents see that and they gain a new perspective about their children because they see they are, to some degree, capable of loving, caring, and attending. It's just very difficult for these children to show love to another human being. So parents may gain a brighter attitude about their children.

Debbie: That's true. And sometimes, when we come across a student with ADHD, they are very hyperactive. We show the parents that their child doesn't have to take medicine at their period; they can behave well. And this is a surprise to many parents because sometimes, they will just worry, "My son doesn't take medicine today. Can he come? Maybe he is messing around." But I think by interacting with dogs, the students can behave well, better than they think that they can. I think this shows just like what you said, a new perspective from their parents about their children.

Cynthia: They see that the children are capable of much more than what they were giving their children credit for. But it's because the children are put in an environment where they can succeed. An important part of the environment is the dogs, the contact with the dogs, through designed interaction and play. This presents the children in new ways, calmer and motivated, and shows that they are capable of many things that the parents didn't realize that the children were capable of.

Debbie: Yes.

Cynthia: And it allows opportunity for the children to grow. To gain the skills they need, to learn to be able to control, recognize, and regulate emotions. So it sounds like the animals are a bridge for therapeutic opportunities.

Debbie: Yes, that's true. Anytime I think about not having a dog here, I wonder maybe that the service would not be that successful. Because sometimes the dog's reaction is really reflecting what's going on inside the room to the students. It helps make them present in the here and now. Most of the time the students, when they try and pay attention, they have difficulty with focus, maybe they don't realize what's going on, how they feel, or what they need to do. But with the dogs here, everyone pays attention, and there's motivation [to participate]. I think it's important.

Cynthia:	Having the dog in the room helps them to focus and be motivated because they want to interact with the animal. This is especially important in helping people who are attention deficit.
Debbie:	Yes.
Cynthia:	Anything else that you would like to help people understand about your program and how it's beneficial?
Debbie:	I think, what we are doing here is to reintegrate different models, different intervention theories into our work. To tailor make the needs with different needs and different people. We do AAT with different populations, and we find that animal-assisted interventions for each case, each group, each characteristic need to be tailor made. And this is what we are doing now because we have to assess the needs of the service user. We implement the treatment goal and lots of things. I think with this dedicated planning, we enhance therapeutic impact.
Cynthia:	And with the dogs being such social beings, they can fit into a number of different social situations to serve a variety of populations. That's one of the things I'm so impressed by, is the number and variety of populations that you serve. A therapy dog can be a catalyst for growth and development for different populations of service users. Based on the professional's design of what one child needs or another person needs, the animal can fit well into a designed intervention because the human–animal interaction is a social interaction. So there's many different populations you can serve that have all types of different needs.
Debbie:	Yes. I think the dog already is a very attractive thing. But I think with this thing, because sometimes they are physical, their appearance, their characters, what they do, I think if we understand the dogs enough we can integrate a lot of things into intervention. For example, I teach my students how to be aware of their emotions. And then I teach them how to look at the tails, the ears of the dogs. I ask when they do something, "How does she, the dog, feel? She's happy because she's wagging. Then when you are happy, what should you do?" I will ask my students to realize what's going on in their body by looking at what's going on in the dog's body.
Cynthia:	And they're not so self-conscious to look within themselves because it's fun. You ask them, "What is the dog feeling?" to read the body language of the dog. And then when you ask them, "So what are you feeling?" it doesn't feel like treatment or therapy because they're just associating themselves with the dog.
Debbie:	Yes.
Cynthia:	So they can look at themselves and learn to identify those emotions within themselves and feel comfortable doing that because it was so fun to do, to try and imagine what the dog would be feeling.

Debbie: Sometimes, we do role-play, just like we have a situation, for example, Jessie, the dog was not happy today because she is not able to play with her other friends. Then if you were her, what emotions do you think she might have? Okay, maybe she said she is not happy. Okay, then what should she do? Sometimes, she will whine; sometimes, she will cry. Something like that. Okay, if that were you, what would you do? How do you react? Because sometimes when our students, they have difficulty in emotional control, they will cry a lot, and then they have a fit, they hit people. We show them, our dog handler will tell them, "Okay, if Jessie had this situation, maybe she is sad, but she just sat for a little bit, but won't hurt people." And then we say, "Will you have better alternatives to deal with your emotion?" We will do this kind of bridging, to like, "Okay, oh yeah, I have to learn from Jessie" or "Okay, there is a better alternative." And sometimes we give them the role as little teachers, so they think, "Okay, I should do better than the dog. So I have to behave well." So I think this is interesting; this is very, very beneficial to the students.

Cynthia: Yeah, by having the dog there with the handler you can do the role-plays where you ask the children to have an imaginary storytelling about what the dog would do in a situation. It allows them to project onto that dog, through their storytelling, many ranges of emotions. They wonder, "What would happen to this dog? How would the dog feel?" And then by doing the imaginary storytelling, the role-playing with the dog, it's easier then for them to look within and ask, "Well, what would I do?" or "What would be better choices for the dog in that situation? What would be better choices for myself in that situation?" So by coming up with better choices for the dog, they can then use that exercise to come up with better choices for themselves to control their impulsive behavior or have more prosocial behaviors.

Debbie: Yes.

Cynthia: You must be proud of your program.

Debbie: I think I'm still learning because sometimes, I just think, how can we be more aware or be more thoughtful as a dog? So we can help our students to have better understandings of themselves.

Cynthia: You and I have visited before. You have this really strong feeling that dogs have a lot to teach us, but we humans have a struggle understanding what it is that they can teach us. And I think that's where you're coming from right now, is constantly trying to pay attention and learn as much as we can about what the animals are offering us. If we can recognize that better when it happens in therapy, we can utilize that with our clients.

Debbie: Yes. I think a therapist is a bridge to bring the dogs to the people in need. This is what I'm doing and I'm believing.

Cynthia: Well, thank you so much for sharing your program with us today. I think it's wonderful what you're doing for the dogs in terms of making sure they're well taken care of and get a chance to go out into the world and spend time with people, and how you're helping so many individuals in need who might not otherwise take the steps they need to grow and develop. It's wonderful, so thank you for sharing your program with us today.

Debbie: Thank you for giving me this opportunity to share.

Editors' Commentary for Chapter 14

Debbie Ngai of the Hong Kong Animal Assisted Therapy Association presents, with her staff, social and educational services as an opportunity to play with and socially engage friendly dogs. This reduces the idea of suffering that challenged youth commonly associate with social services and educational training. This at-risk population in Hong Kong is more receptive to getting their needs attended when opportunity is presented to interact with a dog.

Debbie Ngai designed her programs to attend to safety and welfare of both humans and animals. Therapists are trained in animal behavior and communication and on how to integrate an animal into social service and educational provision. The animals are valued as social beings and not as objects for exploitation. Demonstrated care and concern for the animal is an ideal model for challenged youth, who can greatly benefit from this example.

Editors' Commentary for Part III: India and Hong Kong

We learned from the interviews of professionals working in Asia that animal-assisted therapy practice for emotional concerns is a relatively new concept in India and Hong Kong. So why is it important to include these interviews in our book? Because every culture that incorporates animal-assisted therapy has to start somewhere and it is worthwhile to record how and why animal-assisted therapy began. There is a strong negative social stigma in these Asian cultures attached to having an emotional disorder or mental or intellectual disability. Thus, the idea of attending social or psychological services is not popular, and this is true for both India and Hong Kong. These countries have organized social services, with social workers, clinical psychologists, psychiatrists, and nurses who provide care. Yet service providers we interviewed frequently spoke of the difficulty in attracting clientele to utilize social services. This is one of the reasons emotional and social service providers in India and Hong Kong started incorporating different types of animal-assisted interventions to try to attract more people to utilize the social services available.

In Hong Kong, the beginning of animal-assisted therapy seemed to occur to address community welfare needs that involved both humans and animals. Hong Kong therapists addressed how adopting stray or mixed-breed animals to work as social assistants in animal-assisted therapy provided care and nurturance for animals otherwise neglected by Hong Kong society. The interviewees addressed how in Hong Kong there is a need for therapeutic mediums that address serious social and emotional needs in a manner that is attractive to persons living there. They have found that the opportunity to interact with a therapy animal increases motivation to participate in social service programs, which may provide many benefits for people who are socially isolated or socially, emotionally, or intellectually impaired. Currently, only a handful of service providers from a few agencies offer animal-assisted interventions in Hong Kong for emotional and mental health. These service providers, as well as the researchers we interviewed, are tenacious pioneers in their community.

In India, the staff of Animal Angels Foundation is currently the primary provider of animal-assisted interventions for emotional and mental health. Animal lover and psychologist Minal Kavishwar, founder and executive director of the Animal Angels Foundation, recognized how dogs could be a catalyst for motivating individuals to participate in and benefit from much-needed educational, emotional, and mental health services. Minal Kavishwar's work is increasing interest in animal-assisted therapy in India. Gradually, more service providers, from India and other countries, who take her training are starting to incorporate animal-assisted interventions.

Many of the therapists in India and Hong Kong also aspired to bring greater cultural enlightenment to their people, to help their culture recognize the dog or cat as something much more than property to brag about, if a purebred, or something to neglect or disgust, if a mixed breed. There was expressed desire to help people to value the animal as a social being with much to give in the way of companionship and emotional nurturance. Therapists in both of these Asian countries hoped to raise the level of awareness regarding gifts that animals offer that can be of great service to humans for emotional and mental health.

There are many obstacles to further development of animal-assisted therapy in India and Hong Kong. The idea of a family pet for companionship is somewhat uncommon. Unfamiliarity breeds resistance in people to acceptance of dogs and cats as beneficial beings for interaction, especially those animals with a history as a stray animal from the streets. Transporting a therapy animal to a session is difficult since personal ownership of a car is uncommon and other modes of transportation prohibit animals. Since it is not yet widely accepted by emotional or mental health professionals of India or Hong Kong and research on animal-assisted therapy in India and Hong Kong is sparse, funding for animal-assisted therapy programming and research is greatly limited. Despite these many obstacles, and maybe even because of some of them, those who are practicing animal-assisted therapy in India and Hong Kong are very motivated to further the field in that region of the world. Their interest, determination, and passion are contagious. The energy, efforts, and attitude of those in India and Hong Kong serve to remind us in the U.S. not to take for granted the many opportunities we have to practice animal-assisted therapy in our country.